Real and
Imagined
Worlds

Real and Imagined Worlds

The Novel and Social Science

MORROE BERGER

HARVARD UNIVERSITY PRESS

Cambridge, Massachusetts, and London, England   1977

Copyright © 1977 by the President and Fellows
of Harvard College

All rights reserved

Printed in the United States of America

Library of Congress Cataloging in Publication Data

Berger, Morroe.
    Real and imagined worlds.

    Bibliography
    Includes index.
    1. Literature and society.   2. Fiction — History
and criticism.   I. Title.
PN3344.B4   809.3'3   76-27375
ISBN 0-674-74941-3

For D. and S.

Preface

My interest in the subject and approach of this book goes back to my undergraduate years, when I was inspired in social inquiry by that extraordinary teacher, Charles H. Page. Sentiment leads me now to mention several great thinkers and writers to whom I have been indebted since then. They are Thorstein Veblen, Morris R. Cohen, John Dos Passos, Ignazio Silone, and Robert M. MacIver. Though I did come to know some of them, they influenced me mainly from afar and without being aware of it. The references to them in this book are inadequate expressions of my appreciation of their sharp thinking, clear writing, and broad sympathies.

More immediate debts are equally pleasant to acknowledge, especially to Princeton University for providing a perfect setting and many opportunities for study. Several colleagues were kind enough to read all or parts of this book. They are Jerome W. Clinton, Joseph Frank, Alvin B. Kernan, and Dennis H. Wrong. For research assistance, I want to thank Joan Kimmelman, Lucille Rosen, Russell W. Stevens, and Linda J. Tarver. I greatly appreciate the help of Virginia LaPlante of the Harvard University Press.

Contents

Real and
Imagined
Worlds

Approaches
to Social Life

The Novel remains the most prodigious
of literary forms.
— Henry James, *The Ambassadors*

1.

In a letter to an obscure English novelist, Friedrich Engels remarked that Balzac "gives us a most wonderfully realistic history
of French 'Society' . . . from which . . . I have learned more than
from all the professed historians, economists and statisticians of
the period together."[1] Nearly a century later the Leavises affirmed: "It is the great novelists above all who give us our social
history; compared with what is done in *their* work — their creative
work — the histories of the professional historian seem empty and
unenlightening" (7).

How do novelists tell about social life? How far can fiction supplant history or social science, even assuming that Engels exaggerated to make a point? How can the imagined world of the storyteller inform about the real world of experience? What good is the
novel if it merely clothes sociology in narrative, incident, and
anecdote? Recently novelists have explicitly sought to satisfy the
reader's interest in a narrative treatment of nostalgic historical
themes or of current social problems, while social scientists have
introduced fictional techniques to make their work more immediate and palatable to the same reader. Norman Mailer, claiming to

combine the two approaches in *The Armies of the Night,* gave as its subtitle: *History as a Novel. The Novel as History.* Such intersections of fiction and social science or history, far from being recent, have occurred since at least the eighteenth century, when these two approaches to the study of social life achieved their characteristically modern form. Philosophers turned from closed systems of thought to the direct observation of society and widened their study of past and present to include people and movements beyond the royal courts. Similarly, writers of fiction, as Samuel Johnson remarked in 1750, turned to "that experience which can never be attained by solitary diligence, but must arise from general converse and accurate observation of the living world" (143). Novelists and philosophers read each other, and some, notably Rousseau and Diderot, wrote both novels and treatises. In this way the relation of the novel to life, to science, and to what later became known as social science has remained a lively question in the sociology of art forms.

Fiction and Reality

Whatever purpose, function, or value has been ascribed to art, its relation to life or reality has been central to almost every speculation since antiquity. In the era of the novel especially, art is deemed important or serious to the degree that it mirrors or illuminates reality. This notion is now so familiar that its novelty or peculiarity is forgotten. Before it became widely accepted during the eighteenth century, other criteria were more often applied. For example, art was considered valid to the degree that it justified respect for the divine order, for rulers, or for mythical heroes. Closeness to life was only one of many elements in this mode of judgment, but it became the dominant one in the course of the transition from medieval to modern conceptions. Why closeness to life should confer importance on art is not self-evident. A painting, a play, or a novel is not, after all, life itself, and those who appreciate such works are perfectly aware that they are shaped by the vision and technique of the artist. Yet audiences continue to lend themselves to patent illusions, probably because they have no other choice. Neither art nor science can present total reality, so people must be satisfied with a selection and arrangement of it. Readers prepare themselves for a partial presentation and accept the need for compromise. Knowing the novel is a "presentation," in the show-business sense of the word, they nevertheless want it to tell them something about that total reality which no one can encompass. After having written several novels, H. G. Wells in 1911 announced that the goal of the novel is to embrace the "whole of human life." "Before we have done," he predicted, "we will have all life within the scope of the novel." Yet he soon turned from the novel to history. Contemplating his "brave trumpetings" a generation later, Wells admitted: "I never got 'all life within the scope of the novel.' (What a phrase! Who could?)" Around the same time Virginia Woolf was giving thought to "how I shall re-form the novel and capture multitudes of things at present fugitive, enclose the whole, and shape infinite strange shapes." Before them, Zola had already staked out the claim: "all of nature and all of man belong to us."[2]

In selecting the aspects of "all life" to put into a novel, the writer is imposing some sort of order upon jumbled experience, even if he claims to be portraying the very chaos of experience. The order suggests understanding, which is why novels, as E. M. Forster put it in *Aspects of the Novel,* "give us the illusion of perspicacity and of power" (99). This ancient concept of art as compensation has long troubled artists and critics because it plainly implies that art is an illusion and hence in some way inferior to science, which presumably apprehends nature and society more directly. As Plato argued, the work of art is only "at the third remove" from reality and celebrates our emotions, which men ought to control rather than indulge; hence poetry is inferior to philosophy and should be excluded from "a well-governed society" except when it praises the gods or good men (X. 597, 606-607).

Artists have taken several paths to escape this limited choice of serving authority or amusing the populace. Wanting to be taken seriously, novelists in particular have tried to portray life accurately, to create a world that the reader will recognize as much like the one he inhabits even when dramatized to arouse and maintain his interest in characters and events beyond his own experience. The question of whether readers are interested more in the familiar or the exotic has never been satisfactorily answered. One eighteenth-century answer was that the familiar was more interesting. Benjamin Franklin, who in 1744 became the first American publisher of an English novel, Richardson's *Pamela*, remarked of Bunyan: "Honest John was the first that I know of who mix'd Narration and Dialogue, a Method of Writing very engaging to the Reader, who in the most interesting parts finds himself as it were brought into the Company, and present at the Discourse" (72). This intimacy among life, art, and the reader is the achievement of the realistic novel, seeking to show the weakness of men and women, the triumph of events over motives, and the grandeur and tragedy of ordinary lives. In such works authors make an implicit critique of human nature and social life, but do so through the story and the characters, rather than by direct statement of an attitude or point of view. Another method, often combined with the first method and quaintly called "authorial intrusions," is to add throughout the story the author's own comments on the lives he describes, in little essays that enable the author to be a social philosopher of sorts as well as a teller of tales. This emphasis on the critique of society often leads the writer far from the path of plain realism to the point where only the extraordinary or the absurd can fully convey a sense of the repugnance of life. When even the absurd is felt to be inadequate, writers can resort to the exact reproduction of bits and pieces of reality, as in the stream of consciousness method, the documentary approach, or the objectivity of the French "new novel." The ultimate in this trend is the happening, an announced effort to erase altogether the difference between life and art.

All these paths have in a sense tried to bring art closer to life and thereby to make art less of a game, an illusion, or an amusement. "The writer of stories," noted Trollope in his *Autobiography* near the end of a long and successful career of writing fiction, "must please, or he will be nothing" (185). Yet even that cynic added: "And he must teach whether he wish to teach or no." Novelists have been criticized from the beginning for dealing with subjects usually reserved for philosophy, history, and science. In an attack upon Disraeli's didactic novels, James Russell Lowell in 1847 expressed a traditional view of the novel, often repeated since then, when he warned: "We should not be so severe in our exactions of the novel except that it no longer professes to amuse, but to instruct" (103).

But there is no intrinsic reason that the novel should not seek to instruct or to illumine social institutions. Nor is such a goal incompatible with amusement. For two thousand years critics have been quoting, with varying degrees of approval, Horace's advice that literature must both please and instruct. Yet the novel continues to be regarded, even after three hundred years, as an intruder upon the supposedly sacred precincts of disciplines distinguished as much by their pretensions and failures as by their lofty and exclusive claims. One reason for this steady disparagement of the novel is that some of its practitioners and many of its self-proclaimed defenders have mistakenly pitted it against science and history, instead of trying to find the novel's own place among the various forms of knowledge.

Almost from its beginnings in the seventeenth century, modern science has been seen as a threat to literature. At first literary men, like others concerned with ideas and learning, were exhilarated by the expansion of the human imagination and knowledge. Increasingly, however, they found science to be materialistic and dangerous to humane values. More particularly, they regarded science as an encroachment upon the traditional domain of poetry. The novel, developing at the same time as science, was not at first seen to be threatened by it, but fiction was soon assimilated to traditional forms of literature, and its advocates began to share the familiar humanistic apprehension that science somehow displaces letters. The literary response to this challenge was to claim that poetry reveals a higher "truth" than science, or that science and art are after all compatible ways of ordering nature and man's experience, or that the novel can do whatever science does. Thus Balzac believed he was describing and categorizing human beings as zoologists do animals. Realists and naturalists, such as Flaubert, Zola, Frank Norris, and Theodore Dreiser, saw their fiction as objective reports on human behavior. Zola proclaimed the advent of the experimental novel, and today there is the nonfiction novel. These efforts to make fiction look like science are now complemented by an effort to make science look less objective. Thus it is fashionable for humanists to refer knowingly to Werner Heisenberg's principle of "uncertainty" in physics as if it means uncertainty in the ordinary sense. The argument continues in the Snow-Leavis exchange and the writings of Saul Bellow, Susan Sontag, and P. B. Medawar, and even extends to the realm of social science.

Fiction and Social Science

That the novel and social science are two ways of commenting on human behavior and social institutions is known. Less familiar are the specific ways in which these two approaches intersect and diverge. My aim is therefore not to discuss all aspects of either social science or fictional technique, but to show how the novel has contributed to a knowledge of the same landscape upon which social science has focused, but through a different lens.

The novel and social science have similar antecedents in the eighteenth century, both seeking to describe and to explain social behavior in new ways. Fielding and Mandeville exemplified the common approach of the novel and the social treatise. There are two main ways in which the novel deals with social institutions. The first is directly through the events and characters, which can be used to clarify such broad themes as the basis of human association, the differences of culture and race, political power, and social class. The second way in which novels deal with social life is through intrusions that do not necessarily carry the story forward but comment on that story or on life in general. This commentary is concerned with the subjects of social science such as class, law, the status of women, and interpersonal relations. These aspects of fiction make it possible to compare the writing of novels with the writing of history, the content of literature with life itself, and finally the methods of the novel and social science with the scientific method. The response of literature to the challenge of science reveals the appropriate sphere of each.

For the sake of convenience the words "fiction" and the "novel" are used interchangeably. The words "social science," "sociology," and "history" are used in the same free manner, because these more factual or systematic approaches to social life are being compared as a whole to the novel. Indeed, the range of undifferentiated terms includes "science" itself without qualification, for in some senses the comparison goes beyond social life to involve methods of inquiry into any realm. In works of fiction, the discussion is not confined to any particular type, period, or national expression, although the themes and examples come mainly from English and French novels. As to social science, the comparison of its findings with what may be learned about the same subjects in novels relies generally on twentieth-century positivism liberally defined. The method requires many quotations, to clarify the comparison, to give the flavor of the fictional contribution, and to show the constant repetition of ideas over the centuries as discoveries are made anew. In order to show the capacity and contribution of the novel as a genre, the discussion is not limited to the great novelists, like Dickens, Balzac, Eliot, Dostoyevsky, and Joyce, but also includes the lesser ones and even several, like T. S. Stribling, who are rarely discussed in literary histories. The approaches of both fiction and the social sciences to reality are very diverse, so that examples can easily be found to demonstrate propositions about either similarities or differences between them. Though there is no way to prove a thesis statistically or definitively, a wide range of authors, eras, and styles of the novel reveals convincing parallels and divergences.

The novel seeks to apprehend life in a perennial effort to escape the reproach that fiction is trivial and fanciful. One means to do so, the authorial intrusion, is regrettably named because it suggests that somehow it is inappropriate for the author to express himself directly rather than through characters and events. The term also suggests too sharp a distinction between the indirect and direct methods by which the writer comments upon social life in general.

Yet the term is widely used and convenient, as is the more neutral expression "authorial commentary."

This device enables the novelist to describe or to judge human behavior that would otherwise be difficult or impossible to convey. George Eliot began *Felix Holt, the Radical* (1866) by contrasting travel by stagecoach and railroad: the longer journey was filled with adventure, whereas being "shot, like a bullet through a tube, by atmospheric pressure . . . can never lend much to picture and narrative." H. G. Wells described, through his narrator in *Tono-Bungay* (1908), the "new social arts" of an ascending class at the turn of the century learning how to spend money: "With an immense astonished zest they begin *shopping* . . . They plunge into it as one plunges into a career; as a class, they talk, think, and dream possessions" (284, 286).

William Golding, pursuing the thematic method, commented less directly in *The Lord of the Flies* (1955). He led the reader to contemplate human nature, but neither he nor his characters said anything on the subject itself. Instead, the author described such actions as building a fire, holding meetings, killing a pig and offering it to the unknown "beast," all of which he dramatized in such a way as to make them symbolic of primordial human urges and attitudes. Only at the conclusion did Golding refer directly to "the end of innocence, the darkness of man's heart," ideas he had been building to throughout the story.

Such extraordinary reliance upon events, with only occasional hints and cues to invest them with more general significance, is more characteristic of the novels of today than of previous periods. *Lord of the Flies* would be much the same if every trace of authorial intrusion were excised, but a novel by George Eliot could hardly remain unaffected by the same treatment, nor could Dickens' *Hard Times* (1854) carry its theme without the author's open bias toward his characters, his denunciation of industrialism in Coketown, and his frequent admonitions that Englishmen must temper work with play, calculation with spontaneity, and fact with fancy. All these sorts of commentary betray the writer's mistrust of the story itself, the sheer narrative, as a vehicle for conveying the larger meaning that serious fiction seeks to impart in all eras. Mere plot has long been disdained, though writers have differed over which techniques to emphasize in its place. A hundred years ago, Trollope remarked that although plot is the element by which the public judges a novel, he himself regarded it as "the most insignificant part" of the whole. Just a few years ago Alain Robbe-Grillet complained that even for critics the novel is still mainly a "story," although plot itself has long ceased to be the driving force or the framework of the narrative. Balzac, even before Trollope, once paused to defend his effort to explain events: "some people, interested in the plot, will find these explanations tedious."[3]

The narrative of events has declined not only in fiction but also in history and social science, which now stress causation or the connections between events and analysis of character in place of sheer description. The old argument as to which is superior, fiction or history, goes on. Fiction is called superior by some because it permits the writer to create his own facts to fit his purpose; history is deemed superior by others because it sticks to the facts of life itself, which provides more variety and wonderment than can any individual human imagination. Irrespective of these arguments, novelists have increasingly sought to achieve one sort of objectivity or another, in the course of which they have to face, explicitly or not, the issues of probability and verisimilitude.

Sociology of Art

The sociology of art is a branch of the sociology of knowledge. It is concerned more with the relation of artistic expression to other social expression than with its aesthetic quality, just as the sociology of knowledge is concerned more with the relation of a scientific idea or practice to other social institutions than with its validity. The elimination of aesthetic judgment nevertheless is not total, for the sociology of art must concern itself also with the nature and basis of artistic taste even if not with its validity. The reluctance to judge art, however, has troubled artists and critics who might otherwise find more value in the sociological approach. They see it as a form of philistinism, reducing art to the same category as political and economic behavior. In 1870 Flaubert complained that so much attention is given to the life of an author that his genius is not appreciated, that the purpose of a work of art is

thought to inhere in the circumstances of its creation. "History,"
he warned, "will soon absorb all of literature." A generation later
the American critic Irving Babbitt deplored the replacement of
judgment by sympathetic understanding, which he associated
with the growth of democracy. Criticism, he lamented, had in the
previous century tended "to become first a form of history, and
then a form of biography, and finally a form of gossip."[4] In 1956
T. S. Eliot argued that scholarship about literature, which was
transforming criticism, could provide interesting and useful facts
about a poet's time, but that such information was of little help in
understanding or appreciating his poetry. These strictures do not
diminish the value of the sociological approach, which is concerned with art as a social institution and not directly with the
appreciation of literature. The sociology of art has been studied
from various points of view, such as the social origins of forms, the
influence of social conditions on style or subject, and the social
position of audiences or artists. Thus far, however, the effort to
state general principles about art has met with little success; most
such principles hardly go beyond asserting that art emerges from
or is a reflection of social life. Nor are general sociological theories
helpful, for they are often obscure, pretentious, and irrelevant to
the arts.

The search for general principles in the sociology of art has
been unsuccessful in the century and a half since Hegel first pointed out the difficulties of this approach. "General formulas," he
observed, are mainly "precepts and rules" designed to improve
writing, and are therefore no more than "trivial reflections" (39).
The other extreme, broad speculations about the nature of beauty,
Hegel found equally unsatisfactory, because they too do not establish the proper scientific relation between the universal or general
statement and its particular manifestations in specific works of art.
The reasons he gave for the failure of the sociology of art are still
pertinent. Such a sociology first requires "an exact acquaintance"
with the innumerable works of art themselves — works that have
perished as well as those that have survived, works in all eras, all
countries and societies, and all art forms (38). This vast knowledge
of art and history needs, in turn, a capacity for comparison and

distinction as well as an ability to abstract and to generalize. Further, works of art "elude" scientific treatment because they emerge from the uncontrolled imagination and therefore resist abstract analysis. Flaubert, for example, insisted that no matter what the scientific approach can reveal — and he did not deny it all value — it cannot explain the individual artist or the specific work. He affirmed instead the role of individual talent and will as well as of absolute values, even while rejecting the old notion that works of art "fell from the sky like meteorites." T. S. Eliot expressed a similar view when he observed not only that knowledge about a poem's origin is unnecessary for its appreciation but that "too much information about the origins of the poem may even break my contact with it."[5]

Hegel did not despair on account of such difficulties. He pointed out that art belongs to the realm of thought, which requires learning and expression; that art has technique, which can be apprehended and transmitted; and that art is a representation, whose appreciation by an audience requires not only a feeling about what is represented but also an attitude toward the idea that representations themselves have value. Since art is thus embedded in social life, art is neither "unworthy" of nor beyond "philosophical consideration," and a sociology of art is both possible and useful (37). The sociological approach must at once distinguish the aesthetic element from other elements of human experience and relate the aesthetic element to the others. John Dewey defended his social approach to aesthetic theory by insisting that the aesthetic "is no intruder in experience from without . . . but . . . it is the clarified and intensified development of traits that belong to every normally complete experience" (46). This interlocking only makes the effort more difficult and perhaps more worthwhile. A generation ago the historian of art, Meyer Schapiro, lamented the absence of general theory in this field. Only a few years ago Malcolm Bradbury, discussing sociological approaches to literature, found the same lack in that domain.[6] Fortunately the absence of general theory need not discourage more limited and perhaps more useful inquiries.

Common Origins in the Eighteenth Century

Let us always have men ready to give the loving
pains of a life to the faithful representing of
commonplace things.
— George Eliot, *Adam Bede*

2.

Connections between the novel and social science go back, in
Western intellectual history, at least to the eighteenth century in
England and France. Since every idea has its germ in a previous
era, the novel can be traced to the French romances of the seventeenth century, thence to the Spanish romances of the sixteenth
and fifteenth centuries, to the Italian tales of the fourteenth century, to such earlier collections as the stories of the Arabian nights,
and finally back to the Greek and Latin tales of the first century of
the Christian era. The parallels between the novel and social science, however, developed only with their emergence in forms still
recognizable today, as a result of the new approach to knowledge
and entertainment discernible in the eighteenth century.

Scholars, essayists, and imaginative writers in the eighteenth
century began in unprecedented proportions and intensity to ask
systematically why things happen among and to masses of human
beings. They were not content only to record events or to deal with
gods and heroes; they sought patterns of behavior in individuals
and groups, and turned to social institutions as a tool and a subject of inquiry. Imaginative writers, the storytellers, still wanted to
entertain, but more intensely than ever they also wanted to offer
explanations and guides for behavior.

Expansion of Thought

The eighteenth century conveyed a sense of intellectual drive, emotional excitement, and expanding horizons. The impact and impetus of earlier explosions of ideas and social activity, as in science and geography, continued to be felt. Personal relations, social interaction, governmental functions, trade, and speculative thinking gave a feeling of great activity which was expressed in all forms of literature. Both social commentary and the novel experienced the outburst of energy, confidence, and optimism by adopting new ideas and forms. One of these new ideas was for social thinkers and novelists to explain human behavior rather than only to describe, exalt, or criticize it. Here, as in so many other realms, the Scottish philosophers pointed the way. In the work of David Hume, Francis Hutcheson, Dugald Stewart, Adam Ferguson, and Adam Smith appeared many of the themes that animated later social scientists and concerned novelists as well.[1] Historians and philosophers dealt with facts but also sought coherence in the human record and general principles to explain human behavior. The group, rather than just the outstanding individual, became a unit of analysis, as thinkers turned to races, nations, classes, occupations, and religions to illuminate social life. Novelists resorted to these larger units to make the behavior of their characters more credible and understandable. Whereas nature made humankind equal in one sense, human association and organization introduced differences. These differences were no longer to be accounted for by divine influence, climate, and similar immutable causes, but by moral or human causes such as national character, political ideas, and economic status — that is, by social institutions created by individuals and groups.

The idea of "system" gained ground. Social thinkers saw a system in the division of labor and in specialization, which through the interrelation of many wills and actions produced a pattern of life. The counterpart of such a system in the novel was the relating of persons in credible social roles, times, places, and events. Philosophers were abandoning familiar absolutes. Toward the end of the seventeenth century Locke had denied certainty in human affairs and history. Men act, he stated, on incomplete information, that is, on their notion of the probabilities of what they think and do. Indeed, the truth of ideas sometimes depends on how widely they are held, so that the more people testifying to the truth of an event, the more probable it is. Novelists likewise moved toward notions of probability as they rejected unrealistic and incredible events and characters, insisting upon a resemblance to life and reality—in a word, upon probability in their fiction.

Leslie Stephen, in his *History of English Thought in the Eighteenth Century* (1876, II, ch. 12), concludes that philosophical thought and literature then changed to meet new social conditions, but that the novel did not derive directly from philosophy. In exploring how a new creed usually takes hold, Stephen conjectures: "Some Descartes or Kant will lay down a new philosophical system, correcting and supplementing the old. The primary axioms having been modified, all the subsidiary consequences will gradually undergo a corresponding change, until the whole system of thought is gradually wrought into a harmony . . . As men come to take a different view of their position and destiny, they will gradually learn to subordinate their moral and political views to the new teaching, and the artistic expression of sentiment will mold itself upon the new framework of thought."[2] This pattern, however, does not fit the eighteenth-century "revolution in ideas." Rather, a "reconstruction of the underlying philosophy forced itself upon the acutest minds," because the old ideas were no longer serviceable in the face of a growing heterogeneity.

Regarding the arts, Stephen asks this fundamental question: "How far, and in what way, was the imaginative literature of the time a translation of its philosophy in terms of emotion?" His answer is that both philosophy and literature responded to the same changes in social conditions and needs. The novel, creating a new kind of narrative out of old tales and legends, thus satisfied the feeling and taste of an educated middle-class formed by the new social conditions. This "distinct literary class" of readers and writers was "eager for amusement, delighting in infinite personal gossip, and talking over its own peculiarities with ceaseless interest in coffee-houses, clubs, and theaters." Its emergence coincided with a change in the economic position of writers, who found increas-

ing support through sales of books and magazines to this new public, and less from individual patrons. The new social thought and
the novel thus sprang from the same root, according to Stephen,
producing "remarkable analogies . . . between the speculative and
the imaginative literature," especially in essayists and satirists such
as Swift, Pope, and Johnson, and in novelists such as Defoe, Fielding, and Smollett.

Fielding and Mandeville

Confirming Stephen, subsequent attempts to trace eighteenth
century novels directly to this or that philosopher have not proved
convincing, largely because the connections are too general.[3]
There are closer and more numerous connections between essayists and novelists. The French philosopher-novelists Diderot and
Rousseau used both genres to express their views about social life
and human nature. In *Jacques the Fatalist* (1796), Diderot reveals
his admiration both for the English contemporary Samuel Richardson and for a cavalier, instrumental approach to fiction. In
this fictional tract Diderot expresses pleasure at being able to do
anything with his characters: "How easy it is to fabricate stories!"
(4). But he also interjects: "I don't like novels unless indeed they
are Richardson's. I am making up this story and it's going to interest you or not interest you, and that's the least of my worries. My
plan is to say what is true, and I have carried it out" (222). Inspired by Richardson, Diderot uses novels and plays to convey his
own conceptions of morality. Parallels in outlook and style appear
in the fiction of Diderot and another English contemporary, Laurence Sterne. Similarities also occur between Sterne and Adam
Smith. Fielding and Hume bear witness to the convergence of the
novel and history, for they use "a prose narrative to treat problems
of the individual in society, problems of the human character in
time and history," and their technique includes "an individual
narrative voice and point of view."[4]

The convergence of the treatise and the novel is shown best in
Mandeville and Fielding. They share more than other writers that
eighteenth century combination of realism and irony, sometimes

called pessimism, with a zest for life and a pleasure in observing human nature. They regard society as a system of roles ordained not by divine power but by human nature and social needs. Each looks squarely at human passions and the requirements of social stability. Although Fielding sees some benevolence in human nature, while Mandeville thinks that good emerges only from human desires of doubtful morality, both see passions as dominating humankind and are pessimistic about the possibility of improving life by attempts to control it or by appeals to the "better" instincts, which they consider rather weak. The best that people can achieve, Fielding and Mandeville hold, is to find and use the social good that may come of the pursuit of private goals.

The novelist and essayist persist in uncovering hypocrisy, man's continuous effort to make his vices look like virtues. Mandeville defends this effort by asking: "What hurt do I do to Man if I make him more known to himself than he was before?" Fielding, in his novels, seeks also to reveal character by getting at the motives leading to action and its consequences. In "An Essay on the Knowledge of the Characters of Men," Fielding sets out to help the ordinary man detect the hypocrisy of those who affect altruism in order to take advantage of others; his purpose is to "arm" the "innocent and undesigning" against the "artful and cunning" for whom many "systems" have already been invented. In his preface to *Joseph Andrews* (1742) Fielding implicitly defends the novel's emphasis: "Life everywhere furnishes an accurate Observer with the Ridiculous." The ridiculous comes from the uncovering of affectation, which in turn arises from vanity and hypocrisy. Explaining why he introduces such vices into his novel, Fielding remarks, "it is very difficult to pursue a Series of human Actions and keep clear from them." Mandeville in *The Fable of the Bees* refers often to hypocrisy and nowhere more simply than when he calmly asserts, "In all Civil Societies Men are taught insensibly to be Hypocrites from their Cradle." He adds that "to me it is a great Pleasure" to see how men in different "Employments" and "Stations" act while making money, for example dancing masters "gay and merry" at a ball and undertakers "solemn" at a funeral.[5]

Fielding and Mandeville were moved to take notice in different genres of the great villain and confidence man Jonathan Wild. Fielding wrote a supremely ironic novel named for the villain in 1743, and Mandeville penned a pamphlet, *An Enquiry into the Causes of the Frequent Executions at Tyburn,* on related issues of crime in 1725, a few months before Wild was finally apprehended. Claiming only a "uniformity" between them rather than a "direct influence" by Mandeville upon Fielding, Malvin Zirker has noted similarities in the attitude toward the treatment of crime expressed in this pamphlet by Mandeville and in a pamphlet by Fielding entitled *Increase of Robbers,* published in 1751.[6] Wilbur Cross has suggested that Fielding also tried to say similar things about crime and society in this essay and in his novel *Amelia* (1751).

Fielding and Mandeville are both concerned with the corruption of language attendant upon hypocrisy. F. B. Kaye has drawn attention in *The Fable of the Bees* to Mandeville's capacity to make an abstruse analysis concrete, using a style that has "idiomatic and homely vigor" (I, xxxviii). Fielding deals still more directly with this subject, as Glenn Hatfield has shown. Both participated in the eighteenth century attempt to simplify language in order to arrive at the truth and to reach an audience less accustomed than earlier ones to poetic flights and moralistic rhetoric.[7]

Fielding is a novelist who, regarding himself as a "historian," takes his authorial commentary very seriously. Mandeville is an essayist who, interested in generalizing about behavior and institutions, gives specific examples that reveal a novelist's imagination.

Fielding intrudes upon his story regularly and shamelessly. He introduces each book of *Tom Jones* (1749) with an essay on novels, writing, and that particular book. In the essay introducing book 9 he explains that he regards these interludes as "a kind of mark or stamp" distinguishing his "genuine" "history" from "monstrous romances." Perhaps more important, he asserts that anyone who can manipulate paper, pen, and ink can write a narrative, but that it takes knowledge, observation, and reflection to write these essays; he thus protects himself against imitators who cannot think. George Eliot, more than a century later, intruded into ch. 15 of *Middlemarch* (1872) an introductory comment on Fielding's tendency to intrude. She attests to his greatness as a "historian" but regrets that she cannot follow his example because people in her day have less time, novelists' "digressions" are less interesting, and she herself has too much to do "in unravelling certain human lots" to extend herself over the "universe."

To Fielding, as to his contemporaries, the variety and excitement of life were worthy subjects. Personal enjoyment, self-indulgence, and the idiosyncracies of ordinary people were by then more acceptable not only socially but also as themes for literature. Fielding discusses the fictional treatment of good and evil in his introduction to book 8 of *Tom Jones*. Since novelists are writing about the private lives of ordinary people rather than the public lives of great ones, he points out, they do not have documents to prove the truth of the events they portray. For this reason, the novelist must stay within the bounds of probability or his story will not be believable. This necessity is the greater when the novelist is "painting what is greatly good and amiable" which, Fielding implies, is not easy to believe. Evil, on the contrary, is found more credible, so that the novelist describing it need not worry so much about probability. "Knavery and folly," Fielding asserts in the spirit of Mandeville, "will more easily meet with assent." Such a conclusion met with the assent of the novelists themselves, who were often accused of dwelling on evil in order to make their fiction interesting while summarily punishing evil at the end in order to make their fiction acceptable. Defoe in his preface to *Moll Flanders* (1722) thus admits that his readers may find his heroine's vices more interesting than her penitence, but he hopes that some readers will nevertheless be "much more pleas'd with the Moral, than the Fable."

Such skepticism is congenial to Mandeville, who expressed it earlier and even more intensely than Fielding. Mandeville, too, is interested in pleasure, excitement, and activity. Though he never goes so far as to call the consumption of goods and self-indulgence virtues, he plainly insists in *Fable* that, to build an "opulent, knowing and polite Nation," people must be encouraged to engage in trade and expand their horizons, which will bring wealth, advance knowledge and the arts, enlarge desires, refine appetites, and increase vices (I, 184-185). No wonder that Stephen remarks in *Essays* that "Mandevilles are the inevitable antithesis to an over-strained asceticism" (295-296). In his essays Mandeville allows his ardor and imagination to lead him into using novelistic techniques, as Fielding allows his serious fictional purposes to influence him to adopt the essay. Like the novelists, Mandeville is interested in the way individual people are related to various social classes. He writes about honor, pride, and avarice; poverty and wealth; personal and national character. Mandeville's main point about the individual and society is that the individual cloaks his selfish motives with claims to honor and altruism, and that at least some of this selfishness is conducive to the material prosperity of society — hence Mandeville's subtitle to *The Fable of the Bees: Private Vices, Publick Benefits*. He does not, he notes in the preface, "dignify these few loose lines with the Name of Poem . . . and I am in reality puzzled what Name to give them." So he modestly settles on "a Story told in Dogrel." The "story" of the bee-hive is manifestly about England, for as Mandeville explains in the preface, the country "represented here . . . must be a large, rich and warlike Nation, that is happily governed by a limited Monarchy." Again like the novelists, Mandeville wants to "expose the Unreasonableness and Folly" of people, particularly of those who are "greedy" for the material comforts of an industrious and wealthy social order but who are "always murmuring at and exclaiming against those Vices" that have been "inseparable" from such a social order. Like the novelists, he feels his "story" or "fable" needs buttressing, which he supplies in essays and "Remarks" corresponding to authorial commentary in a novel.

Mandeville's novelistic techniques give added interest to his "story told in dogrel." The foremost illustration of these techniques is his recourse to the fable itself to analyze and judge individual behavior and social institutions. The lesser techniques are equally interesting. Consider the subsidiary fable he invented to explain the "origin of moral virtue" in his "enquiry" published anonymously in 1714, nine years after the first appearance of the "story told in dogrel."[8] According to his imaginative reconstruction, rulers and moralists created two classes of people, those who presumably could not and did not want to control their animal passions, and those who persuaded them to do so by flattery. Because rulers found force insufficient to make men "tractable," they had to find a way to make the ruled "believe, that it was more beneficial for every Body to conquer than indulge his Appetites, and much better to mind the Publick than what seemed his private Interest." These "Lawgivers and other wise Men" persuaded the people to "disapprove of their natural Inclinations" by offering them a reward. Having few rewards to offer that would not be costly to themselves, the moralists "were forced to contrive an imaginary one" — flattery. They told people that they were above the animals because of their rationality. Having thus by "Flattery insinuated themselves into the Hearts of Men," the moralists, who sought to "civilize Mankind," next taught honor and shame. Honor was good, shame bad and to be avoided. They taught men that as "sublime Creatures," they must regard it as shameful to concentrate on gratifying the appetites they shared with the animals. Realizing how difficult men would find it to subdue their natural appetites, the moralists and civilizers taught that to do so was "glorious" and to fail to try was "scandalous." To induce "emulation" as a spur to morality, the moralists next divided mankind into "two Classes, vastly differing from one another." Mandeville's ironic tone shows that he regards the distinction between these two classes as illusory. The one class "consisted of abject, low-minded People, that always hunting after immediate Enjoyment, were wholly incapable of Self-denial, and without regard to the good of others, had no higher Aim than their private Advantage . . . But the other Class was made up of lofty, high-spirited Creatures, that free from sordid Selfishness, esteemed the Improvements of the Mind to be their fairest Possessions; and . . . aimed at no less than the Publick Welfare and the conquest of their own Passion." The first class wanted to be like the second. In a later essay, Mandeville drops the irony and speaks plainly: "Honor in its Figurative Sense is a Chimera without Truth or Being, an Invention of Moralists and Politicians" (*Fable,* I, 98). Thus does Mandeville the essayist offer a secularized fable resembling the Biblical Garden of Eden and anticipating the Marxian idea of class differences designed to make the exploited accept their condition for the material benefit of the exploiters.

Mandeville also introduces dramatic situations and fictional characters to illustrate his points. Arguing that sexual differences in modesty are the result of education rather than nature, he gives as an example: "*Miss* is scarce three Years old, but she is spoke to every Day to hide her Leg, and rebuked in good Earnest if she shews it; while *Little Master* at the same Age is bid to take up his Coats, and piss like a Man." To illustrate the point that well-bred people may satisfy their lust most fiercely so long as they follow custom, he distinguishes between a "brute" and a "gentleman." The brute proposes immediate sexual intercourse to a woman, she flees, and he is ostracized from the polite world. But a gentleman, having the same inclination, first persuades the lady's father that he can support the daughter "splendidly," then gets her to like him through flattery and presents. She "resigns her self to him before Witnesses in a most solemn manner; at Night they go to Bed together," where she allows him to do what he pleases and he get what he wants "without having ever asked for it." Thereafter they act as normal human beings, with no shame, and the "fine Gentleman . . . need not practise any greater Self-Denial than the Savage" (I, 72-73). To illustrate emulation in clothing, which morality bids one avoid, Mandeville cites a "Laborer's Wife," various tradesmen, a "cholerick City Captain," a "phlegmatick Alderman," and a "beardless Ensign" (I, 129-131). One of his best anecdotes is a "Scene of Life" in which a "spruce Mercer, and a young Lady his Customer" engage in polite banter ending in his getting his price at her expense. Mandeville explains their different goals and motives, then describes how politely the tradesman hands the client from her coach to his shop. He encourages her to state her commands, which he never contradicts. In this way, they get on agreeably, going from trifles to business as he applies his stratagems to her ignorance, desire, and vanity, with the result that she thinks she has bought a bargain while paying the regular price or a higher one (I, 349-352).[9]

Belonging to adjoining generations that overlapped only slightly, Mandeville and Fielding were not quite contemporaries; Mandeville was already dead when Fielding's main works appeared. Fielding, however, makes interesting references to Mandeville in *Amelia*. Captain Booth and Fanny Matthews meet as prisoners in jail. He tells her how a friend who laughed at religion and virtue saved his life, showing a degree of goodness seldom revealed even by those professing religion. She agrees that religion and virtue are only cloaks for hypocrisy. "I have been of that opinion," she says in a deliberate pun on the name, "ever since I read that charming fellow Mandevil." Booth hopes she does not agree with Mandeville, who held that love results from such base impulses as pride and fear. Fanny says that although she found Mandeville convincing, "if he denies there is any such thing as love, that is most certainly wrong" (bk. 3, ch. 5). Self-righteous about evil and agreeing that Booth's wife Amelia is wonderful, the two are shown by Fielding to be building up to an affair, which they consummate when Fanny bribes the jailor and she and the Captain go to bed. All of this suggests that Mandeville struck a note which Fielding as well as Fanny found convincing. Later, Booth and Amelia discuss the same subject without mentioning Mandeville. Booth tells his wife that "all men, as well the best as the worst, act alike from the principle of self-love. Where benevolence therefore is the uppermost passion, self-love directs you to gratify it by doing good." But where a governing passion like ambition or pride suppresses benevolence, a man is left unmoved by the miseries of others. Amelia finds this unacceptably cynical, feeling confident that Dr. Harrison, Booth's virtuous friend, could convince him that "there are really such things as religion and virtue" (bk. 10, ch. 9). It thus appears that Booth and Fielding either accept Mandeville's basic principle or deviate little from it.

State of Nature and the Social Contract

The nature of humankind was an important subject to Mandeville and Fielding and to their predecessors and contemporaries. This concern led many thinkers — theologians, philosophers, and novelists — to consider natural law, the state of nature, and the social contract. As Leslie Stephen remarks, the eighteenth century appealed to the simplicity of nature in an effort to understand the relation of the individual to an increasingly complex society. In order to show the character of that relationship more clearly, Defoe attempted to re-create a "state of nature" in *Robinson Crusoe* (1719). In an essay as well, *A Treatise Concerning the Use and Misuse of the Marriage Bed,* ch. 11, Defoe contrasts custom and nature. Custom cannot justify a social practice; it is the "usurper of the throne of reason." Defoe puts the difference plainly: "Custom is a tyrant; nature is a just and limited government. Custom is anarchy and confusion; nature is a regulated monarchy, and a well-established constitution."

From medieval times the "natural law," devised mainly by theologians, appealed to a set of obligations above those created by rulers and limiting even their vast secular powers. It led to the notion of "natural rights" as a complement to civil duties, and then to the supposition that men in a "state of nature" came together in a "social contract" in order to lay the foundations of social order and political order through government.[10] These ideas reached their highest form and gained wide acceptance during the seventeenth and eighteenth centuries, when the novel itself was developing in England and France. Thus theology, philosophy, and many novels posited the isolation of the individual from society in order to discover the basis of human nature, to allow the individual to work out his relationship to God and humankind without the accumulated laws and customs of the past, and to show how society itself must have been created. The supposed state of nature revealed men to be insecure and their lives, in Hobbes's phrase, "solitary, poor, nasty, brutish, and short" (97). Self-interest made each person willing to join in the protection of the security and rights of all in order to protect his own.

For a long time the state of nature was held by critics of the notion to refer to an actual historical condition or era and hence to be insupportable because of the lack of evidence. More recently the state of nature has been accepted as a reasonable device to explain the establishment of social order, to define individual obligations, and to defend limitations on government. Locke, one of the most influential theorists of the state of nature, was aware that historical accounts always reveal men already under government. The idea of the state of nature came about not as an historical fact but as a means to make sense of other things found in history.[11] The state of nature and the social contract are thus historical "fictions" designed to reveal human nature, and the novels seeking the same goal are fictional "histories." Novels such as Aphra Behn's *Oroonoko* (1688) and Defoe's *Robinson Crusoe* examine human nature, as do the philosophical treatises and the travel reports on "primitive" societies which stimulated so many novelists.[12]

Didactic Forerunners of the Novel

As it developed in the seventeenth and eighteenth centuries, the novel was connected also to the moralizing literature of the era. New interpretations of Defoe and Richardson show how the novel emerged from Puritan allegories and from later "guide" or "domestic" books of a secular character.

There was much moralizing in the stories of the early eighteenth century. The reasons were many. First, thinkers often saw a moral crisis in the new religious beliefs, such as deism, which shook older faiths. Exploration, scientific investigation, and ideas of individual rights and obligations accompanied the challenge to tradition. All these unsettling tendencies persuaded many thinkers that a secular morality had to be devised to compensate for the loss of fidelity to, and even knowledge of, the Bible despite the growing literacy. Though much of the moralizing literature referred to the Bible, religious tradition was declining as a guide to belief and conduct. Second, writers of various kinds of stories who sought to entertain their readers with details of love, crime, and the passions found it prudent to justify such treatment of ordinary lives by interjecting exhortations to virtue and ending their fictions with its triumph. Some writers resorted to fiction to make moral preachment more acceptable, and others resorted to moral preachment to make fiction more acceptable. The preachments needed an attractive package, and the novel needed to be more than mere entertainment. Third, the novel found many readers among women and youth, two large groups thought by moralists to require guidance in a time of moral uncertainty.

Paul Hunter has explored the relationship between the early novel and Puritan thought and literature, especially in the prose works of Defoe. Puritan writers applied to historical biography the metaphors of the "spiritual warfare" between good and evil, the "journey" from earth to heaven, and the "wilderness" through which humankind must pass on the journey. To such "spiritual biographies" were slowly added fictional events to epitomize human experience, making allegories out of personal histories. Bunyan's *The Pilgrim's Progress* (1678) is such a fictional fusing of precept and example based on imaginary events. The next important step in overcoming the Puritan opposition to fiction and the acceptance of the novel came with Defoe's *Robinson Crusoe* which, according to Hunter, launched the modern novel while remaining close to Bunyan's fictional allegory. Benjamin Franklin, who had lived through this period of the early eighteenth century and commented on its literary trends while they were still fresh in his experience and memory, also compared Defoe and Richardson to Bunyan, at least in method.[13]

Among the seventeenth-century literary forms that influenced the structure of the novel, the conduct book or guide literature was one of the most important. The domestic conduct book, as it has also been called, offered guidance on attitudes and behavior chiefly concerning marriage, relations between husband and wife, and running a household, including raising the children, managing the help, and domestic economy. Many were directed to the problems of single women. To make such books more interesting, authors began to introduce dialogue and characterization, though these were subservient to the didactic purpose of the work and to the Biblical illustrations in it. Many English conduct books were written by women and presumably for them. As these books developed, they acquired heroes and heroines, incident and anecdote, and other elements of character and story such as were later combined to form the novel proper in the eighteenth century.[14] Some conduct books, reflecting the attitudes and interests of writers such as Mandeville and Fielding, pointed to human weakness and pettiness. The relation between the conduct book and the novel was illustrated by the novelistic aspects of Eliza Haywood's conduct book, *The Tea-Table* (1725), as well as by the guidance offered in a proper novel of nearly a century later, Jane Austen's *Pride and Prejudice* (1813).

The full title of Haywood's conduct book is *The Tea-Table: Or, a Conversation Between Some Polite Persons of Both Sexes, at a Lady's Visiting Day. Wherein are Represented the Various Foibles, and Affectations, Which Form the Character of an Accomplished* Beau *or Modern* Fine Lady. *Interspersed with Several Entertaining and Instructive Stories.* The author, noting in a preface that people are too ready to believe ill of others, assures her readers that her book does not refer to "any particular Persons, or Families." Her purpose is only to show the "foibles" that prevent otherwise good people from earning respect, in the hope of persuading the reader "to correct any of these Solecisms in Humor." The story concerns guests at a tea, but unlike most such domestic entertainments, which are given over to gossip, this one is more serious. One lady, Brilliante, reads a story she has written entitled "Beraldus and Celemena: Or, The Punishment of Mutability. A Novel," which is then discussed by the company. A gentleman, Philetus, points out the usefulness of such stories, which "cloath Instruction with Delight" and thus achieve their good effect almost without the readers' awareness that they are being edified. He is interrupted by the arrival of a lady wearing a "new Suit of Cloaths," and serious talk ends as the subject turns to dress. Several guests leave because they are not interested in the new subject, and the author endorses their attitude (1-3, 19-20, 46-51).

In *Pride and Prejudice,* Austen frequently includes advice on domestic affairs reminiscent of the conduct books of a much earlier time. Elizabeth is pleased that her sister Jane has enough "composure of temper" not to reveal to others that she is falling in love. Their friend Charlotte, like a character in a conduct book, warns against being too guarded: "If a women conceals her affection with the same skill from the object of it, she may lose the opportunity of fixing him . . . There is so much of gratitude or vanity in almost every attachment, that it is not safe to leave any to itself."

Among the early novelists, Samuel Richardson was probably closest in spirit to the writers of conduct books. He ran the gamut of the form, composing a book of letters in 1741 to guide young women, several didactic novels in the form of letters, and a collection of morals and maxims extracted from these novels. Richardson was one of the writers concerned about the decline of morality and religion. In a postscript to a later edition of *Clarissa* (1751) he asserts that he seeks to stem the tide of "general depravity." He has "lived to see scepticism and infidelity openly avowed . . . the great doctrines of the gospel brought into question: those of self-denial and mortification blotted out of the catalogue of Christian virtues" (IV, 553). His *Familiar Letters* (1741) to guide young women were published under the title: *Letters Written to and for Particular Friends, on the Most Important Occasions. Directing Not Only the Requisite Style and Forms To Be Observed in Writing Familiar Letters; But How To Think and Act Justly and Prudently, in the Common Concerns of Human Life.*[15] Even before completing the book, he had already begun *Pamela, or, Virtue Rewarded* (1740) in the same vein. Specific themes in the *Familiar Letters* were the bases for episodes in the novel. Letter 62 is entitled: "A young Woman in Town to her Sister in the Country, recounting her narrow Escape from a Snare laid for her, on her first Arrival, by a wicked Procuress." Letter 138 is called: "A Father to a Daughter in Service, on hearing of her Master's attempting her Virtue." The enduring connection between the didacticism of the conduct book and the novel is seen in Trollope's comment over a century later in his *Autobiography* about the moral value of novels: "A vast proportion of the teaching of the day comes from these books . . . It is from them that girls learn what is expected from them, and what they are to expect when lovers come; and also from them that young men unconsciously learn what are, or should be, or may be, the charms of love" (183-184). Although novelists have since been increasingly reluctant to offer explicit advice on conduct, their works still reveal what may be expected of various sorts of people in certain situations.

Low Status

As a new form of literature intended for a broader audience, including young women and men, describing the private lives of plain people rather than the public lives of the great, and offering counsel without hesitation, the novel did not quickly win the admiration of the guardians of literary taste and morality. These characteristics of the early novel, coupled with the prominence of women as authors, subjects, and readers, assured it a low intellectual and social position. Like sociology later in the nineteenth and twentieth centuries, fiction in the seventeenth and eighteenth centuries was on the defensive, seeking to prove its intellectual and social value. This was the case in France and England at the time that the novel was developed there. Later, when it was introduced into North America, the novel had to go through similar stages of opposition and defense. Edith Wharton recalled that as a child she was required to ask her mother's permission to read any novel, and it was usually not granted. Looking back decades later, she saw "little reason to regret" the prohibition, for it denied her "the opportunity of wasting my time over ephemeral rubbish" and "threw me back on the great classics." The introduction of the novel into Egypt only a half-century ago led to the same sequence of opposition and defense.[16]

Although the novel in France and England soon became a popular success, it took a century or so of development, down to perhaps the second quarter of the nineteenth century, for it to be accepted on its own ground by the critics and guardians of taste. Marguerite Iknayan, examining the literary position of the French novel from 1815 to 1848, has found that its success with the public was clear at the beginning of the period but that its reputation among critics was still low. Poor literary technique, insufficient attention to morality, the prominence of women as writers and readers, and concentration on the ordinariness of private lives instead of the nobility of public life were the reasons advanced by critics to justify their poor opinion of the novel. During this period, however, as Iknayan shows, the novel itself changed, and its reputation began to rise. The novel improved in quality more than other genres did; its purely quantitative place in the total literary output improved also, and important writers resorted to it more often and with less hesitation. To be sure, there were still attacks, such as that by the influential critic Nisard who, despite his praise of Sir Walter Scott, derided the novel as the chief offspring of the time's "double need to write quickly and to read quickly." But increasingly critics found the novel "an instrument for social betterment." The reliable history offered in Scott's novels was reassuring because it instructed. By 1839, the critic Chasles hailed the novel as the "maître" in all Europe, having wiped out epic poetry, absorbed philosophy, and dethroned the pamphlet. In 1862 a novelist, Octave Feuillet, was finally admitted to the French Academy for his work in this genre (64, 61, 72, 84).

In surveying the opposition to the English novel from 1760 to 1830, John Taylor has found a similar derogation of it and for about the same reasons as in France. Before the end of the eighteenth century, some critics already saw the novel's themes as banal, its day nearly over. Again it was Scott "who did most to establish the novel on a moral basis with the reviewers and with the public (97).[17] As late as 1833 an American publisher, in an advertisement for his own list of novels, admitted there was some "force and plausibility" to the argument that novels were "injurious, or at least useless," but insisted that this applied only to individual works rather than to the "species." The advertisement held that novels were "admitted to form an extensive and important portion of literature . . . and are appealed to as evidence in all questions concerning man." A generation later Trollope could still refer to people "who regard the reading of novels as a sin" or an "idle pastime" and novelists as panderers "to the wicked pleasures of a wicked world."[18]

With the best work of such fine writers as Fielding, Defoe, and Sterne being included in the attack upon the novel, the lesser examples of the new fiction were derogated all the more by the guardians of literary taste and public morals. Both contemporary and recent arguments have held that much of eighteenth century fiction was so poor as to deserve its reputation. Robert Mayo, analyzing the fiction published in English magazines, finds it was not of the high caliber assumed by critics of twentieth-century mass culture. This early magazine fiction, he insists, "exhibits in abundance those very qualities of daydream, poverty of feeling, and separation from life as known to its readers that are usually laid at the door of the modern novelist. . . The cleavage between popular and cultivated taste was serious, therefore, even in the middle years of the eighteenth century, and what we seem to witness in the succeeding 150 years is not the disintegration of a homogeneous literary culture, but the gradual extension, on its lower levels, of an amorphous one, among a large reading public which previously had no literary taste at all" (356-357). A contemporary view of such fiction, by Coleridge, resembles the critique of various kinds of recent escape literature and of television as well. Referring to the "devotees of the circulating libraries," Coleridge in *Biographia Literaria* asserts: "I dare not compliment their *pass-time,* or rather *kill-time,* with the name of *reading.* Call it rather a sort of beggarly day-dreaming," for which the reader "furnishes . . . nothing but laziness" and the writer supplies through print "the moving phantasms of one man's delirium, so as to people the barrenness of an hundred other brains afflicted with the same trance or suspension of all common sense and all definite purpose" (I, 34). Earlier, Samuel Johnson had already warned in *The Rambler* of Mar. 31, 1750, that novelists must be cautious because their "books are written chiefly to the young, the ignorant, and the idle, to whom they serve as lectures of conduct, and introductions into life." Johnson is apprehensive that the novel's necessary selection of events from real life familiar to its "easily susceptible" readers might include much more that could induce admiration of evil. This danger is more important to Johnson than are the technical and literary problems of the new genre.

In *Northanger Abbey* (1818) Jane Austen, writing around the same time as Coleridge, amused herself and her readers with extended comments on the novel, including its connections with women, indicating its low status and inferior quality. She begins ironically: Catherine Morland is entirely too normal, too plain, and too lacking in conventional talents to be a proper heroine. Her reading of the popular Gothic novels of the day, such as those by Ann Radcliffe, predispose her to expect such horrors in life. When the horrors do not appear, it is noted in a combined authorial commentary and rumination by Catherine that such novels exaggerate human nature and real life and that the people of the English Midland region are neither angelic nor fiendish.

Despite this criticism of one sort of novel, Austen vigorously defends the form itself. When in bk. 1, ch. 5 she has Catherine reading novels with a friend, Austen adds defiantly, "Yes, novels," and refuses to join novelists who derogate novels either by not permitting heroines to read them or by allowing them to do so with disgust. "Alas!" Austen continues, "If the heroine of one novel be not patronized by the heroine of another, from whom can she expect protection and regard?" She proposes that novelists should "leave it to the reviewers to abuse" their work. "Let us not desert one another," she pleads, "we are an injured body. Although our productions have afforded more extensive and unaffected pleasure than those of any other literary corporation in the world, no species of composition has been so much decried." Banality is eulogized, while novels, so often superior in revealing human nature, are read apologetically by young women who would proudly admit to reading the *Spectator*, although its fictional papers are far below the level of novels. Yet Austen herself derides novels for going on endlessly about unimportant matters. She describes the Thorpes in a few lines, confiding to the reader: "This brief account of the family is intended to supersede the necessity of a long and minute detail from Mrs. Thorpe herself, of her past adventures and sufferings, which might otherwise be expected to occupy the three or four following chapters." She is joking about the poor novels rather than about the fine ones she insists need defense. Nearly a century and a half later another novelist, Ellen Glasgow, was annoyed by novelists of her time who disparaged their art. "It would be astonishing," she writes in one of the prefaces collected in *A Certain Measure,* "if we had not grown used to the almost daily exhibition, to watch the agility with which modern novelists spring up to discredit the art they have attempted to practise."

Women and the Novel

The connection between the novel and women which began even before the eighteenth century has persisted to today; some of the specific issues raised then are still under discussion. In 1928 Virginia Woolf was asked to speak on women and fiction. The more she thought, the more involved the connections seemed and the outcome of her meditations was *A Room of One's Own* (1929). Its theme is that women, repressed through the ages, could not produce good literature or thought. To do so, they need intellectual and financial freedom: "money and a room of one's own," with a lock (186, 188). This by no means settles the matter for Woolf, who plainly states, "women and fiction remain, so far as I am concerned, unsolved problems" (4). One of these problems is the vast gap between the importance of woman in fiction and her unimportance in life: "She dominates the lives of kings and conquerors in fiction; in fact she was the slave of any boy whose parents forced a ring upon her finger" (74-75). This complaint was already made by Jane Austen. Woolf asks another question: "Why was one sex so prosperous and the other so poor? What effect has poverty on fiction? What conditions are necessary for the creation of works of art?" (42-43). Good as are the novels of Austen, the Brontés, and George Eliot, would they not have been better, Woolf asks, if their authors had had money (the exception being Eliot), a private place to write instead of the sitting room of the middle-class home, the freedom to move about in the world, and the independence to concentrate on their work instead of having to alter their values "in deference to the opinion of others"? Because these authors would meet criticism if they dared to think or write, their novels suffered a "flaw in the centre that had rotted them," namely the need of the authors to bend to the values of men (p. 129).

Almost seventy-five years earlier George Eliot herself, when beginning to write fiction, had criticized "Silly Novels by Lady Novelists" (1856). Concentrating on women's bad novels for their lack of acquaintance with any class below the landed, their superficial solutions to real problems, their fake piety and gentility, and their ignorance of history in historical novels, Eliot nevertheless points out that women can and have produced "the very finest" novels which "have a precious specialty, lying quite apart from masculine aptitudes and experience." She does not blame society for the bad novels, for fiction is among the freest of all the arts, but "it is precisely this absence of rigid requirement which constitutes the fatal seduction of novel-writing to incompetent women." Such novels are "very far below" the "ordinary intellectual level" of women but are likely to be praised because to some critics it is proof of superiority that a woman can write "*at all.*" Eliot inveighs against the tendency to overpraise the work of a woman with no talent while the woman of talent or even genius soon "receives the tribute of being moderately praised and severely criticized." Somewhat earlier, Madame de Staël had voiced a similar complaint about the strangeness of men's judgment of women writers and thinkers: "They tolerate degradation of feeling in women if it is accompanied by mediocrity of intellect, while they cannot forgive genuine superiority in a woman of the most perfect integrity."[19]

In *Northanger Abbey* Jane Austen treats the genre of the novel playfully and seriously in turn. On several occasions she refers to the novel in relation to men and women. In bk. 1, ch. 7, Austen's impressionable and modest heroine Catherine timidly asks an opinionated and disagreeable young man, John Thorpe, if he has read *Udolpho*. "Udolpho!" he answers haughtily, "Oh, Lord! Not I; I never read novels; I have something else to do." When Catherine suggests he might find it interesting, John replies that he would not read a novel except by Mrs. Radcliffe. Hesitantly, Catherine tells him, "*Udolpho* was written by Mrs. Radcliffe." This unfavorable and ignorant view of novels expressed by John, perhaps the least attractive character in Northanger Abbey, is in sharp contrast to the informed and favorable opinion in bk. 1, ch. 14, by Henry Tilney, the most attractive male character. Catherine mentions *Udolpho* to him, adding, "But you never read novels, I dare say?" He answers that he has read all of Mrs. Radcliffe's works: "The person, be it gentleman or lady, who has not pleasure in a good novel, must be intolerably stupid." Perhaps still thinking of John, Catherine remarks that she thought young men despised novels. Henry replies that it would be surprising if they did, "for they read nearly as many as women. I myself have read hundreds and hundreds." In bk. 1, ch. 3, at the very first meeting between Catherine and Henry, who fall in love and marry, he affects to be concerned that she will not write of him favorably in her journal. When she says she does not keep one, he professes disbelief that she does not indulge in "this delightful habit of journalizing which largely contributes to form the easy style of writing for which ladies are so generally celebrated." Catherine doubts that "the superiority was always on our side." More seriously, Henry admits, "In every power, of which taste is the foundation, excellence is pretty fairly divided between the sexes."

Austen reserves her strongest comment for an unusual authorial intrusion in ch. 3, rejecting Richardson's view expressed in *The Rambler* of February 19, 1751. He had warned that young women were becoming too aggressive in courting: "That a young lady should be in love, and the love of the young gentleman undeclared, is an heterodoxy which prudence, and even policy, must not allow." She treats this attitude with subtle contempt in describing the first meeting of her heroine and hero. Catherine likes Henry and thinks of him as she prepares for bed. The narrator cannot determine whether Catherine actually dreams of him but hopes not, for if the "celebrated writer," Richardson, is correct that a young lady must not declare her love first, then "it must be very improper that a young lady should dream of a gentleman before the gentleman is first known to have dreamt of her."

In *Sanditon,* a novel Austen began shortly before she died, she returned to Richardson on this subject. Again a young man and woman are discussing novels. He likes those that "exhibit the progress of strong Passion . . . where we see the strong spark of Woman's Captivations elicit such Fire in the Soul of Man as leads him . . . to hazard all, dare all, achieve all, to obtain her." The young woman remarks that her taste is different. Austen then explains that the young man "had read more sentimental Novels than agreed with him." In the works of Richardson and others his "fancy had been early caught by all the impassioned, and most exceptionable parts," which showed "Man's determined pursuit of Woman in defiance of every opposition of feeling and convenience" (106-108). This is the crux of Austen's objection to the notion that a woman must not fall in love until the man declares his love: he may pursue her even against her wishes, but she may not even acknowledge her feeling of love until he permits her by declaring his.

In *Northanger Abbey,* bk. 1, ch. 5, Austen deals further with male writers and editors, the novel, and women. She describes the progress of Catherine and Isabella's friendship to include the reading of novels together and then launches into a defense of the genre. Her examples of fine but undervalued novels are all by women, to which she contrasts the overpraised "abilities of the nine-hundredth abridger of the *History of England,* or of the man who collects and publishes in a volume some dozen lines of Milton, Pope, and Prior, with a paper from the *Spectator,* and a chapter from Sterne." In taking on the admired and influential *Spectator* (1711-1714) of Addison and Steele, Austen drops her usual critical style, often described as "gently ironic." She insists that, although young women are still, after three-quarters of a century, proud to admit to reading that periodical and are apologetic about reading the recent fine novels of Maria Edgeworth or Frances Burney, it is unlikely that a "young person of taste" would find anything in the *Spectator* that is not disgusting. This is because, Austen concludes, its fiction so often includes "improbable circumstances, unnatural characters, and topics of conversation which no longer concern anyone living; and their language, too, frequently so coarse as to give no very favorable idea of the age that could endure it." Austen clearly believed that by the end of the eighteenth century women had improved fiction technically and morally far beyond its state as represented in the male-dominated and still overpraised *Spectator.*

True to her disdain for even the best periodicals current in her lifetime, Austen never published in any of them. These periodicals, especially the ones by and for women, had great importance in the history of English fiction. Mayo, for example, asserts that though the evidence is not copious, a "revolution in taste" occurred between 1690 and 1740 which made novels and romances acceptable among classes of readers that had ignored or disapproved them. In this change, the periodicals "necessarily played only an accessory role," but insofar as the change "is reflected in the history of journalism, it seems to have been accomplished by the various periodicals for women." Moreover, women's magazines significantly influenced the journals that sought a "general acceptance" among both men and women throughout the eighteenth century.[20]

The low quality of fiction in these magazines and of the novels pubished separately kept the genre in low repute. The many women writers and readers, as well as the prevalence of themes of love, courtship, marriage, gentility, and moral uplift, all identified the novel with women, reinforcing the low intellectual status and the moral suspicion of both the entire genre and the entire sex. Taylor shows that in England, novels were decried along with the increasing education and freedom for women. The novel and women's freedom, both innovations of the eighteenth century, reinforced each other. Iknayan proves the same for eighteenth century France, where "the novel was best suited to those of underdeveloped mental powers, and it was chiefly to women that it was relegated, both for the writing and the reading" (52-53).

Ian Watt, in relating the novels of Defoe, Richardson, and Fielding—the beginnings of the modern novel—to changes in philosophical ideas and social institutions, has shown the relevance of women's status to many aspects of the novel. Courtly love was first transformed in England, where freedom of marriage choice for women also developed, although economic realities generally made marriage both more important and more difficult for women. The rise of literacy and leisure in the middle class, extending to women, produced a readership for newer genres, like the novel, which also sought to attract women readers by dealing with their interests in love, private rather than public affairs, and congenial values of the suburban mode of life. Watt thus enlarges upon, specifies, and relates ideas about the modern novel put forward by earlier writers. He goes back also to Madame de Staël, who related the novel to the status of women mainly in its themes, although she found the low repute of novelists to be justified insofar as they ignored all feelings except love.[21]

The identification of women, love, and marriage with the novel has endured to our own time, as Virginia Woolf's essay shows. More than a century after Defoe, Richardson, and Fielding, a novel by Trollope showed the power of these themes in a very different era. In *The Way We Live Now* (1875), which critics have regarded as concerned primarily with the impact of commerce on the gentry, the place of courtship is formidable.[22] No fewer than seven women are involved in affairs with more than that number of men, at various levels of the social scale, with varying degrees of success according to different criteria. Women are still not choosers, even though they express preferences boldly, unlike the restrictions binding them in Austen's novel earlier in the same century. Marriage being more important to women, they still run after partners within the limits of custom. Men continue to deceive women, break pledges, and are more insensitive when they pursue women than women are when they reject men; as a result, women are still the victims. George Eliot's authorial comment in *Middlemarch,* ch. 29, about Casaubon's satisfaction with Dorothea as his wife was still timely: "Society never made the preposterous demand that a man should think as much about his own qualifications for making a charming girl happy as he thinks of hers for making himself happy." Although Hardy expressed some modern ideas about courtship and marriage in *Jude the Obscure* (1895), a generation earlier in *Far from the Madding Crowd* (1874), ch. 20, he had summed up, in an authorial intrusion, the difference between the aims of men and women in these relations. Describing Bathsheba's lack of interest in marrying Boldwood despite his ardor and generosity, the author implies that in marriage women seek security while men seek sex: "It appears that ordinary men take wives because possession is not possible without marriage, and that ordinary women accept husbands because marriage is not possible without possession." A biological view is also expressed by T. S. Stribling in *Birthright* (1922). His mulatto hero has the notion that the superiority of the white race stems from the fact that its women earlier enjoyed an increase in their "power of choice" in marriage. "So deeply ingrained" is this principle, the narrator adds, "that almost every novel written by white men re-volves about some woman's choice of her mate being thwarted by power or pride or wealth, but in every instance the rightness of the woman's choice is finally justified" (277). Interesting as these ideas may be in respect to the novel, it would be difficult to demonstrate any of them. Love themes continue in the novel, as do questions about it. In the 1920s E. M. Forster observed in *Aspects of the Novel,* "If you think of a novel in the vague you think of a love interest," but he made no serious effort to indicate why (85).

Joyce M. Horner in the late 1920s, studying the connection between women novelists and the feminist movement in the eighteenth century, argued that women have a special talent or position that fits them particularly for writing novels. Women have a peculiar ability to observe themselves clearly and to stick to the real and the probable even while daydreaming. They are incapable, concomitantly, of transcending their own motives and of imagining things beyond reality. They therefore have become novelists rather than the "seers of visions and dreamers of dreams" (143). According to Woolf in *A Room of One's Own,* the special quality of women's literature comes from the fact that a woman had to write in the "common sitting-room," where her "sensibility" was refined as she observed "personal relations," character, and emotion. But the constant interruptions also made it easier to write prose and fiction, which require less concentration than poetry and drama (115-116). Excluded from many domains of life, regarded as inferior intellectually and inconsequential with respect to most values and activities, women had to pay attention to these limitations and criticisms. They were thus moved to respond "with docility and diffidence, or with anger and emphasis," and in either case were diverted from the artistic task itself (129). Long before either of these two comments were made, Elizabeth Hamilton, novelist and philosophical writer, remarked in 1808 that women were not so active in society as men were and could therefore better observe the detail and variety of life. Knowing the home, they gained better insight into "the mind and disposition" of people. Madame de Staël held that women have more sensibility, morality, and refinement than men. Where they were not recognized for these qualities, civilization — and literature particularly — was inferior and coarse. She found that the high regard for women in England led to those domestic virtues, happiness, and refinement which made both men and women in that country able to produce good novels: "The life of women is the main reason for the inexhaustible productivity of English writers in this *genre*."[23]

The identification of women with art has persisted. William Dean Howells cautioned "the man of letters" that he "must make up his mind that in the United States the fate of a book is in the hands of the women . . . They are far better educated, for the most part, than our men, and their tastes, if not their minds, are more cultivated" (21). The philosopher Morris R. Cohen made the same observation in *American Thought*, but found that this "monopoly" of women had "conventionalized most forms of contemporary American culture." Women like to be in fashion, prefer to see life portrayed sweetly, and "have little opportunity to cultivate the disinterestedness and objectivity that are necessary for genuine critical appreciation" (31).

The Middle Class, Individualism, and Privacy

The connection between women and the novel raises issues of love and other relations between the sexes, domesticity and privacy, individualism, and their connection with the middle class. Woolf's notion of "a room of one's own" raises the economic issue of women's status. Her explanation for the high number of women novelists is that middle-class women in the eighteenth century were literate and intellectually active, observed manners and emotions in the home, needed a genre relatively impervious to the interruptions in their domestic setting, and found that writing could bring money. Woolf goes so far as to suggest that this phenomenon of the middle-class woman writer was more important in history than the Crusades.

The relation between the novel and middle-class values or the middle class itself has long occupied literary and social historians but has still not received a definitive treatment. It can mean that the writers of novels, as Woolf suggests, were themselves in the middle class. Or it can mean that readers of novels were in the middle class. It can mean that the characters portrayed in the novel were of the middle class. Or it can mean that the novel served the middle class by promoting its attitudes, values, and material interests.

The novel's relation to individualism and privacy, themselves connected, is fairly clear. At some time in the eighteenth century or earlier, individualism and privacy were values of the bourgeoisie, a class that had begun to emerge in Europe as early as the thirteenth or fourteenth century, which lived in towns and cities, engaged in commerce and manufacture, and sought freedom from certain economic and political restrictions of an earlier socioeconomic system. The bourgeoisie came to be known as the middle class, but they became the ruling class in the sense that they exerted more economic and political influence than any other class. Meanwhile, the broad values they espoused became known as human values rather than merely as bourgeois values or interests. By the eighteenth century, and certainly by our own time, it made no sense to attribute everything that had happened since the thirteenth or fourteenth century to the triumph of the values of the middle class, which had surely not stood still for over five hundred years.

Individualism and privacy were values or attributes that spread to increasing numbers of people in England and France, to other parts of Europe, and to some of their overseas colonies in the seventeenth and eighteenth centuries. To the extent that individualism and privacy became valued, significant, and socially acceptable outside the small ruling groups and the sections of society they regarded almost as equals, these two interrelated values extended to people who constituted the middle class. The middle class occupied a large, sometimes unclear, and changing area between the poorest, least powerful people and the richest, most powerful ones. Individualism meant that each person, no matter how low in the social scale, was worthy of self-development, capable of assuming responsibility for his or her own actions, and equally free —up to varying points depending on the philosophical position advocated—from the traditional restraints imposed by collectivities such as the state and family. Although religion was one of these traditional restraints, a new religious doctrine, Protestantism in its several forms, likewise encouraged individualism. The novel of the eighteenth century showed the influence of this powerful idea as much from a religious and moral standpoint as from an economic one — perhaps even more.[24] It showed — in language, story, character, and setting — that the lives of ordinary people were worthy of recording with fidelity to the realities of those lives, even if particular incidents were often selected because they were unusual and hence likely to be more interesting. Many writers of the time remarked on this new kind of fiction-writing. Samuel Johnson in 1750 called novels "familiar histories" in which, for example, anyone might read of an "adventurer" who is "levelled with the rest of the world" (144). In 1795 Madame de Staël described the action of novels like those of Richardson and Fielding: "These events are invented, but the sentiments are so natural that the reader often thinks that it is he himself he is reading about under another name." In a review of Jane Austen's *Emma,* Sir Walter Scott in 1815 pointed to a "style of novel" that had arisen in the last twenty years which avoided the "wild variety of incident" and "romantic affection." The "substitute for these excitements," he continues, is "the art of copying nature as she really exists in the common walks of life, and presenting to the reader, instead of the splendid scenes of an imaginary world, a correct and striking representation of that which is daily taking place around him."[25]

Madame de Staël also connected individualism with privacy. Claiming that readers are interested less in plot than in the feelings of the characters, she asserts, "this disposition results from the great intellectual changes that have taken place in man; he tends more and more, in general, to fall back upon himself, seeking religion, love, and thought in the deepest recess of his being." These impulses and the customs of domestic life are portrayed in English and German novels. To show the place of privacy in eighteenth century life, Madame de Staël elaborates a distinction between ancient and modern liberty. Liberty in ancient Greece and Rome, which were small communities, revolved around the actions of the state and the citizens' share in this public power. Liberty in modern republics, which are much larger in population, means the "respect for private life and private wealth . . . everything that protects citizens' independence of the government." With the improved organization of social affairs in modern times, the individual no longer needs so much the "common power" of government. "Since private life easily provides many pleasures, the government is no longer called upon to serve people's personal concerns." She sees possible disadvantages in this change, such as that the modern state cannot depend on patriotism in the way that the ancient state could, nor can it depend on popular interest in public affairs when privacy is valued so highly. "This possibility of existing apart from public affairs is for most men . . . a great blessing. This calm, unknown to the ancients, is an advantage of large associations of men and offers an added opportunity for happiness to the variety of human natures." To put her points in today's terms, the growth in population, the division of labor, the establishment of representative institutions, the rise of individualism, and the spread of personal wealth have made privacy possible and attractive for people at all levels of society, even for those who can contend for governmental power. This satisfaction with private, domestic interests Madame de Staël saw in the France and England of her time. In England, particularly, according to her, domestic virtues, the family, love between men and women, and the elevated status of women were the impulses to and the ingredients of the novel. "It is the English, in short," she concludes, "who have transformed novels into works of morality in which obscure virtues and destinies can find grounds for exaltation and create a kind of heroism for themselves."[26]

The novel's setting in privacy and domesticity supported the individualistic notion in the eighteenth century that there was a liberty beyond political liberty, a capacity for development and for responsibility in all human beings, and a right of all persons to improve themselves, guided by religious works and their secular successors, the conduct books. Such tendencies in fiction gave the novel a low reputation in critical circles. Iknayan points out, concerning the novel in France even in the early nineteenth century, that "the very subject matter of the novel put it in a low position:

how could a genre which treated of private life be as noble and elevated as those which dealt with public life?" (56). Philosophic thought paralleled, if it did not influence, the novel. The social contract theorists and writers on political economy, from Locke to Adam Smith, sought to build a theory of human affairs upon a basis that stressed voluntary and private action, self-interest, and the conception that public issues are not mysterious entities beyond human control but the sum of the concerns of individuals who make themselves count in the world of affairs. In the middle of the nineteenth century this notion was still echoing, as in Trollope's authorial intrusion in *The Warden* (1855) ch. 15: "What is any public question but a conglomeration of private interests?" A century earlier, in the midst of the novel's change in this direction, Fielding had already made the point about public and private lives. In the introductory chapter to book 8 of *Tom Jones* he observes that if the "historian," as he calls the novelist, sticks to real people and events, he may sometimes "surprise" the reader with "marvellous" events but not tax his credulity by including the "incredible." When the historian or novelist resorts to inventing fictions, however, he may include "incredible" events. Here Fielding distinguishes between the historian of "public transactions" and the historian, like himself, of "scenes of private life — a phrase Balzac also used as a title in *La Comédie Humaine*. The historian of public transactions has records and testimony to corroborate the events he relates, but the historian of private life has no such evidence to adduce concerning the people and events in his "history" and must therefore "keep within the limits not only of possibility, but of probability too"; else he will not be believed.

In recent years literary and social historians, seeking to widen both disciplines, have assumed rather than shown the connections between art and society, uncritically turning into a cliché the notion that art reflects social influences. This has been the fate of the idea that the novel is a middle-class form. Although the novel's connection with realism, individualism, and privacy suggests that it may have some connection with the middle class, the precise connection has yet to be demonstrated. Diana Spearman, in fact, rejects the claim that the eighteenth century novel was a new form and that it somehow derived from social life. Arguing that the English novel existed before the middle class, she shows the continuity in literary form. By calling into question the degree to which the middle class had triumphed during the rise of the novel, she casts doubt on whether Defoe, Richardson, and Fielding actually portrayed the middle class or expressed its values. Her position is that whatever influence social institutions exerted on the novel, other influences were stronger, such as the accident of the appearance of great writers and the capacity of the literature of one era to shape that of the next. In short, what Spearman calls the "theory of the middle-class novel" proves unsubstantiated.[27]

Other social and literary historians have questioned the assumptions linking the middle class to the novel. Alfred Cobban, for example, disagrees with the widely held view that the bourgeoisie triumphed over the aristocracy and ended feudalism in the course of the eighteenth century. He shows that the bourgeoisie was far from homogeneous, that the "middle class" is an unsatisfactory term for differing groups acting across several centuries, and that feudalism was not abolished in the eighteenth century. As for the middle-class novel, Mayo shows that the novel was criticized even in eighteenth-century English magazines which regularly published fiction and presumably also expressed middle-class tastes and values. Warning against oversimplification, he concludes that "prose fiction was clearly viewed with suspicion by important segments of the bourgeois reading audience." Frederick Karl also sees the English novel as critical of the "predominant culture" at the same time that it "seemed to bow to the tastes and needs of the new bourgeoisie." Warren Roberts comes to the conclusion that the eighteenth-century French "moralistic" novel was created by the "aristocracy."[28]

"Middle class" has become a moral concept. Institutions have changed, but the term has remained constant in an almost exclusively pejorative sense, meaning attitudes, in whomever found, such as smugness and self-satisfaction, or moral rectitude with hypocrisy. Not being rulers, the middle class are not feared; not being poor, they do not deserve sympathy. The middle class is thus used to represent what anyone who discusses art happens to dislike. In *For a New Novel* the novelist Robbe-Grillet relates "narrative" in fiction to an "order" which is "linked to an entire rational-istic and organizing system, whose flowering corresponds to the assumption of power by the middle class" (32). Such nonsense reflects a bias: Robbe-Grillet does not like narrative or the middle class, so he links them.

If the novel and the middle class are to be connected, the terms must be clarified and the social and literary history must be ana-lyzed. In seeking the origins of the novel in its eighteenth century form, greater account must also be taken of influences other than social class—influences that may be no less "social" than class. One approach is that taken by Scott in 1815, on the basis of his own experience as a novelist and critic. In his review of Austen's *Emma* he attributes the changes wrought in fiction to literary hab-its and tastes. Before 1800 or so, he observes, the novel was ex-pected to "tread pretty much in the limits between the concentric circles of probability and possibility." Not allowed to go beyond possibility, the writer usually went beyond probability. He satis-fied the readers' curiosity about "new, striking and wonderful" events outside their ken and their desire to read about virtue and elevated sentiments even if they could not themselves reach such heights. These two sources of interest and emotion were used so frequently by writers that readers tired of them. The material available for novels, Scott continues, became "stale and familiar." Accordingly, writers sought new sources of interest; they avoided the exhausted "splendid scenes of an imaginary world" and of-fered the reader instead "a correct and striking representation of that which is daily taking place around him." Dealing with people and events within the ken of readers, novelists now had to do more than merely describe what everyone knew. No longer able to use exaggerated incidents and pure sentiments, novelists had to sub-stitute "depth of knowledge and dexterity of execution" in pre-senting events and characters familiar to readers. In this way, according to Scott, the novel changed. Scott resorts not to pro-found notions of class but to familiar matters of public taste and the author's needs, to issues of literary influence and technique. The easy connection of the novel and the middle class thus be-comes far less convincing.

Human Association and Culture in the Novel

I describe not men, but manners; not an
individual, but a species.
— Henry Fielding, *Joseph Andrews*

3.

The vast and diverse fictional treatment of social institutions and human behavior can be divided into two main groups: the expression of broad social themes through character and event, or specific authorial commentary on social issues. The first group of novels explores such themes as the basis or origin of human association, the contrast of cultures, political power in its widest sense, and social classes. Although several more themes could be added, these suffice to illustrate the capacity of the novel. Certain novels could easily be included in more than one category; indeed, compressing them into one category makes them seem narrower than they really are. Silone's *Bread and Wine* is a political novel, though it plainly reaches beyond a broad definition of politics and deals with the erosion of man's relation to man in authoritarian systems and also treats the Italian peasantry in a way similar to Balzac's study of the French peasantry a century earlier. Such limitations to any classification should lead to caution in their application without deterring the effort to establish useful categories.

The Basis of Human Association

One of the most enduring fictional devices is the imaginary voyage to a strange island. Novelists using this device differ in their intentions, as do critics in their interpretations. The voyage novel has been viewed traditionally as a travel or adventure story and as a religious allegory. Another way of looking at these novels is as "experiments" in Zola's sense, designed to place men in their pristine condition in order to see what "original" human nature is like and how men come together to create a society. In this sense the voyage novel is like the eighteenth-century social philosopher's concept of the "state of nature"; indeed, the two devices play the same role in these different genres.

Defoe's *Robinson Crusoe* is the most famous and most interpreted example of voyage fiction. Recently the French writer Michel Tournier has rewritten the Crusoe story from a different point of view. A comparison of these two versions shows not only how each uses the novel to illuminate the origins of human association, but also how the two authors, separated by two and a half centuries, differ in their treatment of the original condition of man. Two other novels on a similar theme, a shipwreck that lands a group of youths on an island, treat it in quite different ways, *The Coral Island* (1858) by Robert Ballantyne and a century later *Lord of the Flies* by William Golding.

Defoe's Robinson Crusoe has two paramount feelings or impulses as he contemplates his isolation from all human society and from virtually everything that society has created: fear and a zeal to improve his position. His fear is translated into precautions against possible attack and a longing for human companionship, as when, on learning from Friday that there are seventeen white prisoners on the land he has come from, Crusoe immediately begins building a boat to enable him to join them and then to escape. Crusoe's zeal for increasing his comfort by applying his ingenuity and labor to the available resources is subject to various economic analyses, as shown by Maximillian Novak, who insists that Defoe's works, including *Robinson Crusoe,* embody not capitalist free enterprise and individualism but older ideas of mercantilism. There is no ambiguity, however, about Crusoe's social ideals, for even as he gets his bearings on the island, he begins to think and act like a Western and Christian man. His attitudes and needs impel him to recreate Western technology as he knew it with the means at hand, that is, the land as well as the tools and equipment he is able to salvage from the wreck. With the arrival of Friday, he recreates Western society in miniature — its economy and government, its religious and ethical values. What Western man had available in society, Crusoe now makes available to himself in isolation, recapitulating on the island the development of technological and social forms from the ancient Near East to the Western world of his time.

Both to Crusoe and to his creator, Defoe, the state of nature is not acceptable but must be improved. The reason is that even in the state of nature man already has needs and desires, which he soon, in the seventeenth century conception that shaped Defoe's thought, bends to fit his ideas about the world as expressed in religious myths and obligations. G. A. Starr and Paul Hunter have shown that *Robinson Crusoe* is related to the Puritan "spiritual autobiography" and "providence literature" of the seventeenth century. Without derogating *Robinson Crusoe* as a travel story of special economic meaning, Hunter shows that it "is structured on the basis of a familiar Christian pattern of disobedience — punishment — repentance — deliverance" (19) and that it is a guide or conduct book, seeking to persuade readers to moral and virtuous behavior, a form that was one of the foundations of the novel itself. The state of nature was thus not a condition to be desired but a device and a test. It was a device for the novelist, to enable him to express his views of man and society by setting up a test for his characters, an extreme situation, which would show how deep is man's religious faith and how effective his ingenuity.

Robinson Crusoe is a Zolaesque experiment or test designed to reveal original human nature. This kind of test is vitiated, however, because Crusoe brings to the island a fully equipped spiritual and intellectual heritage and the remnants of a technological one. Although the island is in a state of nature, so to speak, Crusoe himself is not. The experiment therefore tests not man's original nature but the capacity of Western man to survive in an extreme situation. Crusoe's success and his obvious superiority, in Western terms, over the native "savages" and Friday testify to the potency of the social order from which he comes. Defoe vividly displays the differences among men and societies: Crusoe in a state of "civiliza-tion," Friday more truly in a state of "nature." Yet these exem-plars of contrasting social orders have a stock of attitudes and sym-bols in common, upon which Defoe draws in order to bring them together to carry out their varying roles.

Defoe must presume such a common stock if he is ever to bring off the experiment at all. Crusoe, after twenty-five years alone, realizes that he needs help to escape the island and resolves to "get a Savage into my Possession" (I, 231). When several savages finally appear, he tries to save one who is being pursued by others. In the course of this combination of selfishness and humanity — "I was call'd plainly by Providence to save this poor Creature's Life" — Crusoe is able to communicate with the savages. Crusoe places himself between Friday and his pursuers and calls to him. Friday looks back, appearing to Crusoe to be "as much frighted" at him as at the pursuers. Crusoe "beckon'd with my hand to him, to come back" (I, 235) after Crusoe shoots one of the pursuers dead. Friday does not move, appearing to Crusoe to be too afraid: "I hollow'd again to him, and made Signs to come forward, which he easily understood . . . [I] gave him all the Signs of Encouragement that I could think of, and he came nearer and nearer, kneeling down every Ten or Twelve steps in token of acknowledgment for my saving his Life: I smil'd at him and look'd pleasantly, and beckon'd to him to come still nearer; at length he came close to me, and then he kneel'd down again, kiss'd the Ground . . . and taking me by the Foot, set my Foot upon his Head; this it seems was in token of swearing to be my Slave forever" (I, 236).

How can two such different creatures understand each other's tones of voice and gestures? How does Crusoe know the way that savages display fright? How is it that Friday understands Crusoe's beckoning with his hand? How does Friday agree with Crusoe as to what are "Signs of Encouragement," or what gesture is a "token of acknowledgment" and what ritual a "token" of subservience? This concord of symbols and meanings reveals a common ground of unexplored communication despite the considerable differ-ences between Crusoe and Friday. Defoe's story shows in the end that the test or experiment to discover original human nature unaffected by society cannot be carried out because man cannot be imagined in a state of nature with absolutely no stock of ideas and understandings drawn from some kind of human association, however limited. The device of the state of nature is usable as an hypothesis in social or political thought, which may abstract for various purposes. The novel, however, cannot abstract in this way; it must touch the concrete, the specific, the particular, even if they are invested with symbolic meaning of a broad kind. The state of nature simply cannot be described. The novelist must portray distinctive characters and events, while the state of nature is a social void that offers none. Though such an abstract concept may be useful in social science, it cannot serve the novel.

There are many differences between Defoe's Crusoe of 1719 and the Crusoe of 1967 in Michel Tournier's version of the story, *Friday, or the Other Island,* though both tales are set in the latter half of the eighteenth century. In Defoe, Crusoe is the quintessence of rational man, and such elements of nonrationalism as he exhibits are related to a belief in God and religious obligations and are themselves tied to reason. In Tournier, Crusoe is at first the same sort of rational man and a Quaker. The key to their differences is in the relation of each to Friday. In Defoe, the savage is inferior to Crusoe in all respects, and both know it and act upon this basis. In Tournier, the relationship starts out in the same way, but gradually Crusoe comes to see Friday as possessing a greater natural wisdom and a beauty worth emulation and admiration. The later Crusoe turns away from formal Christianity, Western technology, the spirit of enterprise, and the desire to control nature, moving toward a religion of man in which he himself is a kind of creator, toward a sexual and spiritual union with the island itself (whereas there is no sex to speak of in Defoe's story), and an appreciation of nature and brotherhood. Crusoe, in Tournier, remains the superior in respect of sheer power but in little else. In short, Defoe's Crusoe is a product of eighteenth-century Western optimism and self-confidence as Europe expanded geographically and intellectually and saw the triumph of its ideas of order, precision, and work. Tournier's Crusoe, though he lives in the eighteenth century, is a product of twentieth-century Western pessimism and doubt concerning its inherited values; he reaches out for a different relationship with nature and men. In this sense, the two novels deal not only with the basis or origin of human association but also with the contrast of cultures or races.

Defoe enables Crusoe to fit Friday into his own scheme of things, but Tournier's Crusoe does not find it so easy. Because the earlier Crusoe had no doubts on the point, he did not have to make resolutions; the later one writes in his journal: "I must fit my slave into the system which I have perfected over the years" (138-139). He takes steps to do so, as his predecessor did, and concludes that the slave's submission is actually "too complete," except for his devilish "bursts of demonic laughter" (144-145). When Tournier's Crusoe goes to another part of the island, his absence makes Friday think himself "his own master and master of the island" (149). He chooses to wander off too, which makes Crusoe "recognize that beneath the show of submissiveness, Friday possessed a mind of his own, and that what came out of it was profoundly shocking and subversive of discipline on the island" (154). The old order is upset; Crusoe sees not only that he has failed to fit Friday into the system but that the slave is an "alien presence" who threatens to destroy it (156). This is exactly what Friday inadvertently does when he throws burning tobacco into Crusoe's cave, his storehouse of food and ammunition, the source and symbol of his dominion. In the ruin, Crusoe realizes that "the cultivated island had begun to oppress him almost as much as it had Friday." He really hoped for this release and for Friday to "show him the way to . . . a new order which Robinson longed to discover." Crusoe becomes a "wanderer, foot-loose and timorous," bound in his companionship to Friday, in whose disdain for work and exclusive concern for the present he sees an "underlying wholeness, an implicit principle" (180-182).

By reversing Defoe's Crusoe-Friday relation, Tournier attaches a different significance to the state of civilization, the state of nature, and the nature of man. Writing centuries after Defoe and aiming to point a different moral, Tournier is more aware of historical stages and invests Crusoe's actions with deeper meaning. He hovers over Crusoe, observing his moods and movements, reporting and interpreting them to the reader. Defoe, writing in the first person as Crusoe himself, takes a more casual stance between his main character and the reader. Defoe's Crusoe is not solemn about killing a goat who is feeding a kid, except to say that it "griev'd me heartily" (I, 70); his grief does not deter him from killing and eating the kid itself when he finds he cannot domesticate it. When Tournier's Crusoe, in a fit of fatigue, fear, and anger, cudgels a goat to death, the author steps back and gravely marks the event: "It was the first living creature Robinson had encountered on the island, and he had killed it" (19). Similarly with Crusoe's start on his journal, Defoe has him turn to it calmly after arranging his goods and building a table and chair, while Tournier's Crusoe "nearly wept with delight when he traced his first words on paper. In performing the sacred act of writing it seemed to him that he had half-retrieved himself from the abyss of animalism into which he had sunk, and returned to the world of the spirit" (46). Tournier's stages occasionally take an anthropological turn, as when Crusoe learns to milk his goats: "Like mankind at the dawn of history, he had passed through the stage of hunting and gathering into that of tilling and stock raising" (49).

Solitude is an affliction to both Crusoes, but with a difference. In Defoe solitude causes a desire for company for its own sake and for the pragmatic purpose of aiding escape. In Tournier solitude is so devastating that it leads Crusoe to doubt the usefulness of his labor and drives him to sexual union with the earth itself. The earlier Crusoe finds companionship in God, the later one in nature.

Though he craves company, Defoe's Crusoe also fears other human beings. His craving is often expressed in a desire for mere conversation, so that it is sometimes easy for him to speculate that thinking to himself and speaking to God in prayer might be "better than the utmost enjoyment of humane society in the world" (I, 157). Tournier's Crusoe, however, longs so much for companionship that he fears neither man nor animal nor plant; "he must," as the author puts it, "consummate his marriage with solitude, his implacable bride" (44). Unlike Defoe's Crusoe, Tournier's finds companionship in the very island itself, whose shape appears to him to resemble a woman's in an attitude of "submission, fear,

and simple abandonment" (48). Ultimately he has sexual intercourse with a tree, and then with the earth, which gives birth to a
new plant from his seed. Meanwhile, he becomes less and less satisfied with his improvement of the island. As he finishes a major
task, he wonders whom it is all for, who will respond to the new
achievement. He senses another kind of person growing within
him who will not need work, order, discipline, and achievement —
and then comes his union with plant life and the beginning of the
new humanism he learns from Friday.

To Defoe's Crusoe, religion and God are Western and Christian: he thinks of God, reads the Bible, repents, and prays. But he
can also take a rational attitude toward ordinary events. Unable to
explain the growth of some grain, Crusoe regards it as a miracu-
lous work of God. When he then learns how the seed found its way
to such a place, he confesses that "my religious thankfulness to
God's Providence began to abate" (I, 90). While there is much
religion, there is little sex in Defoe. As Crusoe remarks, on the
island he is away from "all the Wickedness of the world" and has
no "Lust of the Flesh" (I, 148). In Tournier, religion is mixed with
sexual desire and nature. Crusoe sees in the "offspring" of his
union with the earth the realization of a promise in the Song of
Songs. As a result of this sexual union strengthened by the Biblical
blessing, the earth becomes more human and Crusoe more a part
of nature, until upon waking one morning, he discovers that his
beard "had begun to take root in the earth" (130). Though Defoe's
Crusoe feels his dominion over the island, he never has the idea
that he is the Creator or in any way resembles Him. Tournier's
Crusoe, on the contrary, is a kind of Creator himself; he is not so
easily distinguished from God and the earth, which he marries. In
a sense, he lives the Bible, in that Tournier regularly shows analogies between events in his life on the island and events in the Bible.

In Defoe, Crusoe is Western man exploiting the land and con-
quering it, while in Tournier he yearns for and achieves unity with
it. This difference extends to both Crusoes' relation to Friday.
Defoe's Crusoe begins as the superior and never changes. Tournier's Crusoe begins in the same way but soon seeks with Friday a
unity not unlike that which he achieves with the earth. There is an

irony in the relation between the two in Tournier. In Defoe, the
relation is simple: Crusoe is dominant and it never occurs to either
one that they might approach equality. In Tournier, however,
Crusoe comes to appreciate Friday's superiority in his organic relation to animals and land and seeks to emulate him and adopt his
ways. Approaching equality with Friday, Crusoe is therefore capable of jealousy. He is enraged to come upon Friday having intercourse with the earth in Crusoe's own sacred spot. Because his
earth is "sullied, outraged by a Negro," Crusoe beats Friday "with
all his white man's weight and strength." Friday pleads for his life,
and Crusoe leaves off beating him, suddenly realizing that he has
been enacting "the first murder in recorded history, the murder of
all murders." "Who was he, then? Was he the avenging arm of
Jehovah, or was he marked by the curse of Cain?" (167). Through
Biblical analogies, Crusoe comes to forgive Friday.

There is a final irony in Crusoe's relation to Friday which reveals the different meanings extracted by Defoe and Tournier
from the ending of the state of nature as civilization comes to the
island in the form of a European ship and sailors. Defoe has Crusoe return happily to England with his servant-companion Friday,
who is killed on one of their later travels. Tournier has Crusoe
decide to pass up the chance to return to the state of civilization
and the world of "usury, dust, and decay" in favor of remaining
on the island with Friday in the "eternal present" (226). When the
ship sails away, Crusoe is shocked to find Friday nowhere on the
island: he has departed with the British seamen. Desperate and
fearful, Crusoe comes upon the boy who was the ship's cook on the
departed vessel. The young, blond Christian boy has elected to
join Crusoe, who names him Sunday. Now they are eternal company for each other. Thus Tournier suggests that the roles are
reversed: the black savage in tune with nature chooses civilization,
while the European man is joined by a Finnish boy in the state of
nature, as another phase of the great cycle seems to begin.

Allegorical and realistic voyages in fiction, with various purposes and lessons, have long fascinated authors and readers alike.
In the twelfth century a Spanish Arab philosopher, Ibn Tufayl,
developed a similar theme of the solitary inhabitant of an island

who builds a perfect philosophical and religious system, in contrast to the mixture of weakness and evil he finds on a visit to a settled island, which he then quits for the lonely purity of his own place. Shakespeare's *The Tempest* is an enduring example of the device of placing a superior European on an island which he commands and to which others from civilization come with good and bad intentions.[1] The Crusoe story is a special variant whose appeal continues in modern times, as Tournier's version attests. *The Swiss Family Robinson* (1813), written mainly by Johann Rudolf Wyss, has been very popular. Muriel Spark's variant, *Robinson* (1958), tells of two men and a woman who survive an airplane crash on an island in the North Atlantic. Robinson, a recluse who lives there with a Portuguese boy, helps them and then disappears amid signs that he has been murdered. The three voyagers quarrel, thinking each other the murderer. Robinson reappears, and the three return to England on the boat that regularly puts in at the island. The contrast is made between Robinson's peaceful, lonely existence and the suspicious quarreling among the involuntary intruders. They bring only trouble and do nothing constructive during their months on Robinson's island.

The voyage-shipwreck novel has used not only the solitary surviver, to whom the main challenge is loneliness or the need for technological ingenuity, as in Defoe and Tournier, but also the group of survivers, to whom the main challenge is to find a satisfactory mode of association. Robert Ballantyne's *The Coral Island* is an optimistic resolution of this problem, whereas William Golding's *Lord of the Flies,* based in part on *The Coral Island,* is a pessimistic one. Here, as in the Defoe-Tournier pair, the optimistic work is the older, the pessimistic one the newer.

The Coral Island purports to be nothing more than an adventure story with a wholesome, uplifting moral. Three English youths are shipwrecked on an island in the South Seas. They live harmoniously in this idyllic setting for several months. British pirates land and take one of the boys away with them, and together they have extraordinary adventures, some involving natives and Christian missionaries. The boy eventually makes his way back to Coral Island, and all three leave it regretfully to return home.

The youths are the narrator, Jack Martin, aged eighteen, Ralph Rover, fifteen, and Peterkin Gay, fourteen. From the moment they land on the beach, they feel saved rather than lost. They look forward to a life of ease, but Jack, their leader, warns them not to daydream, for "we are wasting our time in *talking* instead of *doing*" (15). They build and work hard, enjoy sport and leisure, and cooperate perfectly; there is abundance and no fear. "I am certain," Jack says, "that none of us wished to be delivered from our captivity, for we were extremely happy" (139). From this idyllic existence it is difficult, if not presumptuous, to extract profound lessons. The boys, Jack says, love each other so much that they never disagree. Religion and work are extolled. Missionaries are portrayed as civilizing the natives, who respond eagerly to Christian teachings. Savagery is shown to be characteristic both of the first natives they see, who beat each other cruelly and even eat one another, and of the first civilized people they see, British trader-pirates from whom they hide.

Only rarely does an incident cause unease. Jack and Ralph come upon twenty pigs asleep under a fruit tree. Jack suggests they kill one or two, but Ralph says they ought to wake them first. Jack disagrees: "If I wanted *sport,* Ralph, I would certainly set them up; but as we only want *pork,* we'll let them lie" (72). The same utilitarian attitude is expressed in a later episode that causes a slight disagreement. Peterkin spears an old sow. The others ask why he did it, to which he replies he merely wanted the skin for a pair of shoes. This ends the matter; all three carry off the sow with no qualms, and later Peterkin makes the shoes.

The treatment of such incidents marks the vast difference in method and probably intent between Ballantyne and Golding, who in *Lord of the Flies,* ch. 8, invests the same event, the killing of a sow, with more pointed meaning for both his characters and his readers. In the first place, the boys plan to serve up part of the pig to placate the "beast," the imaginary animal many of them fear. Golding describes the bloated sensuous pigs, the lean boy hunters, the spears aimed at the sow, her wild rushing about bleeding from the wounds of two spears, and the boys chasing her, "wedded to her in lust, excited by the long chase and the dropped blood." The hunters catch up with the weakened sow in an open place and surround her, each stabbing at her while "she squealed and bucked and the air was full of sweat and noise and blood and terror." Jack spears her throat. "The sow collapsed under them and they were heavy and fulfilled upon her." Jack orders a stick sharpened at both ends; to one end he attaches the sow's severed head, the other he drives into the earth. He orders the carcass held up. In the silence, Jack speaks loudly: "This head is for the beast. It's a gift." Suddenly all the boy run away toward the beach.

Golding's powerful scene suggests the end of man's innocence in killing with sexual overtones. At the end of the story, ch. 12, as British naval officers rescue the boys who are by now divided into hunters and hunted, Golding remarks that "Ralph wept for the end of innocence, the darkness of man's heart." The island is in flames, two boys have been killed, and the others cannot even tell one of the officers how many are left. An officer is disappointed that the group could not live harmoniously. "I should have thought," he tells Ralph, "that a pack of British boys — you're all British aren't you? — would have been able to put up a better show than that." Ralph begins to explain that they did get along well at first. The officer nods in understanding of how it must have been and, assuming their familiarity with Ballantyne's idyll — which the boys themselves mention soon after landing on the island — says sympathetically: "I know. Jolly good show. Like Coral Island."

One of the main differences between Ballantyne's and Golding's portrayal of human association in the state of nature is that in the older, optimistic novel the three youths live harmoniously, whereas in the later, pessimistic one the more numerous group soon divides. In novels like *The Coral Island* the contrast is usually between the civilized people who are shipwrecked and the inferior natives they encounter. In *Lord of the Flies* the contrast and conflict are within the civilized group itself. The boys crash onto the island with their stock of Western, Christian values and attitudes; the harsh life they face quickly erodes the cultivation of millennia, leaving them in a state of nature whose test they fail. Civilization is only a thin layer of concealment; beneath it, what Golding calls the "darkness of man's heart" shows through when human beings are forced to live in extreme situations.

As the boys begin to make themselves apparent to each other after the airplane crash, two of them, Ralph and Piggy, try to bring about a degree of order. They are joined by a more disciplined group, a choir led by Jack. In ch. 1 the boys select Ralph as their leader, who, to placate the loser, concedes that the choir still "belongs" to Jack. Jack suggests that they might be "the army," but Ralph counters that they might be "hunters." They agree. Gradually Jack develops the hunter spirit in his followers and magnifies their function. The others concern themselves mainly with building a shelter and maintaining a fire to attract rescuers. Jack offers a few of his hunters to watch the fire; absorbed in hunting, they let it go out. Accused by Ralph, Jack in ch. 4 makes an unconvincing defense, standing with "the bloodied knife in his hand. The two boys faced each other. There was the brilliant world of hunting, tactics, fierce exhilaration, skill; and there was the world of longing and baffled commonsense."

This division, central to the novel, is embodied in the two groups, their opposing tendencies and their contending leaders. Jack is an aggressive, authoritarian chief. Lifting his spear, "safe from shame or self-consciousness behind the mask of his paint," he shouts a manipulative invitation to the assembled boys in ch. 8: "Listen all of you. Me and my hunters, we're living along the beach by a flat rock. We hunt and feast and have fun. If you want to join my tribe come and see us. Perhaps I'll let you join. Perhaps not." Later in ch. 9, Piggy tells Ralph that Jack's appeal has persuaded several boys. Ralph "uneasily" replies, "Let them go." Piggy starts to observe, "Just for some meat — ." Ralph completes Piggy's disappointed reflection on the boys' susceptibility to the irrational appeal, "And for hunting, and for pretending to be a tribe, and putting on war-paint." The tribe increases under Jack's relentless influence, despite Ralph's and Piggy's efforts to explain the importance of acting like grownups: building a shelter, maintaining the fire, keeping up the hope and work for rescue, and following orderly procedures based on discussion and experience.

Simon, a quiet and introspective boy, learns the truth that the beast is only a dead man. As the tribe engages in a mad ritual, Simon tries to tell them in ch. 9 that the beast is only "a body on the hill." In their madness, the boys take Simon for the beast and strike, bite, and claw him to death. Then Piggy is killed, and Jack leads a hunt for Ralph, when the rescuers come.

Golding uses each of these events and tendencies to convey a set of messages and judgments about human nature and human association. Pursued, Ralph thinks of the boys as savages; soon Golding himself, as author, calls them by the same name. The savage is thus not the native but the civilized boys placed in the condition of natives. Something of this theme appears in Ballantyne's *The Coral Island* when the three boys their hiding place for the first time: "Little did we imagine that the first savages who would drive us into it would be white savages, perhaps our own countrymen" (159). Yet this is only a passing mood in the dominant theme of harmony, work, love, and the strength of Western morality and religion. In *Lord of the Flies* there is mainly savagery, hostility, suspicion, and rivalry. Golding is reported to have stated: "The theme is an attempt to trace the defects of society back to the defects of human nature. The moral is that the shape of a society must depend on the ethical nature of the individual and not on any political system however apparently logical or respectable."[2] Because of their "defects," the boys are unable to create even the veneer of civilization they have known. Although social institutions may make a difference, ultimately individual defects put narrow limits upon the capacities of the social order.

While telling an absorbing story, Golding conveys judgments of human nature and society in a brief space. Social scientists are usually much less successful in describing or explaining the primordial, mythic relationships exposed in *Lord of the Flies*. Other novelists, resorting to lengthy authorial comments, are likewise less successful. John Steinbeck aims to tell something about human association in *The Grapes of Wrath* (1939), where he uses the familiar device of interludes of commentary among narrative chapters. What Golding brings out in the story Steinbeck attempts in historical and sociological description. In ch. 17, for example, he tells how each night the migrant families form a settled community, with a code of behavior based on experience of stops along the road to California, which they dissolve in the morning as they travel on, and then create anew at the next resting place. Steinbeck consciously seeks a Biblical analogy: "Every night relationships that make a world, established; and every morning the world torn down like a circus." As in this simile, Steinbeck's language is not equal to his intention. He also delivers platitudes that somehow, unlike Golding's meanings which are probably no less platitudes, do not impress: "A certain physical pattern is needed for the building of a world—water, a river bank, a stream, a spring, or even a faucet unguarded. And there is needed enough flat land to pitch the tents." These pretentious pieces of wisdom show that a novelist can be as uninspired as a social scientist in expressing his ideas on how human beings create communities. Even the storyteller needs both good ideas and interesting ways of expressing them.

Differences of Culture and Race

The Crusoe novels touch upon another broad category of social themes, the contrast between cultures or races. When Europeans began to make important geographic discoveries in the fifteenth century, their interest grew in the vastly different peoples and cultures they found in the new lands. Soon the novelists took up the themes of explorers, and by the seventeenth century there were many fictional works about the new regions. One of the earliest, anticipating several themes that were to become popular, was Aphra Behn's *Oroonoko: Or, the Royal Slave* (1688). Behn, a playwright, wrote her novels in dramatic form; in this one, through a story of African royalty, she tells of exotic people and places in a romantic style familiar to her readers.

The first part of the story takes place in Africa, where the handsome black Prince Oroonoko falls in love with the beautiful Imoinda. For different reasons, both are sold into slavery in Surinam, where they are reunited. Fearing that promises of freedom will not be honored, Oroonoko leads some slaves in an abortive rebellion.

He is punished and anticipates a terrible fate for Imoinda. He kills her, mutilates himself, is recaptured, beaten and finally killed by dismemberment.

Through this story, its remote locales, and the noble character of Oroonoko, Behn shows something of black life in Africa and a European colony in South America. Oroonoko's perfect character, however, makes him simply a copy of the traditional Western princely hero, whose equal the author claims him to be. Yet the very fact that an uncivilized person can be such a hero is one of Behn's points: savages can be noble even if most of them are not. Another point is the demonstration that Christian society is hypo critical and therefore not entitled to regard itself as superior. Behn shows this much, even though she does not undertake a systematic comparison of the different societies; indeed, her royalty in Africa looks suspiciously like royalty in Europe. Finally, Behn criticizes the more cruel aspects of slavery at this early time, even though she does not go so far as to favor abolition of that institution.

Although the discussion of mankind in the state of nature was already launched when Behn began to write, she made one of the earliest fictional contributions to it. She contrasted African with Christian culture and told her readers their civilization was inferior. Early in the novel the narrator remarks of Africans: "And these People represented to me an absolute *Idea* of the first State of Innocence, before Man knew how to sin: And 'tis most evident and plain, that simple Nature is the most harmless, inoffensive, and virtuous Mistress. 'Tis she alone, if she were permitted, that better instructs the World, than all the Inventions of Man: Religion would here but destroy that Tranquillity they possess by Ignorance; and Laws would but teach 'em to know Offenses, of which now they have no Notion . . . They understand no Vice or Cunning, but when they are taught by the *White* Men" (79-80). Most of the evil deeds in the story are committed by Europeans, emphasizing Oroonoko's humanity and nobility. There is even a hint of the difference between African and European slavery. Oroonoko takes slaves in battle in Africa, whereas in Surinam, himself a slave, he offers his captors a ransom of gold or slaves to gain his freedom. The novel does not condemn slavery among Africans, only their enslavement by Europeans. When Oroonoko despairs of his freedom in Surinam, he arouses the slaves to rebellion by telling them how miserable their lives are but without objecting to slavery on principle; rather, he suggests that the most objectionable features of their enslavement are that their white masters are both different from and inferior to them, that they have been enslaved according to rules alien to their society or according to no rules at all. "And why," he asks the slaves, "should we be Slaves to an unknown People? Have they vanquished us nobly in Fight? . . . This would not anger a noble Heart . . . No, but we are bought and sold like Apes or Monkeys, to be the Sport of Women, Fools and Cowards; and the Support of Rogues and Runagades, that have abandoned their own Countries for Rapine, Murders, Theft and Villainies. Do you not hear every Day how they upbraid each other with Infamy of Life, below the wildest Salvages? And shall we render Obedience to such a degenerate Race, who have no one human Virtue left, to distinguish them from the vilest Creatures?" (173-174). This speech anticipates several themes that emerge in the later history of resistance to Western slavery: that it was more cruel than African or Asian slavery, that the slavemasters were the real savages, and that exploitation by a different race was in itself more reprehensible than exploitation by one's own kind. This last theme has also been prominent in the recent Afro-Asian nationalist struggles for independence of Europe.

A common device of writers who want to portray whole cultures is to compose long novels covering several generations through history or to present a cross section of personalities, occupations, classes and other categories within a more limited period of time. Some novelists do both, others do so in a single volume or in a multivolumed story, and still others resort to a large number of independent yet loosely connected stories and volumes. In England such novels and series have been written by Trollope, Hardy, Bennett, and Galsworthy; in France by Balzac, Zola, and Proust; in Germany by Broch, Mann, and Zweig; in Russia by Tolstoy, Pasternak, and Solzhenitsyn; in the United States by Dos Passos, Faulkner and Glasgow.

The introduction of conflict, a perennial fictional device, has special importance in the novels portraying whole cultures. Through conflict, the novelist is able to show cultural differences just as the social scientist uses the comparative method for the same purpose. The fictional clash, as in Behn's *Oroonoko,* can come when two cultures are from different geographical regions and meet on the territory of one culture. This case is typical of novels of colonialism, such as Joyce Cary's *Mister Johnson* (1939). The clash of cultures may also occur in novels of race relations within a single society and geographical region, as in *Birthright* (1922) by T. S. Stribling, a white author, and *If He Hollers Let Him Go* (1945) by Chester B. Himes, a black author.

In *Mister Johnson* Joyce Cary portrays individual characters of different social groups while revealing the social structure formed by their interrelations and the social changes introduced by their ambitions and values. In the course of the novel, too, Cary illuminates social groups and processes such as the family, bureaucracy, and labor.

The story is mainly about the rise and fall of Mister Johnson, the African clerk to Mr. Rudbeck, the local British administrator of Fada, a small town in Nigeria surrounded by bush country. Seventeen years old and the recent product of a missionary school, Johnson takes seriously the laudatory stories he has heard about the British king and life in England, yet he is not far removed from the African life he now affects to despise as "savage." Besides embodying two kinds of civilization, Johnson is an incurable romantic who loves to express his boundless good will by pleasing the people he likes and receiving their admiration in turn. Already in debt, he gets in deeper in order to marry a beautiful pagan bush girl whom he wants to transform into a Christian "government lady" worthy of his own status. He is treated kindly by his boss, Rudbeck, who is so obsessed with building a road that he has little time to run the office or to curb Johnson's imagination. They even conspire to juggle the cashbooks to provide funds to continue the road, which Rudbeck has justified as certain to increase mobility and trade. Johnson, catching his idol's enthusiasm, helps to obtain the money to find native labor, and to drive the workers. Once the road is finished, trade does increase, but so does crime and disorder. Rudbeck is vaguely uneasy, partly because his beloved task is completed, partly because he is not now so optimistic about the results. Johnson continues his thieving and partying. Rudbeck finds out he has been in collusion with a native chief to collect a fee from those who use the new road. Outraged, Rudbeck fires Johnson, who cannot understand this sudden change after he has worked so hard for his employer and has at least kept the books correctly.

Johnson's troubles mount. His wife threatens to leave him, the native chief with whom he has been in collusion refuses help, and he has no money. In order to throw one more big party, he steals from the store he once worked in. Frightened by the appearance of the owner, a white man, Johnson stabs him to death. Everything gone and facing trial, Johnson does not lose his charitable view of the world. Rudbeck, whom Johnson has forgiven, must judge him but tries to help him. After finding him guilty and sentencing him to death, Rudbeck recommends leniency. His superiors refuse, however, and Rudbeck must now hang Johnson. The clerk understands Rudbeck's position. Afraid but calm, he still has a reserve of pride and courage when every misfortune befalls him. He asks Rudbeck to shoot him quickly instead of having him hanged by a prison official. Rudbeck complies with a dim apprehension of Johnson's reason and then, because he has acted illegally, commits his last act of falsifying records in collusion with his clerk by reporting that Johnson was hanged in accordance with the law.

Cary portrays his characters with skill, showing them as both unique individuals and members of social classes sharing traits with others. They are not stereotypes, yet their group ties help to reveal the springs of their behavior, for Cary presents them sympathetically, even when they are doing mean things.

The most powerful group is the local British administrators, of whom Rudbeck is the most fully drawn. He is aware of his imperial responsibilities but is embarrassed to speak of his job in such grandiose terms. He is kind but distant, prefers outdoor work on the land to office work with pencil and paper, and is human enough to show weakness and to forgive it in others. His new wife, determined to help him, has at first a romantic attitude toward Africa that corresponds to Johnson's attitude toward Christianity and England. She is anxious to show interest in local customs and scenery but makes the kind of joke about status that is acceptable in London and misunderstood in Fada. When her husband introduces Johnson to her as his "right-hand man," she embarrasses the clerk by saying, "Oh, but I expect he's the real boss" (89). Trying to please Johnson but usually puzzling him instead, she exaggerates his favors or misses the point altogether, as when she calls the "lady latrine" he has earnestly built for her "a kind of drawing-room" (90). Visiting the "dungeon of mud" that passes for a prison, she surprises Johnson and the jailer by exclaiming, "What a fine jail you have here—better than we have in England" (99). Eventually she becomes ill from the swift changes she has undergone and must be taken home. When she returns, she settles down more realistically.

Sargeant Gollup, the ex-soldier who owns the local store, is a lesser member of this powerful class of foreigners. Often drunk and brutal, he lacks the administrator's subtlety and predictability in his contempt for Africans, yet he is closer to them in some ways, even to the point of talking to them about his family back home, making no secret of his African mistress, and singing and telling stories with them. He is a jingo, resents the rich, speaks of the sacrifices that soldiers make to civilize "you nigs," and proclaims to the Africans that the God-given task of "the Pax Britannia takes a bit of keeping up" (130). Johnson understands and appreciates these sacrifices.

The class of native rulers is very different from the foreigners who come to Africa to rule on a new basis of authority and force. Although the traditional rulers have ties to the foreigners and even depend on them to some extent, they do not aspire to be like them. In a sense the two groups of rulers compete in exploiting those beneath them. Waziri is the main character of the African ruling class. He resents the new road, fearing that any change will upset the conveniences of tradition. Through Johnson, the marginal man in both camps, Waziri keeps abreast of the foreigners' moves and is able to adjust to them. Thus, having opposed the road, he does not hesitate to collect an illegal tax from those who use it. Waziri is suspicious of everyone, shrewd in self-defense, heedless of the needs of Africans if they do not coincide with his own, self-indulgent, and corrupt in his personal version of the native tradition.

Next in degree of power in Fada are the Mister Johnsons themselves, Africans who have been Christianized, educated in foreign schools, and who serve the British rulers as clerks, messengers, and policemen. Johnson is a beautiful creation of Cary's, a credible and attractive collection of contrasts. As a clerk, he can read and write English, but he brings to the alphabet and numbers his aesthetic preferences for certain letters and figures. The cashbook is more than a dull record to him; it is a sacred symbol of British efficiency and Christian integrity to which he adheres with all his heart. One may be forgiven for stealing but not for inconsistency in the account book. A product of an African town, he marries a beautiful girl from the bush and aspires to make her behave like an Englishwoman. His imagination poeticizes the commonplace and the harsh. Johnson combines art with labor as he cajoles the chiefs to provide road workers, whom he then inspires with his songs giving his own vision of Rudbeck's obsession. He is shrewd and gullible, energetic and lazy, self-indulgent and self-sacrificing. In the clash of cultures taking place within Johnson, the West has already made its dent in African tradition, for he is above all energetic, ambitious, full of schemes, eager for new experience, and convinced of the goodness of his masters' conception of progress. He has already been smitten by what Thomas Hardy calls in *Jude the Obscure* "the modern vice of unrest" (pt. 2, ch. 2). In contrast to most of the other characters, both British and African, Johnson has no visible family or tribal connections in a culture where these are important. He does not even have a first name, only a title. It is as if Johnson's modernism and bureaucratic loyalty to the empire and to the booming town of Fada leave room for no other. Odd as it may seem, Johnson is an African Babbitt, a local booster who believes that a bigger Fada is sure to be a better Fada. He is optimistic, convivial, and generous, just as Sinclair Lewis portrays

George Babbitt entertaining his friends in Zenith: "Babbitt drank with the others; his moment's depression was gone; he perceived that these were the best fellows in the world; he wanted to give them a thousand cocktails" (113). Johnson behaves similarly at parties. For all his eager embrace of Christianity and England and his religious respect for cash accounting, however, Johnson spreads his own exploits in the African way. Spurned and frustrated, he holds his audience at the rest house in thrall: "he has his choice of chairs, fires and meals . . . He is among the most welcome and honored guests in all Africa, men of imagination, the story-tellers, the poets" (189).

The least powerful social group portrayed in *Mister Johnson* are the bush people, who are also the most numerous. Among them are Johnson's wife Bamu, her family, and an old village woman who has attached herself to him as a servant because she was homeless. Cary shows them as individuals but reveals their group position: suspicious of the foreign Africans in the towns, in awe of the white rulers, fearful of their own chiefs. They expect no good of such strangers, who exploit them, and in turn they assume that the strangers are to be exploited for such petty gains as bush people can wring. The road gangs, virtually impressed into service by their chiefs, form a chorus in the background. The least modern of all the groups, they are the ones who construct the symbol of progress and who most quickly absorb and forget the finished road because their lives are the last to be affected by it and they cannot imagine anything except the momentary pleasure and pride they derive from hard labor, drinking, and singing.

Through the interactions of individuals in these four groups Cary reveals the social sructure of Fada and the beginning of vast changes whose extent and results are clear. He shows the differences in the conception of marriage and the family. Among the bush people who practically sell Bamu to Johnson, family roles are closely connected to economic needs. Family loyalty supersedes all other, and Bamu and her family cannot fully recognize Johnson, a stranger, as one of them. So long as he fulfills his economic function, Bamu does her duty, but she cannot comprehend the Christian, romantic idea of marriage that he has created from the scraps picked up about love and loyalty in the English ideal. Cary illuminates bureaucratic agencies and procedures in showing the relation between the local British administrator in Fada and his colleagues in the larger stations and the central administration. All levels protect themselves, the central office by requiring endless reports, and the small posts by evading the excessive regulations that tend to paralyze. The responses of local officials to the conditions of their service vary from resistance, to martyrdom, to mechanical compliance.

The new road is the symbol and reality of change. Rudbeck pushes it through, with Johnson's help, against opposition and indifference. The British administrators are skeptical, fearing the road will only continue the process of breaking up the old tribal organization. The native chiefs fear that the road will only increase crime and vice by bringing riffraff to Fada, who will stay in the new inns. Johnson's imagination is fired by his vision of the road. "Roads are a most civilized thing," he assures a native chief (85). He endorses the British Crown's interest in the Fada road, which will enable the people to go about and see the world. Johnson drives the work gangs fiendishly until the bushmen too become obsessed and see themselves as creating a gigantic thing to match the glory of the sun, the moon, and the very forest through which they hack the road. They celebrate when the first motor vehicle goes over it. A letdown follows. The work gangs break camp and go home. Crime immediately increases, not merely because of the influx of travelers but also because of the unrest among the people of Fada. Rudbeck is proud of the sheer physical achievement that he never thought possible, but he feels himself at loose ends, wondering whether the road will not bring too much harm. The road itself speaks to him: "I am abolishing the old ways . . . I am bringing wealth and opportunity for good as well as vice . . . I am giving you plenty of trouble already, you governors, and I am going to give plenty more . . . What are you going to do about it? . . . You made me, so I suppose you know" (168-169). Cary emphasizes the ambivalent mood: the road may mean progress but it also brings problems. Civilization is inextricably connected with corruption: "There has never been a mail robbery in Fada, and there never will be until civilization and private enterprise are much further advanced" (51). The theme is the same as in Behn's *Oroonoko.*

The *zungo,* or roadside inn, is an accessory to the road in its guilt. It enables travelers to stay in Fada and attracts the residents as well. It symbolizes the unrest, anonymity, and cash nexus of an urban, trading society, while serving as the site for the age-old processes of forming and reforming groups, of storytelling and adventure. The rootlessness and transiency are epitomized in the traders, who bring wanted goods but are themselves contemptible, despite their wealth, for being strangers. But in the *zungo* they thrive naturally; their strangeness is overlooked, taken for granted, and becomes an advantage because the stranger brings new tales. The *zungo* in Fada is like the modern European hotel H. G. Wells portrays in *Tono-Bungay,* peopled by "a vast drifting crowd of social learners" (284). Cary describes the *zungo's* daily turmoil and an emerging pattern of association and dispersion in terms reminiscent of Steinbeck's weaker attempt. As the town enters the afternoon doldrums, the *zungo* is in the process of creating the night's social order: "All these hundreds of people are chattering together with the peculiar lively note of sociability and evening happiness . . . In fact, what seems like confusion is seen to be exactly ordered as a beehive" (180).

Cary's social reporting and commentary are skillfully made a part of the story of the relationship between the two main characters, Johnson and Rudbeck, who are from contrasting societies and different social positions. Cary pictures the conflict of two worlds in these two men, although Johnson and Rudbeck, perhaps because they appear so human, are not stereotypes or symbols set against one another to make a profound point. For all their differences of background and status, Johnson and Rudbeck see many things in the same way, as much because of the former's imagination as of the latter's power. Johnson's peccadilloes accumulate and lead to his end, while Rudbeck controls his own slips and has help in covering them. They both understand the situation that makes Rudbeck sentence Johnson to death. They try to think of ways to comfort each other. Rudbeck asks whether he was too unfeeling at crucial points, such as when he refused John-

son an advance on salary, wrote an unfavorable report on the
clerk, and actually fired him from the road job for taking money
from the users. Johnson reassures Rudbeck that he has indeed
been a kind master and that more kindness would not have
changed things. Facing death, Johnson can still be magnanimous
toward someone superior in status but not in humanity. In this
story of a clash of social worlds, Cary finds a way to make a larger
statement of common humanity.

Several African writers have attacked Cary's portrait of Johnson
and Africa as a "colonialist" exaggeration. It is fortunate, therefore, to have a novel with which to compare it, *No Longer at Ease*
(1960) by Chinua Achebe, a leading African novelist from Nigeria.
Achebe's story is about a more modern African returning with his
Cambridge degree to a Nigeria on the way to full independence.
Some of the themes in *Mister Johnson* are still significant a generation later in *No Longer at Ease*. Although the two main characters differ in personality and the main setting of the later novel is
the capital and central government, they face similar situations.
There remains the overriding conflict between modern goals and
traditional ways, attended by the rise of new forms of wealth and
power, new loyalties, and increasing temptations to corruption in
public office. Their tragedy is the same, for both heroes want to
do what progress demands but become enmeshed almost involun-
tarily in the new and irresistible temptations.[3]

In *Mister Johnson* the leading character is an African moving
between two worlds. The African world he has come from, however, is the demographically and culturally dominant one, and in
time it will become politically dominant as well. On the contrary,
the Afro-American in the United States, the subject of *Birthright*
by Stribling and *If He Hollers Let Him Go* by Himes, who is also
on the margin of two worlds, has no prospect of ever becoming the
dominant influence, and even the notion of his autonomy within
the wider system is still inchoate. These two novels are a prelude to
the rapid development of this notion of self-direction in the 1960s.

The main theme of Stribling's *Birthright* is that the most significant differences between black and white are biological and
hence unbridgeable except perhaps through millennia of evolu-

tionary change. The main character is Peter Siner, who has just graduated from Harvard and is returning to his Tennessee village, Hooker's Bend, to teach school and to establish a college for blacks. Approaching the South, he again experiences segregation in trains, restaurants, and hotels. In the "Niggertown" of Hooker's Bend he collects money to buy land for his school but is easily swindled by the white banker, who sends the money to a Christian missionary in Africa. The incident amuses the whites, confirming their belief that you cannot really educate a black, and diminishes the blacks' faith in both education and Siner. His position deteriorates when he is forced into a street brawl with an uneducated black, Tump Pack, over Cissie Dildine, a light-skinned, educated woman who was Tump's sweetheart but is now attracted to Siner. Siner feels alienated from all communities. Cissie tells him that they both, being light-skinned, are too different from "full-blooded" blacks to help them advance. They plan to go North together some day. Meanwhile, Siner takes a job as secretary and intellectual companion to old Captain Renfrew, also a Harvard alumnus, who has helped the Siner family. This promising relationship proves unsatisfactory because there are quickly-reached limits to the Captain's willingness and freedom, in the South, to ignore the racial difference between himself and his fellow alumnus. Cissie also proves only a temporary support, for she tells Siner that she cannot marry him because she is his moral inferior, which he assumes means that she has been known to steal from her white employer. Peter now develops and tests his plan to improve understanding between blacks and whites. He approaches some blacks lounging and cavorting in the sunshine and admonishes them to work hard to gain self-respect and the respect of other races. Amused, they offer just as cogent reasons why they should continue to relax. He tries to convince a white employer that blacks should be paid decent wages and their pilfering not be tolerated, but the employer misses the point. In despair, Siner decides to go North alone and abandon Cissie, even though she is now in jail for theft on a charge brought by the son of her employer, who was angered when she refused to do his bidding. She is also pregnant by her accuser. The black community rallies to her support, but

Siner remains aloof. Tump Pack frees her from jail and is killed while doing so. Her employers are angered by their son's action and refuse to press charges, so Cissie remains free. Siner has a sudden insight and change of heart: Cissie's "wrongs" do not really affect her basic character, for morality is relative to the needs and capacities of each race. He marries Cissie, and they go to Chicago where he will take an executive job previously offered him. Understanding the bioracial nature of character and morality, Siner is happy with Cissie as she is.

Stribling reveals a curious mixture of equalitarianism through his special interpretation of Darwinian theory and of racism through his emphasis on biological determinism. Because he regards black-white differences as largely unbridgeable, he dwells on them whether they are big or small. He is careful to call people mulattoes, quadroons, or octoroons, since degree of whiteness or blackness is important. He remarks that on railroad trains blacks are noisier than whites; they have a special smell; black women hold an apple in the palm of the hand as they eat it, while white women hold it in their fingers; black men are more lavish than white men in their appreciation of women; black and white grief is different; black homes are poorly lit; blacks are soft-hearted and cannot concentrate on material progress, whereas whites take a hard and instrumental view of things; black morality differs from white morality because black biology is different and morality is only what biological nature requires of a race if it is to be healthy and to thrive. Stribling is also saying that blacks with white "blood" are very different from full-blooded blacks, although at times he suggests that it does not much matter, as at the end of the novel when Siner realizes that he came out of Harvard as he went in: a black. The emphasis of the story, nevertheless, is upon the importance of degree of whiteness or blackness, and Stribling argues that the best course for the blacks with "white blood" is to seek individual solutions that separate them from the mass of blacks. This is what Siner and Cissie do, after making a brief effort to advance the black race. The implication is that people like them are or soon will be "acceptable" to whites, at least in the North, and hence need not remain in the black community even if they could lead it. Stribling suggests that blacks like Siner cannot lead. His education has so alienated and bewildered him that he feels he cannot "understand his people," the blacks (287). Belonging to the white world, he finds that blacks have a "weird morality" (302). When swindled by the white banker, Siner, with his college education, does not understand the process nearly so well as does Tump Pack, the uneducated black whose mind is uncluttered by books and the partial acceptance of whites. This is another aspect of Stribling's biological idea: Tump's instinct and inherited mother-wit, his "birthright," are superior to Siner's education; it is the superiority of nature over nurture.

Stribling explicitly deals with Darwinism, which was viewed with hostility by the guardians of public morality in the South, although the Scopes trial in Tennessee did not occur until 1925, three years after the publication of *Birthright.* When Siner is in the employ of Captain Renfrew, he notices that the old man's library has many books on religion and cosmology, all of them proving the truth of the Bible. Siner wonders why so intelligent a man should have no scientific books published after the decade of 1880-1890, "when Charles Darwin's great fructifying theory, enunciated in 1859, began to seep into the South" (182). Later, Siner figures out the reason that Captain Renfrew's only book on evolution is called *Darwinism Dethroned:* the Captain's library is a form of "special pleading against the equality of man." Siner expounds an equalitarian interpretation of Darwinism, that from this "great hypothesis" of the "great biologic relationship of all flesh, from worms to vertebrates, there instantly followed a corollary of the brotherhood of man." Stribling offers this analogy in bringing Christianity up to date and making it compatible with the new science: "What Christ did for theology, Darwin did for biology, — he democratized it. The One descended to man's brotherhood from the Trinity; the other climbed up to it from the worms" (219).

Though he thinks the brotherhood of man was proved by science, Stribling also sees ineluctable differences between the races. He attributes fundamental importance to a racial difference in the status of the sexes, itself another biological distinction. Siner comes to realize that all attraction between the sexes in Nigger-town is physical, that the black man's strength permits the black woman no freedom of choice in selecting a mate. But the "progress of any race" depends precisely on the degree to which women have this power, because only women select on the basis of spiritual and mental qualities. "For millions of years," Siner muses in biological terms, "these instinctive spiritualizers of human breeding stock have been hampered in their choice of mates by the unrestrained right of the fighting male. Indeed, the great constructive work of chivalry in the middle ages was to lay, unconsciously, the corner-stone of modern civilization by resigning to the woman the power of choosing from a group of males" (78). Later, Siner ponders the point more directly: "The history of the white race shows the grad-ual increase of the woman's power of choice," whereas his "own race was weak and hopeless" because it did not have this concep-tion of love between the sexes (277).

Stribling thus uses his story to bring together a hodgepodge of nineteenth century extensions of Darwinism to social life, biologi-cal determinism, populism, and twentieth century liberalism of a sort. What is interesting is not the validity of these ideas—many of them confused, quaint, and questionable—nor the quality of the novel as art—since it is not very good— but the use of fiction to popularize ideas about personal behavior and social institu-tions. The broadest such notion Stribling expounds is the biologi-cal function of morality. In another statement Siner, reflecting on his happiness with Cissie as they sail northward from Hooker's Bend, speculates on the difference between white and black mo-rality. Conceptions of good and evil "are merely those precepts that a race have practiced and found good in its evolution. Morals are the training rules that keep a people fit." Since races have a different biological nature, they have different needs and morals. Stribling introduces a hint of the noble savage: "If the black race possess a more exuberant vitality than some other race, then the black would not be forced to practice so severe a vital economy as some less virile folk." He is claiming that because nature, not so-cial institutions, has endowed the black race more liberally with physical strength and the capacity and will to reproduce itself, it can afford to practice a morality that does not place so high a value on work, thrift, sexual regulation, protection of the individual, and perhaps even life itself. Ultimately, blacks are to be judged by a different standard, for, "there is no such thing as absolute morals" (307-308). Although he couches these ideas in terms of moral relativism, which is usually associated with ideas of racial equality, Stribling's tone, his ideas, and the story itself leave no doubt that the black race is regarded as inferior. Despite his apparent sympathy for the Southern black exploited by the white, Stribling's form of racism is hardly distinguishable from that of the white South generally. He has, however, made two interesting controversions. Just as he uses Darwinism to affirm the equality of the species when others use it to reach the opposite conclusion, so he uses moral relativism to affirm the inequality of the races when others use it to undermine that idea.

Difficult as it is to exemplify such ideas and abstractions in a story about individual human beings, Stribling tries hard to do so, but without great success. At times Siner is portrayed as superior to full-blooded Negroes because he is educated, at times he appears inferior for the same reason, and almost always he is alienated from all groups. He is different from and the same as all blacks. He is entirely acceptable to whites, entirely unacceptable, and acceptable in varying degrees, depending on their social position and the specific relationship. Stribling is not consistent in using character and events to demonstrate the abstractions Siner expresses, although individual people in specific situations do not necessarily conform to general ideas about social life.

The effort to induce conformity weakens *Birthright* as a work of art. Robert Penn Warren has argued that Stribling's concern with abstractions prevents him from getting "too close to his material" because such fidelity would interfere with the broader "truths" about social life he wants to convey. Warren criticizes Stribling for making a misleading comparison between "a noble Negro . . . and a white society considerably less than noble." Treating Stribling as a social critic and advocate as well as a novelist, Warren claims that he is "too absolute in his definition of Southern character" and fails "to understand the historical context." Stribling, Warren concludes, is a "propagandist" interested not only in portraying and criticizing white-black relations in the South but also in prescribing what they should be.[4]

Stribling himself in *Birthright* criticizes art that is propagandistic. As Siner reflects on Captain Renfrew's library, he criticizes "Southern orthodoxy" for its lack of "sincerity" in holding to religious views supporting traditional social arrangements: "All attempts at Southern poetry, belles-lettres, painting, novels, bear the stamp of the special plea . . . Peter perceived what every one must perceive, that when letters turn into a sort of glorified prospectus of a country, all value as literature ceases . . . [The South] is a lawyer with a cause to defend. And such is the curse that arises from lynchings and venery and extortions and dehumanizings, — sterility; a dumbness of soul" (219-220). It is this uncompromising, uniform characterization of Southern life that arouses criticism, especially among Southerners. Critics of the South, however, do not rise to defend Stribling; they cannot accept his Darwinism with its equalitarian turn or his version of racism. Consequently, he alienates serious critics of almost every social and literary persuasion. Although he was popular with the general reader in his time and his books sold well, he is all but forgotten today.

In *Birthright* the two dissatisfied main characters look forward, right after World War I, to getting out of the South; they see the North as a place where they can live in dignity, where the clash of cultures, even if it continues to exist, will not prevent them from pursuing their own lives as they like. In *If He Hollers Let Him Go,* by the black novelist Chester B. Himes, the blacks have already migrated from the South to California, where many of them are integrated into the defense industries of World War II, but prejudice and discrimination still mar their lives. Old patterns persist in the new region, Los Angeles, and even in the new wartime workplace, the shipyard, where much of the story takes place. One of the problems is precisely that the relationships are new and unsettled. Blacks and whites have migrated to Southern California from the South since the 1930s, and their numbers have multiplied since the beginning of the war emergency in 1940. Everyone knows that Los Angeles cannot become a replica of a Southern city, yet the whites do not accept quick and far-reaching change, while the blacks do not accept the old ways of the South.

The story concerns Bob Jones, a black man in his mid-twenties from Cleveland, who has reached the position of leader of a small team of blacks employed in a Los Angeles shipyard. Though he is tall, powerful, and handsome, with some college education, a good income, and the prospect of marrying the daughter of one of the richest and most influential Negroes in the state, Bob is apprehensive and uneasy. He is afraid that the whites' racial hatreds and fears, exemplified in the confinement of Americans of Japanese descent in concentration camps, must one day challenge him personally, and that his response will doom him. Himes shows the relations between blacks and whites on the job, where friction exists because, although there is supposed to be equality, the whites use their greater power to hold down the blacks, who in turn will accept this discriminatory treatment only up to a point that is not clear to either group. Racial contacts on the job are complicated by sex, for some of the white women are excessively suspicious of black men, hostile, or coy and teasing.

Bob has trouble with two whites especially. One, Johnny, knocks him unconscious in an argument during a lunch-time crap game. Bob vows to kill Johnny and actually trails him several times to scare him. The realization that a white man can be afraid of a Negro makes Bob laugh in disbelief but also gives him a sense of power. His relation with the other white, Madge, has the opposite effect: it makes him feel helpless and drives him to do things he regrets because they almost ruin him. Madge is alternately hostile and sexually inviting on the job and off. At work, she insults him gratuitously, he responds, and his supervisor demotes him on Madge's complaint. This makes him vulnerable to the military draft. Bob is comforted by Alice, his girl friend, who convinces him to do what is necessary to get back his higher job. They plan to marry, and Bob feels at ease for the first time, as he comes to agree with Alice that they can live their own lives pleasantly by avoiding painful racial situations. Examining a new task on the ship, he discovers Madge sleeping in a cabin. She is in one of her inviting moods, but Bob wants to get away. They hear voices of people passing outside, so she locks the door and fights him to keep him from opening it. Inevitably, someone in authority wants to enter the cabin to inspect and becomes suspicious because it is locked. Bob tries again to open the door, but Madge screams she is being raped by a "nigger." Workers force open the door, drag him out, and beat him. In the ship's hospital room he learns that his greatest fears have been realized: he is under arrest on a charge of rape with no more evidence than the word of a white slut he angered by rejecting. He escapes and is caught. The president of the shipyard appears in court and reports that Madge has patriotically agreed not to press charges in the interest of avoiding racial trouble and keeping up defense production. Assuming Bob's guilt, the president berates him for not living up to the trust placed in him and for letting down his race after receiving such fine employment opportunities. Because a gun was found in Bob's car, he faces another charge. The judge proposes to ignore it if Bob will go into the army. Two hours later, with two Mexican Americans in the same situation, he has been inducted.

At the end of Stribling's *Birthright,* the black couple leave the South for Chicago where, the author intimates, they will be able to live in dignity. In Himes's *If He Hollers Let Him Go,* the blacks have already moved out of the South, but the improvement of their situation does not keep pace with the advance of their expectations. In this novel, by a black author writing a generation after Stribling, the couple find that the white world intrudes on them, now that they are in contact with it in a new region and on a less familiar basis, perhaps even more so than in the South. In ch. 19 Bob suddenly realizes: "No matter what the white folks did to me, or made me do just in order to live, Alice and I could have a life of our own, inside of all the pressure, away from it, separate from it, that no white person could ever touch." He is wrong, at least in this novel.

In bringing the races into closer contact under new and uncertain conditions, Himes is not interested chiefly in showing the differences in their modes of life. Instead of dwelling on the clash of cultures, he emphasizes the clash of wills and ambitions, the competition for power, goods, and dignity based on skin color. The clash, in a sense, follows from the fact that blacks and whites now have the same goals, but whites do not recognize that blacks are entitled to conditions which would enable them to realize these goals or even to entertain them. Bob contemplates the demands whites make of blacks to be proud of their race while continuing to "worship your white fathers" and to accept the limits whites place upon blacks. He fears that even though whites are "sitting on my brain, controlling my every thought, action, and emotion," he cannot crawl into this niche, but must rebel because the whites have also instilled in him the "jive" about "liberty and justice and equality." He concludes that American society has inculcated in him an expectation of fairness and a sense of ambition so firmly that discrimination cannot eradicate it: "That was the hell of it: the white folks had drummed more into me than they'd been able to scare out" (ch. 18).

This ambivalence Himes reveals in Bob's alternating resolve and despair. Dressing for work, he says: "Something about my working clothes made me feel rugged, bigger than the average citizen, stronger than a white-collar worker—stronger even than an executive. Important too. It put me on my muscle." At other times he feels impotent. Hearing a black baby sucking at his mother's breast, he thinks, "if they really wanted to give him a break they'd cut his throat and bury him in the backyard before he got old enough to know he was a nigger." Seeing a vaudeville show with white acrobats and black singers and dancers, he reflects on how "the white folks were still showing everybody how strong they were and how we spooks were still trying to prove how happy we were" (ch. 1). He is not content with the limits placed on his ambition and freedom: "Anyone who wanted to could be nigger-rich, nigger-important, have their Jim Crow religion, and go to nigger heaven." But he would prefer to be a leaderman at the shipyard if only he "could be a man" (ch. 18). Occasionally he thinks about the differences between black and white nature: "We're a wonderful, goddamned race . . . Simple-minded, generous, sympathetic sons of bitches. We're sorry for everybody but ourselves; the worse the white folks treat us the more we love 'em" (ch. 1). This kind of desperate comparison approaches Siner's observation in Stribling's

Birthright: "[Negroes] lacked the steel-like edge that the white man achieves. By virtue of his hardness, a white man makes his very laws and virtues instruments to crush and mulct his fellow-man; but negroes are so softened by untoward streaks of sympathy that they lose the very uses of their crimes" (290).

Himes reveals the black person's sense that white people and institutions overwhelm him. Bob envies the whites their exemption from this particular form of external domination. As he contemplates killing a white man in ch. 5, he feels relaxed and powerful: "I felt just like I thought a white boy oughta feel; I had never felt so strong in all my life." He experiences such confidence only occasionally; usually he has a sense of doom, either that he will do something to ruin himself or that white trickery will accomplish it. All contacts with whites are dangerous to him, even those that do not immediately appear to be so. In ch. 9, a white woman freely enters a black hotel bar and starts "performing": "She could get everybody in the joint into trouble, even me just sitting there buying a drink. She was probably under age anyway; and if she was she could get the hotel closed, the liquor license revoked, probably get the manager in jail. She could take those two black chumps flirting with her outside and get them thirty years apiece in San Quentin; in Alabama she could get them hung. A little tramp— but she was white."

The need for constant caution is an obsession to Bob and all blacks. They must observe the white man steadily and accommodate to his moods. Walking downtown, Bob passes a newsstand and sees "rows of white faces on the magazine covers." Trying to buy cigarettes in a drugstore, he is kept waiting while the "little prim-mouth girl" serves all the white customers first. He passes a movie house and sees "just a lot of white faces on the marquee billboards" (ch. 9). On the job he is humiliated: "The taste of white folks was in my mouth and I couldn't get it out" (ch. 14). Even the blacks' own struggle against white domination is itself dominated by whites. At a party a white liberal grills Bob about strategies for black advancement. In anticipation of a theme of autonomy more characteristic of the 1960s, Himes emphasizes Bob's resentment: "I wasn't going to have this peckerwood coming down here among my people, playing a great white god, sitting on his ass, solving the Negro problem with a flow of diction and making me look like a goddamned fool in front of my girl, when all I could do around his people was to be a flunky and get kicked in the mouth" (ch. 10). The word "white" itself becomes a synonym for power, arrogance, provocation. Encountering difficulty with a succession of white guards as he arrives at work, Bob observes, "The white folks had sure brought their white to work with them that morning" (ch. 2).

The black's sense of being overwhelmed, controlled, and tyrannized by white persons and institutions alienates him from America even as he seeks equality in it. When things go well for him, Bob is proud of his role in war production. He first wants the Japanese to win, but later feels "included" in America and is stirred by the importance of the war to his country. As he is battered on the job and off, Bob loses this confidence in America; by the time he is falsely accused of rape in ch. 21, he is afraid of America, not of its violence or its mobs, the admittedly ugly aspects of our national life, but of its supposedly virtuous features: "American justice. The jury and the judge. The people themselves." Irreconcilability of the races thus emerges as a main theme. Bob tells a white liberal that blacks and whites can live and work side by side yet go on hating and fighting each other. A Southern white woman puts the matter in Biblical terms reminiscent of Stribling's *Birthright*. California liberals may use different terms, but the subtle language and allusions do not much reduce the distance and hostility whites impose on the relation between the races.

Political Power and
Social Class in the Novel

A great writer is, so to speak, a second government.
— Aleksander I. Solzhenitsyn, *The First Circle*

The two themes of the basis of human association and the contrast of cultures or civilizations are related to the differences in political power and social class. Politics in its broadest sense refers to the relations among power, moral ideas, and social institutions, as illustrated both by Ignazio Silone's *Bread and Wine* (1937) and by another of T. S. Stribling's novels, *Fombombo* (1923).[1]

Political Power

Silone is concerned above all with the moral issues of power as they apply to the two corrupt totalitarian movements of modern times, fascism and communism. People and governments corrupt each other, so that the purely moral blame attaches both to the rulers and the ruled, although the latter, as the victims, evoke sympathy for their suffering and for the innocence of at least some of them. At times Silone suggests that the city is more corrupt than the country; at other times he indicates that they are equally corrupt, for peasants are no more willing than workers to undertake a personal commitment to moral action rather than to mere political rhetoric, which Silone sees as the ultimate requirement for community. He lays a special responsibility upon intellectuals in this regard and finds them seriously wanting.

All of these issues Silone manages brilliantly in a simple story simply told. Pietro Spina, a revolutionary of middle-class background, returns to Italy from exile to resume the task of building the revolutionary movement against the Fascist regime which, morally bankrupt, is on the point of declaring war on Ethiopia. To recover from illness and to disguise himself because he is wanted by the police, Spina dresses as a priest and goes to the village of Pietrasecca. He enters the life of the small community and learns over again the ways of the peasant. Feeling better, he is about to return to underground work when he learns of some youths who approach revolution by wanting to put into effect Mussolini's early socialist ideas. Spina enlists one of them in his conspiracy and goes to Rome, where he lays aside his disguise and looks up his old comrades to help him find one promising worker to join him in the villages. He finds only despair and disillusion in Rome. Resuming his disguise, Spina returns to the countryside. There the Fascist declaration of war on Ethiopia arouses the worst instincts of the peasants, who respond to the regime's rhetoric in a spirit of selfishness and pathetic greed. Spina hopes in vain that mobilization for war will at least bring the peasants out of their isolation and ultimately into some kind of moral cooperation. Saddened, Spina resolves to go into exile again but first visits his old teacher. Don Benedetto inspires him with a new and realistic faith and sends him a young man to help in revolutionary work. The regime meanwhile cracks down on Spina's friends, murdering some and arresting others. Warned that the police are closing in on him, he flees to the mountains. He is followed by Cristina, a devout woman who has worshiped him as a saint and wants to take food and clothing to him. Lost and exhausted, she cannot find Spina. She calls his name and hears in response the howl of the wolves. As night falls, the wolves come closer; she makes the sign of the Cross.

Silone has stated that both his fiction and his essays have much in common: "The same effort at understanding has constituted, I think, the underlying purpose of both my essays and my novels;

the form may differ but the same basic theme is common to them all."[2] In addition, Silone has treated much of his fiction as scholars and social critics have treated their analytical studies; that is, he has revised three of his novels, including *Bread and Wine* itself. In revising this novel, Silone notes in his new preface that he has removed only "secondary elements and affairs of only contemporary concern," while giving more attention to the "fundamental theme." Thus, the second version is similar to the first in plot, even though many pertinent events, dialogue, and authorial commentary did not survive the revision. Silone suggests in the preface that he was further moved to revise *Bread and Wine* in order to mitigate the effects of his "state of mind" in the political excitement of the time of its writing, a state of mind in which he was "more prone to exaggeration, sarcasm and melodrama than to calm narration." In general, he feels, "the writer moved by a strong sense of social responsibility" is liable to such emphases and to giving a "purely external description of things, while the events in the inner life of characters are what count in literary works." The new version of *Bread and Wine* carries out this new attitude of the author toward the appropriate balance in fiction among story, character, commentary, politics, and affairs at the moment of writing in relation to the moment written about. The basic intent and meaning of the novel has not changed, although the first version contains more explicit political commentary. Silone intends it to be so, as shown by the preface to the new version. Another clue to his attitude comes from an essay: "Critics who see me primarily as some kind of sociological or political writer, with all the limitations that such an assessment implies, have never been to my liking. For the one thing that has always truly interested me is the fate of man, his involvement in the complex machinery of the modern world, at whatever latitude or longitude."[3] The sociopolitical meaning of *Bread and Wine* derives from the fact not that Silone is "some kind of sociological or political writer" but that he has convincingly posed in his fiction the deepest moral issues facing man in society.

Silone describes the mutual corruption of rulers and ruled in Fascist Italy in the very first scenes of *Bread and Wine*. The old teacher-priest Don Benedetto awaits some of his former students, now in their thirties, on the occasion of his seventy-fifth birthday. Contemplating recent changes that have spread from the city to the countryside, he reflects that truth itself, which used to move in the opposite direction, is no longer even tolerated. Like the hemp which farmers can no longer sell to the city, it is also "expensive, primitive, and crude; while hypocrisy is smooth, always up-to-date, and not only cheap but profitable." Don Benedetto has withdrawn from life's affairs not because he is old but because his fellow priests will not tolerate his liberty of spirit. Even his family, except for his aged sister, have abandoned him, resenting his failure to acquire the influence he could have had with the "authorities" and which "he might have used to their advantage in an age in which honest work was useless without influence and wire-pulling." When several of the young men arrive, the talk is dispirited, revealing them to be already "aged cynics" actively or passively corrupt. One of them, an ambitious local priest, says he is writing an article on "The Scourge of Our Time." He is annoyed when Don Benedetto asks if it is about war and unemployment. Those are "political questions," the young priest replies, whereas he is writing of spiritual matters; from his point of view, the scourge of our time is "immodesty in dress."

This disappointment in what young men have become is repeated when Cristina and Bianchina, two very different women who love Spina, talk about the fate of their schoolmates. Incoronata is still waiting for an opening to teach in a provincial school; sleeping with the prefect's chauffeur did not help. Anita is poor now, but her "family dignity" requires that instead of working in an office, she "stay at home and rot, waiting for some rich landowner" to marry her. Colomba, who married a station-master, a widower with three children, "has practically become the family servant." Evangelina was entranced by the Fascist dictator, found an unemployed worker to marry her when she became pregnant, and now runs a Fascist girls group (73-75).

Don Benedetto regrets that his pupils have been unable to develop their essential qualities, which when they "entered the world" were "side-tracked, suppressed, thwarted, corrupted." He asks them "what is this new Fate that prevented you from being what you wanted to be? What is this obscure and pitiless destiny that has played havoc with your generation?" (14-16). Later Spina asks: "What would happen if men remained faithful to their youthful ideals?" The local pharmacist gestures to suggest it would be the "end of the world" (150). But life in general is a disappointment, Silone shows, for people cannot come to know each other trustfully. A young peasant who hides Spina and gets him medical treatment asks: "You work, you buy, you sell, you rent, and you need papers and recommendations. You go abroad to work, and see lots of officials and meet a lot of people. But is that a way of knowing them?" (24). The doctor himself, who was Spina's fellow pupil under Don Benedetto, comments: "All our life is lived provisionally. We think that for the time being we must adapt ourselves, even humiliate ourselves, but that it is all just temporary, and that one day life, real life, will begin. We get ready to die, still complaining that we have never really lived" (31). Despite such despairing remarks, the novel is filled with good people, such as Don Benedetto, Spina, Cristina, and Bianchina. Spina, helped in his time of need at the risk of his friends' personal safety, muses on the goodness of the peasant and the doctor: "You had to have faith in friendship" (33). All these good people, however, are powerless. The possessors of land and the holders of power in state and church are exploiters and oppressors. Spina, at least, wants to end this injustice, not simply to improve the material conditions of life for the masses (bread) but to help them achieve a new morality (wine). He tells one of his friends that revolutionaries must not deal with superficial, political issues, for what is needed is "conversion" in the old sense, "a new way of living." He continues: "At heart every revolution puts this elementary question afresh: What, it asks, is man? What is this human life?" Revolution must not be merely a way to change exploiters. Rather, "for the poor people revolution stands for . . . liberation, a need of truth and simplicity" (283-284).

Much of *Bread and Wine* demonstrates hopelessness. Life is corrupt. To seek change has two disadvantages: it makes life "provisional," a continual preparation for something else, and change

itself is difficult, elusive, and in the end is likely to be insubstan-
tial. Silone's recommended way of life is the same in this novel as
in his essays: struggle for the true and simple. Spina tells his friend:
"You can be a free man under a dictatorship. It is sufficient if you
struggle against it. He who thinks with his own head is a free man
. . . Even if you live in the freest country in the world and are lazy,
callous, apathetic, irresolute, you are not free but a slave . . . Liberty is something you have to take for yourself" (32). Thirty years
after *Bread and Wine* Silone wrote an essay, "Rethinking Progress," which considers the problems brought on by the "welfare
state." Corruption of another sort accompanies such economic
progress, and the old opposition between state and society persists,
even if in a slightly different form from the one it took in the poverty Silone wrote of in his novels. The essay reaffirms his view of
the "direction in which the hope of progress lies. All one need do is
to hold fast to the ancient and well-tried criterion: in every age
and in every kind of conflict, progress is to be found only in what
promotes the freedom and responsibility of man individually and
in his complex relationship with his fellow human beings."[4]

Although Silone portrays working-class characters favorably, it
is to peasants and intellectuals that he gives most attention. The
moral question he raises about peasants is their corruption through
poverty, whereas the question for intellectuals is the corruption of
their talents through alliances with power holders.

Bread and Wine is a study of peasant life rather like Balzac's
The Peasants. Indeed, Silone's peasants sometimes resemble Balzac's as in the description of peasants who are cheated regularly by
their rulers and in turn rob other poor people: "The manner of
several of these poor peasants, their way of laughing and talking,
betrayed craftiness, an animal-like selfishness; they looked like
habitual thieves and pilferers" (109). Silone takes up various aspects of peasant life, such as domestic and community life, or economic conditions and the peasant's response to them. Far from
ennobling the peasants or romanticizing their existence, Silone
shows them to be shrewd and calculating but also stupid and gullible. Mostly, the peasants seek to accommodate to the system that
engulfs them and to gain whatever petty advantages it can yield.

They are willing to sell their very souls for such gains, though there are so many others ready to do the same that it avails little: "There really are too many souls," one peasant says (108). The portrait of the peasants is filled out with descriptions and authorial comments about their hard labor and hard play, quarrels and superstitions, births and funerals, simple customs and subtle attitudes. At a sign, "Rubbish May Not Be Dumped Here," is a pile of litter and garbage which, the author comments, "did not indicate any great respect for hygiene on the part of the inhabitants of Pietrasecca, but at least it proved that they could read." Other questionable symbols of modernization are not lacking. The peasant Sciatàp got his name from repeating the only English phrase he had learned, "Shut up," during years of slaving for a fellow villager in New York who sold coal and ice. "Thus," the author observes, "the phrase . . . passed into local idiom . . . the solitary example of a modern, foreign culture grafted on the ancient culture of the peasants" (55).

Though he finds that peasants from various countries have much in common, Silone is describing the peasants of a certain part of Italy in a particular time, a time of mobilization for war against Ethiopia. Spina, the revolutionary disguised as a priest, contemplates the different types of peasant even within Italy, all sharing an unlimited "capacity for suffering" and a life of "isolation." Now a bankrupt government, resorting to the "bloody diversion of war," finds it necessary to conscript these people and so to bring them together and end their isolation. Spina wonders whether this process, designed for evil, may not result in some good: "One knew how mobilizations of the hungry and poverty-stricken began; how they ended no man could foretell" (193). The response of the masses at this early stage is not promising. The civilian and military minions of the regime organize demonstrations to whip up the war spirit. Women are thrilled. Mothers of dead soldiers are suddenly remembered with small honors. Ordinary people are intoxicated by their own rhythmic chanting as they are diverted from the brutality and suffering of war by the thought of the material gains they may be able to realize. Under the impact of government propaganda, even some of Spina's revolutionary friends applaud the war and think of profit.

Silone stresses the difference between the village and the town. He does so mainly in symbols which suggest that the countryside is productive, exploited, natural, and simple whereas the city is exploitive, artificial, and pivotal to a repressive government. Spina reproaches himself for having ceased to be a peasant: he can neither forget the soil nor return to it. Thus the country is made to seem sympathetic, even though Silone does not explicitly assert its superiority and indicates that city workers are in fact more reliably revolutionary than peasants. Somehow, the greater exploitation of the peasants makes radicals expect more of them, which in turn brings on greater disappointment when the peasants display only ineffective hatred of their exploiters. Above all, Silone is determined not to romanticize the peasants, about whom all his novels, from first to latest, are written. In a foreword to his first novel, *Fontamara* (1930) Silone advises the reader: "This story will seem loud in its contrast with the picturesque image that southern Italy frequently assumes in literature." In Fontamara, he warns, there are no woods and few birds, the peasants curse rather than sing, and they even abuse the few saints they adopt.

Peasants and intellectuals are the most numerous characters in Silone's novels, and he is equally stern with both groups. Morality and power are Silone's main concerns in human relations, and intellectuals have a different place in such matters from the one occupied by peasants. *Bread and Wine* shows the conflicts and dilemmas intellectuals face with respect to both the exercise of power and its organization.

Spina, as an intellectual revolutionary, is ironical, ambivalent, self-deprecatory. He forces himself to judge his own actions and motives mercilessly. As a professional revolutionary, he senses that his idealism has been compromised by his political role. Indeed, his decision to end his exile and throw himself into underground work is the result not of a rational calculation but of a need to live at "such a pitch of intensity" that he could avoid thinking of his betrayal, a need to keep himself from examining his conscience. Nor was his original impulse to become a revolutionary a rational calculation; like the impulse of his comrades, it had come from his "moral condemnation" of the society in which he grew up. Back in the underground he faces this dilemma: he cannot ignore the suffering of the poor and retire from politics, nor can he go on accepting as supreme the interests of the revolutionary party, with its intrigues and lies (86).

The gap between ideals and life itself, Spina tells a religious woman about to enter a convent, is the source of all evil. Anyone who rises above animal instincts, he tells Cristina, retires to a monastery or convent. "Do you not think," he asks her, "that this divorce between a spirituality which retires into contemplation and a mass of people dominated by animal instincts is the source of all our ills?" (80). In a sense, *Bread and Wine* tells of Spina's resolve to break this pattern, to rise from animality, and to live and work among the masses. Cristina, whom Spina respects for her selflessness and idealism, reveals the limitations of her path of renunciation of this world when she defends her family's refusal to sell to peasants, at a price they can afford, land that would be safe from the floods that regularly destroy their houses. "One must be content with one's lot," she tells Spina (104).

On the organizational side, the difficulties are equally serious. Spina feels deeply the contradiction between the revolutionary party's opportunism and the attractive ideals it proclaims. He declines to compromise with society only to find himself in a party that defends its immorality by calling truth and justice "petty-bourgeois prejudices" (81). Ideals are an embarrassment to those who deal in power. The popular lawyer and orator, Zabaglione, a former socialist, and now an amiable cynic in the service of the Fascist state, complains that youngsters take things too literally when they expect capitalism to be destroyed simply because the regime claims the "corporate state" will replace it: "No regime ought ever to be taken literally, otherwise what would the world come to! Suppose a French citizen took it into his head to live according to the Declaration of the Rights of Man! He would end up in prison . . . There ought to be a rule that a country's constitution only concerns lawyers and older persons who understand the meaning of discipline and sacrifice, and must be rigorously ignored by the young" (149).

The sharpest and most poignant expression of the organizational dilemma occurs when Spina, in Rome, visits Uliva, a friend of student days, a violinist, and a revolutionary who has been in prison and is now removed from politics. Uliva laughs at Spina's invitation to return to work among the masses. He agrees that the "situation" is serious but insists that the masses are "cowed" and "corrupted," that even Fascism has changed from a "movement" to a "bureaucracy." "But what is the opposition?" he asks Spina. "Another bureaucracy that aspires to totalitarian domination in its turn, in the name of different ideas and on behalf of different interests." As he continues in this pessimistic vein, Spina interrupts: "Uliva, you're raving. You have been one of us, you know us, and you know that that is not our ideal." Uliva answers with weary finality: "It's not your ideal, but it is your destiny. There's no way out." To Spina's protests, Uliva replies that "every new idea . . . is crystallized in formulas so that it may be propagated . . . Thus every new idea invariably ends by becoming fixed, inflexible, parasitical, and reactionary." An intellectual, he insists, cannot adapt himself to a totalitarian regime. Unlike a worker, who can separate himself from such questions, the intellectual cannot escape taking a stand: he serves power or must oppose it and die. Uliva meets the dilemma by offering a formula for the intellectual's withdrawal: "I do not believe in progress, and I am not afraid of life" (174-177). He can face life without benefit of illusions, partly because he is even less afraid of death than of life. Death is indeed his fate, for soon Spina learns that Uliva, preparing explosives to blow up a church, died accidentally by his own hand in his apartment. Later, Spina shows that he too has adopted a form of withdrawal as his personal solution to the bureaucratic dilemma. He listens to the long confession of a young revolutionary who was forced to become a police informer. "If I were the head of a party or a political group," Spina says compassionately, "I should judge you according to the party statutes . . . But I am not, or am no longer, a political leader. I am just an ordinary mortal, and, if I am to judge another man, I can have nothing to guide me but my own conscience" (264).

Silone discusses the relation between intellectuals and power in works other than novels. In an interview as late as 1970, Silone referred to the "pact" between the rulers of the Soviet Union and certain Western intellectuals. He called this pact a "hybrid compromise of mutual aid between a political power and a spiritual power," according to which the intellectuals proclaimed the totalitarian state a noble, humanitarian, democratic achievement while Stalin, Khruschchev, Brezhnev and their Communist minions gave the intellectuals not only certain "material benefits" but assured "contact with the masses" and the illusion of leading a movement for progress in tune with history. By this pact, the intellectuals regularly protested repression in the West while maintaining silence about the labor camps in Siberia. In exchange, Communist critics hailed their works as art. With the rise and repression of intellectual dissenters in the Soviet Union itself, known to the world, Silone saw the end of this pact at least for the near future.[5]

The bureaucratic dilemma that Silone treats in novels was the subject of analysis by a number of social scientists earlier in this century. Robert Michels typified the pessimistic approach to politics when he concluded, in agreement with some other analysts of his time, that each group ascending to power would be corrupted by its exercise. "The socialists might conquer," he warns, "but not socialism, which would perish in the moment of its adherents' triumph" (408).

Silone likewise discusses, in many works of various genres, this general problem of power. In *The Story of a Humble Christian*, a different kind of work from *Bread and Wine*, he asks whether a man who becomes disillusioned with and leaves a religious or political movement can ever return to it when it appears to be reformed. His answer is no. The dissenter, once he stands outside the movement, never sees its truths except as defenses; he cannot recover his innocence because he has been freed of the "intellectual influence of the closed society" (33). And the movement itself cannot really reform, according to Silone. The "formalized ideology" in the service of a bureaucracy cannot even in a crisis return to genuine freedom: "a river never returns to its source—I'm sure of that, at least."[6]

On a less philosophical level, Silone poses the issue for Spina of how to convert the masses to an honorable way of life and to socialism. Having rejected traditional radicalism as opportunistic and bureaucratic, Spina decides he must befriend those people he would convert. Exile has made him impatient; he sees the urgency of action: "The facts of dictatorship must be confronted, not with the words of liberty, but with the facts of liberty" (130). His new contact with the peasants has demonstrated that there is a season for everything, and this is the season to build a moral way of living to oppose the immoral life under fascism. In deciding how to begin and how to work, Spina expounds and exemplifies a new technique of underground activity: no propaganda; friendship and mutual teaching and learning between a revolutionary and his "contact"; an end to the notion of the superiority of workers over peasants; a concern for the truth, wherever it may lead; and a rejection of action for the sake of "appearances."

When Spina meets peasants and workers, however, he is disheartened. He asks a peasant if he has "ever suffered from lack of liberty" (114). Misunderstanding Spina's reference to politics, the peasant answers that there is too much liberty—for boys and girls. Spina asks another peasant if he "agrees" with the unjust political arrangements in the countryside. "Agreeing" has nothing to do with it, the peasant replies. "Facts are one thing and words are another" (127).

Speech and silence are used to good effect in *Bread and Wine.* Words, rhetoric, and oratory are associated with power and exploitation, silence and deafness with natural goodness and repose. Silence brings people together, rhetoric is a barrier that alienates them. When Spina meets a young peasant, he tells him, "How I should like to stay here with you in silence, all night, sitting round this pool, as we are now . . . There is a kind of silence in which the . . . thick shell of fiction and prejudice and ready-made phrases which separate man from man, begins to crack and open . . . In no century have words been so perverted from their natural purpose of putting man in touch with man . . . To speak and to deceive (often to deceive oneself) have become almost synonymous . . . Therefore it is perhaps better to keep silent and to trust the silence" (154-155). The novel offers many examples of the corrupt speech of national and local Fascist authorities. When the Fascist troops came to arrest Zabaglione, they were so entranced by his speech that they left without arresting him. The carabinieri came next and gagged him, but his gestures were so expressive that they looked away to avoid being persuaded; and he was kept gagged even while being interrogated.

Silence is thus more expressive than speech. It is also a weapon for the peasant against his tormentors. As *Bread and Wine* begins, Don Benedetto hears noises from the road outside his home, where he finds a shepherd, with his donkey and dogs, blocking the path of an automobile. One of the passengers, in the uniform of a militia officer, angrily shouts and gesticulates to the shepherd, who gesticulates back to show he's a deaf mute. Don Benedetto greets the visitors and introduces them to the shepherd, who suddenly addresses the guests, "Why didn't you tell me you were going to see Don Benedetto?" Much later in the story, when Spina, disguised as a priest, is trying to make contact with individual peasants to convert them to humanist socialism, he is attracted to a young man who looks at him intently. Spina talks to him and asks his view of things. The young man leads Spina to his humble home, silently offers him a snack, as Spina continues to talk. The innkeeper finds Spina, whose welfare she has made her own responsibility, and calls him to dinner. Spina declines, saying he is not hungry and wants to continue the discussion with his young friend. "But haven't you noticed," she remarks, "he's deaf and dumb and only understands signs?" (112). Watching the young man's eyes fill with tears, Spina tells her to return to the inn. He remains with his friend, now both silent, until nightfall.

The religious overtones of such encounters are confirmed by other events and symbols of a religious character in the novel. The main symbol is suggested by the title. Bread stands for humanity's material needs, wine for it spiritual needs, the two elements that are necessary to a decent community. Poverty, Silone seems to say, makes the moral life difficult for most people to achieve, but wealth without morality does not raise humanity above the animal level. Silone offers an even more explicit interpretation through Spina, who is given bread and wine as a family mourns a dead son. "The bread is made of many grains of corn," he tells the father.

"Therefore it stands for unity. Wine is made of many clusters of grapes, and therefore it stands for unity, too. Unity of similar, equal, and useful things. Hence also it stands for truth and brotherhood, things that go well together" (311).

The practical and the spiritual—the political and the religious—are joined in Spina himself. He is a political man who tries to be moral, a revolutionary dressed like a priest who returns to the countryside to convert people politically only to find himself called upon, because of his guise and his manner, to minister instead to their religious and spiritual needs. Women take him to be a saint, even Jesus, and when he hides in a hayloft, Silone directly makes the analogy with the child in the manger. Spina himself tells his old teacher, Don Benedetto, that it was a "religious impulse" that made him a revolutionary. Indeed, he goes about his revolutionary work in a religious way, concerned more about moral than political questions, insisting that political activity is not a matter of spreading "new formulas, new gestures, or shirts of a different color," but is rather, in the "old expression," a matter of "conversion" (283). Silone explains the "southern Italian, Catholic" sense of spiritual comfort in the presence of a priest. In a revolutionary movement, a priest's role is similar to that of a chaplain in an army: "Would a peasant, even an atheist peasant, advance to the attack if he did not know there was a chaplain in the rear? The presence of a consecrated person in the revolutionary ranks is welcomed in the same way. It gives a sense of greater security"—a protection against harm and an assurance that one's side is right (156-157).

Silone draws another politicoreligious analogy. The political movement and the religious movement both become ends in themselves, seeking to protect the interests of the organization at the expense of the ideals that gave rise to it. Uliva, the disillusioned revolutionary, blows himself up preparing explosives to destroy a church where the Fascist regime has been planning a ceremony. A local parish priest defends the church's failure to condemn the war against Ethiopia: "The Church is an old, a very old lady, full of dignity, respect, traditions, bounden rights and duties," and it cannot risk adventures and indiscretions (237). Don

Benedetto, ostracized by and alienated from local and central church authorities, is more forthright: "The spirit of the Lord has abandoned the Church, which has become a formal, conventional, materialistic institution, obsessed with worldly and caste worries" (242). In 1962 in an interview, Silone described himself as Spina might have described himself: "Now I consider myself to be a Socialist without a party and a Christian without a church."[7]

Silone has continued to deal, in imaginative works and essays, with bureaucratic corruption and morality, but he has turned his attention more recently to the ill effects of affluence rather than of poverty. Affluence is not a new interest for him. Even while he was writing about the poor peasants of Fontamara in 1930, he heard his Swiss friends complaining about the vulgarity, superficiality, and boredom they attributed to middle-class status. The welfare state, with its "bureaucratic paternalism," has corrupted those formerly corrupted by poverty. The "old Adam" in us, remarks Silone, has confounded the hopes of reformers who thought that human behavior would be made moral by increasing consumption or changing institutions. As to what can be done about corruption, Silone offers the same guidance in his fiction as in his essays, whether the corrupting influence is poverty or affluence. In *Bread and Wine* Spina observes to Cristina: "He is saved who frees his own spirit from the idea of resignation to the existing order . . . Spiritual life and secure life do not go together. To save oneself one must struggle and take risks" (290-291). This is how Spina lives in the novel. In an essay thirty years later, Silone makes the same modest point: the direction in which hope lies is the promotion of "freedom and responsibility of man individually and in his complex relationship with his fellow human beings."[8]

In the 1920s, following World War I, American social critics heightened their attack upon certain institutions. Domestically, they criticized the national passion for material goods, as revealed in the growth of advertising and salesmanship, industrial expansion, and civic pride based on business values. They condemned American business and government for intervening in Latin America, as exemplified in several marine landings just before World War I, and for making profit out of war by the sale of munitions. Always on the alert for current issues to portray and discuss in fiction, the novelist T. S. Stribling combined all these themes in a weak yet interesting novel, *Fombombo,* published in 1923.

Thomas Strawbridge, a munitions and hardware salesman from Keokuk, Iowa, goes to Venezuela to sell guns. Committed to capitalist values and patriotism, he seeks advice from the American consul, who simultaneously warns him that the law prohibits the sale of guns to private individuals and helps him to get in touch with General Fombombo, the leader of an insurrection in control of the Rio Negro area. The American Babbitt and the local Latin tyrant get on well. Strawbridge joins the campaign to enlarge the general's domain because, to sell him guns, he must see the soldier's needs at first hand. The salesman accidentally becomes a hero on the field of battle and falls in love with Fombombo's beautiful wife, whom the general has neglected in favor of his mistresses. Now Fombombo is challenged by another soldier, while still another rebel leads a group of poor, simple, desperate people of the area who look to the foreign hero, Strawbridge, to deliver them from exploitation. Strawbridge remains loyal to his first sales prospect, Fombombo, who unfortunately goes down to defeat and is killed. As Strawbridge tries to escape the confusion with the dead tyrant's wife, he receives a letter from a former follower of Fombombo commissioning him to deliver munitions to the victor. But the letter bears a postscript from the leader of the poor announcing that he has just killed Fombombo's killer and has set up a new regime in the Rio Negro to ensure peace, justice, and prosperity.

In the course of describing the political life of this region of Venezuela, Stribling dramatizes one main issue: whether the supplier of the means should concern himself with the ends to which another puts them. Stribling poses the question in an unusual way, for in his novel the salesman, far from denying his complicity in the use of his product, proclaims it. Only when the users point out the implications of his eagerness does he begin to suspect the complexities of his sales approach to the morality of means and ends.

Strawbridge comes to General Fombombo with an attitude that puzzles the Latin tyrant. The supersalesman indicates an interest in Fombombo's plans for conquest in order better to serve his future needs. He quotes his boss back home: "When you sell a man, you have really gone into partnership with him. His gain is your gain." The general draws an implication that makes the salesman slightly uneasy. "I see," he says. "Because I am going to buy some rifles from you, you ask me what cities I am going to attack next." Strawbridge hesitates, then plunges into the moral abyss: "If you're going to use my guns, I'm partners with you in your . . . er . . . expansion. That's American methods, General; that's straightforward and honest" (53-54). This argument is one usually advanced by radical opponents of the makers and sellers of munitions; it sounds odd coming as a sales pitch from a representative of what in the 1930s were called "merchants of death." The same point is explored later when a local enemy of Fombombo is puzzled by Strawbridge's claim that he must help the tyrant by going to the battlefield to understand his customer's needs better. "But why is that, señor?" he asks about this tie between supplier and user, or means and ends. "If you sell a man anything, it is his. He has it. You have sold it." In reply, Strawbridge concedes that the use of the product is the buyer's affair. "But," he reaffirms, "perhaps with my expert knowledge I can show you how to use it better." He warms to the idea: "When you buy anything from me, gentlemen, you are not buying just my goods, you are buying human service! . . . You are buying the best in me to cooperate with the best in you, and between us we'll make this world a better world to live in." This kind of capitalist moral fervor still puzzles the precapitalist mentality of his listener, who again draws the uncomfortable implication: "For example, señor, if I wanted to buy a dirk to cut Lubito's throat, you would come and cut it first to see what kind of knife I should use?" Again Strawbridge pauses, then plunges into agreement (122).

Stribling thus tries to explain to the American reader the consequences of American sales logic in a tyranny in another society. He carries the effort through his salesman's meetings with various people who inform him of local conditions. Immediately on Strawbridge's arrival in Caracas, the capital, he is lectured by the American consul on the endemic insurrections. Later he is given further details by the manager of a British estate from which General Fombombo confiscates such resources as he needs. Describing the lofty promises and base activities of successive tyrants, the manager offers his judgment of the people: "The trouble is in the stock . . . scrub . . . scum. You can't make any decent government out of this . . . manure" (145). Fombombo's public relations aide, a black man, gives a local viewpoint to correct Strawbridge's American notions about "the people" and the structure of power in Latin America: "When you say 'everybody' you are speaking as an American, of your American middle class. That is the controlling power in America because it is sufficiently educated and compact to make its majority felt. We have no such class in Venezuela. We have an aristocratic class struggling for power, and a great peon population too ignorant for any political action whatsoever. The only hope for Venezuela is a beneficent dictator" (31). He presents his boss as an idealist: "It is his dream to create a super-civilization here . . . He will be wealthy; the whole nation will be wealthy . . . but what lies beyond wealth? . . . *Pues,* he will found a government where men can forget material care and devote their lives to the arts, the sciences, and pure philosophy" (34-35).

As the American salesman travels over the general's terrain, he finds only suspicion, repression, forced labor, unhealthy villages, and arbitrary rule. "Is this the beginning of Fombombo's brotherhood devoted to altruistic ends" he cries out (39). The general's public relations man gives him the answer he has already heard: yes, these harsh means will lead to noble ends.

All that he sees confirms the salesman's sense of American superiority in its freedom, efficiency, and cleanliness. The author, however, regards this sense as unwarranted or naive, and he portrays Strawbridge as blundering through to at least a minimum of understanding. In a village store, for example, he tries to convince the clerk that if he tidies up the place and displays his goods attractively in the window, he will increase profits and get ahead personally; all he needs is to give the "joint a prosperous, up-to-date look." The clerk explains that looking prosperous and up-to-date will only mean more taxes, so they keep their goods out of sight. The American salesman suddenly understands the "squalor and filth" he has seen: "It was an intentional filth, chosen to escape governmental mulcting" (83, 85). But he is still puzzled by the Latin American governments' discouragement of business, so different from the North American government's total dedication to increasing business. "Your market has got to be open," he tells Fombombo's public relations aide, "and it's got to be protected before you get any real big volume of trade" (93). This became the American message in "foreign aid" after World War II in many parts of the world.

Stribling takes his salesman's education a step further into the morality of sexual relations. In love with Fombombo's wife, Strawbridge becomes uncomfortable about extramarital affairs when he sees the tyrant with his new mistress, a young girl he has taken from a peon. Strawbridge has known about the general's mistresses, but his discomfort becomes unbearable only when he sees them together. The general's openness and the salesman's discomfort are the occasion for an authorial commentary on the distinction between "North American chastity and Venezuelan laxity." Turning to these broad cultural differences, Stribling points out that the North American has his shortcomings but seeks to conceal them, while the Latin American does not mind revealing his own. The North American is not being hypocritical, since he does not intend to deceive anyone, nor is anyone deceived. He simply does not want to offend others by parading his own vices before them: "To be seen openly sinning is to make of oneself a public nuisance." By keeping his vices secret, the Anglo-Saxon avoids paining others. "Taking us all in all," Stribling concludes in a sophisticated argument to his presumably puritanical readers, "perhaps America's greatest gift to the world is the peccadillo of low visibility" (105). Stribling implies, but does not make plain, that different cultures have their own logic for exposing and concealing their peccadillos. "Low visibility" — the more recent cliché is "low profile" — changes from culture to culture.

Fombombo's combination of politics and the contrast of cultures in the Americas has since been followed in novels about Africa. One of the best is Evelyn Waugh's *Black Mischief* (1932), in which an Englishman advises an Oxford-educated African dictator who seeks to modernize his country rapidly. Paul Theroux's *Jungle Lovers* (1971) comes even closer to *Fombombo,* describing an American insurance salesman's adventures in the dictatorial and revolutionary politics of Malawi.

Social Class

Social class is the last of the four major social themes in the novel. From almost any point regarded as the origin of the novel, as far back as the early seventeenth century, writers use it to portray manners and morality, that is, the conduct and attitudes of characters in different stations of life. As socialist ideas developed through the nineteenth century, novelists began to use class differences in a more directly political way. The sheer portrayal of such differences, however, is not necessarily associated with radical ideologies. Even in novels which do make the association, writers often portray the lower or the working classes not merely because they want to criticize the upper or middle classes. In the delineation of social power and prestige, including their unfavorable consequences, most novelists have continued to use mainly upper- and middle-class characters and to explore their individual history and psychology. Novelists also show the families and social classes to which the individuals are connected, but the focus is usually on the dramatic experiences of the individual rather than of the group. Perhaps the very structure of the novel as well as popular tastes require this focus.

Balzac is a favorite novelist of Marxists because he places economic relations at the base of class differences in interest, conduct, and attitude. In *Les Paysans,* he describes how large-scale farming in postrevolutionary France was becoming like large-scale industry with respect to management, the market, and risk. He gives details of management by stewards, who occupied a position between the aristocratic owners on one side and the smallholders and peasants on the other, the two main classes in competition and combat. It was this struggle between rich and poor, Balzac notes in the novel, that he undertook to describe in this portion of his vast work. The Marxist critic Georg Lukacs has called *Les Paysans* a "masterly picture" of the destruction of the peasant smallholding, comparing the novel to one of Marx's analytical studies. Balzac, he asserts, "presents in literary form the same essential development of the post-revolutionary smallholding that Marx described in *The Eighteenth Brumaire*" (21, 35).

There are several other instances in which a novel and an analytical study are alike in their treatment of social class. Edgar Mittelholzer, a Guyanese novelist, tells a story of class and color in *Sylvia* (1953). One of his characters, an Englishman married to a woman of black and Indian parentage, explains to his light-skinned daughter why she must marry a man of color and of good family, in the process describing the class-color-nationality mixture that governs life in the capital of what was then British Guiana. A similar explanation is given in an analytical work by the social scientist Raymond T. Smith. The novelist's need to clarify implicit differences of class or race is shown in Mittelholzer's reference to a light-skinned man's employment as overseer on a sugar estate. He helps the North American or British reader appreciate the significance of this fact by a parenthetical explanation that "the sugar-estates employed only white men as overseers," implying that the young man could "pass" as white (35).

Another such pair, in which the novel again antedates the analytical study, is John Galsworthy's *The Island Pharisees* (1904) and C. F. G. Masterman's *The Condition of England* (1909), which quotes the novel. Galsworthy contrasts the physically robust but insensitive middle class with the unhealthy lower orders. Concentrating on the middle class, he describes their contented isolation: "All was marvelously sane and slumbrous. Everything—the soft air, the soft drawl, the shapes and murmurs, the rising smell of wood-smoke from fresh kindled fires—was full of the spirit of security and of home. The outside world was barred off. Typical of some island nation was this nest of refuge—complacency was born and bred there; men grew quietly tall, fattened, and without fuss dropped off their perches; ideals flourished blandly, as sunflowers flourish in the sun, and, when the sun goes in, fall asleep" (147).

Masterman, in much the same critical mood, sees England as exploitative, opulent, vain, and complacent.

Many other English novelists successfully portray the social classes as they guide their heroes and heroines through the vicissitudes of social existence. In Jane Austen's works social class and money are always important to the romances and marriages she chronicles. In *Emma* (1816), for example, Austen shows the relations between the gentry and working farmers, and also touches upon tradesmen and poor laborers. Class or social position is clearly based on property, birth, and manners, as exemplified by George Knightly, who is well-born, has a large estate upon which he works, and is careful not only to avoid drawing attention directly to his exalted place but also to show appropriate solicitude for the deserving among the less fortunate. Thomas Hardy, in *The Mayor of Casterbridge* (1886), to name only one of his novels, connects his characters' attitudes, speech, and conduct to their social class and their particular trade. He also reports on economic conditions such as the corn laws and speculation in commodities. At the end of the nineteenth century a social critic, Vida Scudder, made an interesting comparison between the classes portrayed by two novelists, Dickens and Thackeray: "The two authors, taken as a whole, give us a bird's-eye view of the entire social structure. One begins where the other ends, and only in rare cases do their provinces intersect. Dickens starts in the depths . . . It is the great world of trade that he shows us, especially of retail trade: the small shopkeepers and peddlers, the dolls' dressmakers, the dancing-masters, also the lower grades of professional folk, nurses, lawyers' clerks, surgeons' apprentices, sextons, and the like . . . They possess no resources, they have no manners. As soon as he tries to enter the world where propriety and pretty behavior rule, Dickens becomes absurd. Not so with Thackeray. Manners are his one solace in a dreary world . . . The drawing-room and the club are his arena . . . Though Dickens and Thackeray live in the same city, and work in a way on the same material, their worlds barely touch . . . Certain great social omissions are notable in their work. They do not know the agricultural poor . . . Nor is even Dickens fully aware of that silent throng on whom rested the whole social fabric: the productive class . . . The worlds they depict are not uncorrelated, however separate. For the world of Dickens exists that the world of Thackeray may live; makes its gowns, cares for its horses, officers its prisons, provides its food, its inns, its dancing-lessons, its coffins . . . What are the distinctive features of this social order? The first obvious fact about it is that it is filled, rid-dled, created by money: commercial to the core. Dickens' world is absorbed in the making, Thackeray's in the spending, of money" (130-135).

George Gissing is a novelist who often portrays a class between those of Dickens and Thackeray. Concerned also with the effects of social position and money, Gissing shows the drab life of the aspiring poor, people with little money, but not of the lower classes, who were on the edge of respectability and fought to cross the line into that class of mediocre uprightness. His short stories, for example, collected in *The House of Cobwebs and Other Stories* (1906), correlate income, speech, clothes, and manners to delineate the same class to which Leonard Bast, an important character in Forster's *Howards End,* belongs.

Forster's story involves three families in differing social classes. The Schlegel sisters, Margaret and Helen, are cultured, intelli-gent, liberal, and eager for experience. They are attracted to the Wilcox family, wealthy and capitalist, whose country house is Howards End, several hours from London. Helen, the younger sis-ter, falls in love with Paul Wilcox, younger son of Ruth and Henry Wilcox, but the affair is broken off. Margaret and Ruth become intimate friends, the older woman being an inspiring example of wisdom to Margaret. At Ruth's early death, she informally leaves Howards End to Margaret. The Wilcoxes ignore the mother's wish and keep her note a secret. Henry Wilcox, now a widower, falls in love with Margaret and persuades her to marry him. Meanwhile the Schlegel sisters have become acquainted with Leonard Bast, a poor clerk whose cultural pretentions they encourage. Leonard's wife, Jacky, who trapped him into an unhappy marriage, turns out to have been the mistress of Henry Wilcox, and so the circle connecting the three families is complete. Margaret is sympathetic to the strengths and weaknesses of the Wilcoxes, while the more impetuous Helen is repelled by them and more sympathetic to the Basts. Out of guilt for her own advantages and in a rejection of conventional values, Helen spends a night with Leonard and becomes pregnant. Henry characteristically expects Margaret to understand his own extramarital affair but criticizes Helen for hers, while Margaret finds it possible to tolerate both, though she is more critical of her husband. When for various purposes they are all drawn to Howards End, Henry's son Charles self-righteously attacks Leonard, who dies of the combination of a weak heart, the blow from Charles, and symbolically the books that fall on him in the scuffling. Now the Wilcoxes too are shattered. Charles goes to prison. Henry becomes ill, cannot sustain his old values, and reaches toward a new morality when Margaret moves him and Helen into Howards End. Helen's baby is born there, beloved even by Henry. Helen and Henry, opposites, come to understand and like each other. Henry makes a will, leaving his money to the remaining Wilcoxes but Howards End—now encroached upon by London—to Margaret, just as his first wife Ruth did before all these trials and renewals of faith.

A fine and capacious novel, *Howards End* has several themes, only one of them being the confrontations of different social classes.

The novel's epigraph is "Only connect . . ." The idea appears in several places in the novel, most prominently when the narrator describes, in ch. 22, Margaret's mood and intention as she becomes engaged to Henry, whose limitations she recognizes: "She would only point out the salvation that was latent in his own soul, and in the soul of every man. Only connect! That was the whole of her sermon. Only connect the prose and the passion, and both will be exalted, and human love will be seen at its height. Live in fragments no longer." The main connections are made by Margaret. Through marriage she connects the Wilcoxes and the Schlegels, Henry and Helen, the older and younger generations, practicality and idealism, the living Henry with his dead wife Ruth, whom Margaret comes increasingly to resemble. The Schlegel sisters too connect Leonard Bast with the Wilcoxes—although Mrs. Bast and Henry Wilcox had their own liaison—a connection that leads to tragedy. This theme of connection, incidentally, also appears in Silone's *Bread and Wine,* whose title symbolizes prose and poetry, practicality and idealism.

Another theme or message in *Howards End* is that personal relations count most in life. In ch. 4, Helen tells Margaret that the Wilcoxes are not "genuine people," that even Paul, with whom she had a brief meeting of minds, was afraid of emotion and friendship. Margaret, in the same mood, says that she and Helen have never known that "great outer life" of the Wilcoxes in which "telegrams and anger count. Personal relations, that we think supreme, are not supreme there." But she has some doubt, suspecting that the "outer life . . . does breed character," while "personal relations lead to sloppiness in the end." Drawing on her observation of Paul during their personal crisis, however, Helen is confident that "personal relations are the real life, for ever and ever," and that Paul, living the "outer life," had "nothing to fall back upon." The lesson is driven home, in ch. 36, when Helen is pregnant at Howards End and Henry brings along a doctor, Mansbridge, to examine her. Margaret refuses to admit the two men, telling her husband: "It all turns on affection now. Affection. Don't you see? Surely you see. I like Helen very much, you not so much. Mr. Mansbridge doesn't know her. That's all. And affection, when reciprocated, gives rights. Put that down in your notebook, Mr. Mansbridge. It's a useful formula."

In this scene in ch. 36, Forster illustrates another theme of the relations between the sexes when the two women occupy Howards End against the men. As Margaret keeps them out, the narrator comments: "A new feeling came over her; she was fighting for women against men. She did not care about rights, but if men came into Howards End, it should be over her body." When in ch. 37 the Schlegel sisters see their furniture in the Wilcoxes' Howards End, they agree in their dislike of the drawing room. "It's a room," Margaret remarks, "that men have spoilt through trying to make it nice for women. Men don't know what we want — ." Helen interrupts, "And never will." Margaret, more moderate, replies: "I don't agree. In two thousand years they'll know." Earlier, just before Margaret and Henry marry, she learns of his affair with

Jacky Bast ten years ago. Unable to understand how he could yield to such a temptation, she doubts she can marry him. "Men must be different," she feels. "Are the sexes," the narrator asks in ch. 28, "really races, each with its own code of morality, and their mutual love a mere device of Nature to keep things going?" After Margaret and Henry are married, although she is clever and reads books, she does what he wishes and yields even when she is ahead in an argument. "Man is for war," the narrator remarks in ch. 31, "woman for the recreation of the warrior, but he does not dislike it if she makes a show of fight." In an inevitable confrontation, in ch. 38, Margaret tries to make Henry see the connection between his indiscretion with Jacky Bast and Helen's with Leonard Bast: "You shall see the connection if it kills you, Henry! You have had a mistress — I forgave you. My sister has a lover — you drive her from the house . . . Men like you use repentance as a blind, so don't repent."

The three families in *Howards End* exemplify three social classes: the Wilcoxes, rich, capitalist, practical, bordering on the ruling class; the Schlegels, secure if not rich, cultivated, the middle of the middle classes; the Basts, Jacky already beyond respectability and sunk in the lowest class, Leonard on its edge and desperately eager to climb up.

The three classes meet, in ch. 16, in a masterly depiction of both obvious and subtle psychological connections and gaps among them. The Schlegel sisters, having heard from Henry Wilcox that the company Leonard Bast works for is about to fail, invite Leonard to their home in order to warn him to change jobs before losing the one he has. Helen explains herself and her sister to him: "We aren't odd, really — nor affected, really. We're overexpressive: that's all." Male but inferior, Leonard becomes condescending: "The more a lady has to say, the better." Helen, a woman and superior, becomes sharp. "Yes, I know," she says. "The darlings are regular sunbeams." Margaret, less emotional, gets to the point of the visit, Leonard's employers, by asking, "How do you like your work?" This question annoys Leonard because he thinks he has been invited to talk about culture, not his economic position. The Schlegels tell him they have heard his employers will fail. He defends the firm, insisting their information is "quite wrong." Margaret surprises him by exclaiming, "Oh, good!" The narrator comments: "In his circle to be wrong was fatal . . . To them [the sisters] nothing was fatal but evil."

As the sisters persist in discussing business, Leonard becomes increasingly annoyed that he cannot spend these few precious moments with them talking about books. Suddenly Henry and his daughter come in to show the Schlegels two puppies he has bred. Helen is ecstatic, gets down on all fours to play with them, and asks Leonard to join her. This invitation to the frivolous makes him see how sour everything has gone, and he announces he must leave. Still with the puppies, Helen casually asks him to come again. His anger rises: "No, I shan't; I knew it would be a failure." The narrator explains that the earnest Schlegels cannot let the matter rest: "They had attempted friendship, and they would take the consequences." Helen calls Leonard rude; he questions why they want him there at all. "To help you, you silly boy," Helen tells him. Leonard resents condescension: "I don't want your patronage . . . What do you want to unsettle me for?" He appeals to Henry, the only other man present: "I put it to this gentleman. I ask you, sir, am I to have my brain picked?" Henry is sympathetic because he, like Leonard, is put off by the sisters' intellectuality. After playing neutral, Henry agrees with Leonard, calling the situation the Schlegels have created "highly unfair." After Leonard goes, the sympathy that Henry, the most powerful person in the group, has had for Leonard, the least powerful, evaporates. A new alignment takes place. Henry expresses his amused admiration for the way Margaret has managed Leonard. Turning serious, he joins the Schlegels against Leonard, warning Margaret that to treat such people with kindness only encourages them to impose: "You must keep that type at a distance . . . They aren't our sort, and one must face the fact." Margaret explains that she and Helen like Leonard because, despite his limitations, he seeks adventure, and they want to help him "go to the real thing." Henry reverts to siding with Leonard in feeling that the sisters interfere in his life: "Your mistake is this. This young bounder has a life of his own. What right have you to conclude it is an unsatisfactory life?" He adds in a note of condescension to Margaret: "That's where we practical fellows are more tolerant than you intellectuals. We live and let live, and assume that . . . the ordinary plain man may be trusted to look after his own affairs." The idealistic, middle-class Schlegels thus believe in stirring and improving their inferiors, while the practical, upper-class Wilcoxes prefer to leave them to their own adequate devices. The poor themselves prefer both the idealists who encourage their aspirations and the practical rich who leave them some pride.

The main class distinctions in *Howards End* are between the Wilcoxes and Schlegels, and these distinctions go beyond economic position. The two families are fully aware of these differences, though they also see themselves as belonging to the same broad privileged class. Helen, pointing to their common deficiencies in ch. 22, calls both families "the upper classes." The cultural-political differences between them emerge early as Helen admits that the Schlegels have much to learn from the Wilcoxes. Under the spell of her infatuation with Paul, she seems to fall in love with the Wilcox style. "The energy of the Wilcoxes had fascinated her," the narrator indicates in ch. 4. "She had liked giving in to Mr. Wilcox, or Evie, or Charles; she had liked being told that her notions of life were sheltered or academic; that Equality was nonsense, Votes for women nonsense, Socialism nonsense, Art and Literature, except when conducive to strengthening the character, nonsense." She changes her mind, when Paul becomes frightened of their affair, telling Margaret later that "the whole Wilcox family was a fraud, just a wall of newspapers and motor-cars and golf-clubs, and that if it fell I should find nothing behind it but panic and emptiness." From then on the differences became more pronounced. The Wilcox mistrust of the Schlegels comes out most clearly in the younger generation, Charles and Evie. When in ch. 21 Henry and Margaret agree to marry, Charles tells his wife that Margaret "always meant to get hold of Howards End," and he vows to act firmly if the Schlegels worry his father "with their artistic beastliness."

The Schlegels and the Wilcoxes disagree and struggle steadily— over Howards End, which may be a symbol of England itself, over art, the poor, propriety, responsibility — over almost anything that comes up about which it is possible to differ.

The difference between the public and the private summarizes the differences between the Wilcoxes and Schlegels. Practical people are concerned with the outer life, idealists with the inner life. The narrator in ch. 18 says that Henry sees "modern life steadily," while Margaret sees it "whole." With optimism and self-confidence, Henry "never bothered over the mysterious or the private." In the public world, appearances count. When Helen is pregnant by Leonard, the sisters and their younger brother Tibby think about her, Leonard, and the child, but in ch. 38 the Wilcox men hold that Helen's "seducer" must marry her, and if he is already married he "must pay heavily for his misconduct and be thrashed within an inch of his life." The private people, however, as Margaret sees in her moderate way, depend on the public people. "If Wilcoxes hadn't worked and died in England for thousands of years," she tells Helen in ch. 19, "you and I couldn't sit here without having our throats cut. There would be no trains, no ships to carry us literary people about . . . More and more do I refuse to draw my income and sneer at those who guarantee it." Margaret is willing to go far in her recognition of connections. "Some day," notes the narrator in ch. 18, expressing Margaret's rather than Helen's thoughts about Henry Wilcox, " — in the millennium — there may be no need for his type. At present, homage is due it from those who think themselves superior, and who possibly are."

Despite her cautious reservations, Margaret feels the same sense of victory Helen might when, as the story ends, the Schlegels have prevailed. They have Howards End, and Henry, no longer the moralizing tycoon, is living with the two sisters and the illegitimate child of one of them. When Henry announces that he is giving Howards End, the prize, to Margaret, and his heirs acquiesce, the narrator remarks: "Margaret did not answer. There was something uncanny in her triumph. She, who had never expected to conquer anyone, had charged straight through these Wilcoxes and broken up their lives." The triumph is Helen's too, who had most dramatically challenged the Wilcox values, even if, as the story implies, Margaret's more moderate challenge was the more effective. The outer life of power and empire gives way to the inner life of social causes like "temperance, tolerance and sexual equality" contrasted in ch. 4. The Schlegels are public in that they care for public issues or the "Social Question," but in a way different from the Wilcox way. The sisters "desired that public life should mirror whatever is good in the life within." In ch. 37, when Margaret and Helen are at Howards End, love overcomes their initial unease: "They looked into each other's eyes. The inner life had paid."

To the cultural-political gap between the Schlegels and the Wilcoxes, Forster adds a difference about the place of money. When Margaret becomes Mrs. Wilcox and meets her husband's friends, she realizes that even he has no deep affection for them. His friends he made by chance, his investments with care. Money figures frequently in *Howards End;* what counts is more the amount one has than one's place in the productive process that creates capital in the first place. In this relationship, as in others, Margaret is closer to the Wilcoxes than Helen is.

Before they become engaged, Henry Wilcox offers, in ch. 18, to sublet his London house to the Schlegel sisters. Margaret's eagerness to see it pleases him: "I'm glad you don't despise the goods of this world." She responds reassuringly: "Heavens, no! Only idiots and prigs do that." Her attitude softens him; he almost kisses her as the car passes Buckingham Palace on the way to his house. Clearly Margaret's good sense has brought them much closer, but the gap between him and Helen is not narrowed. Helen becomes disturbed when Henry remarks that Leonard's employers are a sound company after all, for the clerk, upon the sisters' advice, has left his job for one paying less money. Helen tells Henry, in ch. 22, that they are responsible for the injury to Leonard. Henry replies, "No one's to blame." Helen's liberal conscience must reject this abdication of guilt: "Is no one to blame for anything?" Henry counters with the broad advice: "Don't take up that sentimental attitude over the poor . . . As civilization moves forward, the shoe is bound to pinch in places, and it's absurd to pretend that anyone is responsible personally." With the complacency that Galsworthy was criticizing around the same time in *The Island Pharisees,* Wilcox denies that there is a "Social Question." "There are just rich and poor," he pronounces, "as there always have been and always will be."

Money is also significant in the relations between the Schlegels and the Basts. The sisters, who have money and culture, seem always to be discussing money with Leonard Bast, while he, having neither, wants only to talk about culture. In ch. 16 the narrator observes that women are "heavy-handed" about money: "They cannot see why we should shroud our incomes and our prospects in a veil." Margaret does not hesitate to talk about money, realizing that having it makes it possible for people to take the risks that make life interesting. "You and I and the Wilcoxes," she tells her aunt in ch. 7, "stand upon money as upon islands. It is so firm beneath our feet that we forget its very existence . . . the very soul of the world is economic." People ought to be honest about it: "I'm tired of these rich people who pretend to be poor." Leonard, who does not like to talk about money, personifies the unfortunate consequences for those who do not have it. When he first meets the Schlegel sisters at a concert and accompanies Margaret home to retrieve his umbrella, which Helen, leaving early, has taken with her, he is impressed by easy, cultivated talk. He, in contrast, must think about the price of the ticket, whether he can do without a program, the umbrella itself, instead of letting himself go on culture. He realizes that to catch up with people like the Schlegels, one must have more than an hour now and then for reading.

Without money or culture, Leonard excites the Schlegel sisters' sympathy because of his lofty aspirations so close to their own tastes. They understand his low origins, "grandson to the shepherd or ploughboy whom civilization had sucked into the town," as they think of him when they see him for the second time. He is among the thousands who have lost rural robustness without acquiring urbanity or culture. Margaret ruminates in ch. 14 on the many who are "wrecked" in the attempt to cross the line from a natural to a cultivated life; less sympathetically, she thinks of Leonard as a "type," with "vague aspirations . . . mental dishonesty

. . . familiarity with the outsides of books." He is described in ch. 6 as a product of a mass society, hoping to "come to Culture suddenly" with little real effort. But the Schlegels are also disturbed by Leonard's inchoate nature. In ch. 5 Forster leaves the reader, as well as the Schlegels, with a sense of foreboding after Leonard's first visit to their house to retrieve his umbrella. Helen is uneasy because they did not invite him into the dining room for tea. The "little incident" as a whole, the narrator remarks, impressed the sisters "more than might be supposed. It remained as a goblin footfall, as a hint that all is not for the best in the best of all possible worlds, and that beneath these superstructures of wealth and art there wanders an ill-fed boy, who has recovered his umbrella indeed, but who has left no address behind him, and no name." Margaret, in ch. 13, voices the same sense of fear when Helen describes unkindly an unexpected visit from Mrs. Bast, who has come looking for her husband "as if he was an umbrella." Margaret is not sure the story is funny: "It means some horrible volcano smoking somewhere, doesn't it?" Helen, who is to be most deeply affected when the volcano erupts, denies that the miserable Basts are "capable of tragedy." Still, Margaret fears such contact with "turmoil and squalor," which the narrator once more calls a "goblin footfall."

Helen differs with all the other main characters about money. She likes it but depreciates it. Leonard tells her, in ch. 27, that since losing his job he cannot appreciate nature or books as he used to because "one must have money." "Well, you're wrong," she responds. He argues that "the real thing's money and all the rest is a dream." Unsympathetically, she tells him that he has forgotten Death, which shows the "emptiness of Money" and which scares the rich, the powerful, and the practical more than it does those unencumbered by money. Helen this night seduces Leonard, loving him out of pity. She decides soon afterward, true to her ideals, that she must accept full responsibility for Leonard's predicament—his being out of a job and his yielding to her desires. Having offered herself, which he takes at her command, she now offers him money, a considerable part of her fortune, which he refuses just as he is evicted for not paying his rent. To help him, she had gone so far as to sell some shares, but her gift of money spurned, she reinvests on good advice and makes a profit out of her altruism, showing that the rich get richer, the poor poorer. Leonard, remorseful on learning that Helen is pregnant, never thinks she might be to blame for that evening, when she was drawn to him by the contrast between his poverty and sensitivity and the Wilcox wealth and crassness. But Helen, the narrator observes in ch. 41, "loved the absolute. Leonard had been ruined absolutely, and had appeared to her as a man apart, isolated from the world." Hostile to those who refuse to recognize their responsibility, guilt-ridden herself and sympathetic to the Basts, she had offered herself to the oppressed man: "She and the victim seemed alone in a world of unreality, and she loved him absolutely, perhaps for half an hour."

Leonard, with neither money nor culture, is treated condescendingly by the other characters in the novel, by the narrator, and even by the author. Yet toward the end he is shown to have a kind of courage, independence, and nobility. As his fortunes wane, he turns to his own family for money, but before the Schlegels and Wilcoxes he maintains a facade of self-control. Helen lectures him about money, but he refuses the money she offers. He is generous toward his wretched wife with whom he has never been happy. He is equally generous toward Helen, taking the entire burden of sin upon himself. Obsessed with guilt, he seeks out Margaret to confess to her, and it is at this moment that Charles Wilcox delivers the blow which kills him.

Helen's attitude is that people like herself must help people like the Basts, but she must do so in her own way rather than his. She borders on what has been recently called "radical chic." In ch. 15 Forster describes similar attitudes at an "informal discussion club" which the sisters attend. One of the members proposes the notion that she is a millionaire about to die and asks the question, "How ought I to dispose of my money?" Others are assigned different roles and argue for different positions. The focus becomes how to help the Basts of this world; various schemes are advanced to give them art, a library, athletic facilities, even to pay their rent without their knowledge. Margaret interrupts: "Why not give him the money itself?" In response to the protests, she argues for a large gift of money rather than "little driblets," the same word Helen later uses to defend her effort to "compensate" Leonard with five thousand pounds. "Money's educational," Margaret continues. "It's far more educational than the things it buys." Replying to the argument that the poor do not know how to manage money, Margaret insists: "Give them a chance. Give them money. Don't dole them out poetry-books and railway-tickets like babies. Give them the wherewithal to buy these things. When your Socialism comes, it may be different, and we may think in terms of commodities instead of cash. Till it comes, give people cash, for it is the warp of civilization, whatever the woof may be . . . It is so slurred over and hushed up . . . Money: give Mr. Bast money, and don't bother about his ideals. He'll pick up those for himself." The "more earnest members" misconstrue her; practical themselves in "daily life," they "cannot bear to hear ideals belittled in conversation." When asked if giving Leonard money would not profit him at the expense of his spirituality, Margaret answers, "he would not gain his soul until he gained a little of the world." The members are not convinced. One "earnest girl" suggests the poor need "personal supervision and mutual help," which in the narrator's words would change them "until they become exactly like people who were not so poor." Thus the members early in this century debate the nature of the poor in a way that social scientists have recently debated the "culture of poverty."[9] At home, Helen asks Margaret what is the "woof" of the world if money is its "warp." She is imprecise: "Very much what one chooses. It's something that isn't money—one can't say more."

Some of Forster's intrusions in *Howards End* bear closely on the theme of social class. The most important feature of these intrusions is that they put forward the views of three people: Forster as author, the narrator as a conservative woman (her sex is not revealed until ch. 28, the last third of the novel), and Margaret as the leading character. Sometimes Forster the author seems to make the narrator appear narrow-minded or ironical in her condescension toward the poor, as in ch. 6, where the narrator refers to the novel in general as avoiding the lower classes: "We are not concerned with the very poor. They are unthinkable, and only to be approached by the statistician or the poet. This story deals with gentlefolk, or with those who are obliged to pretend that they are gentlefolk." The narrator's views come through as a cross between those of the first Mrs. Wilcox and the members of the discussion club. The narrator admires the class of the Wilcoxes because it has built up England, yet she complains of the destruction of beauty by industrial progress. She is sympathetic to the high culture of the Schlegel sisters yet disparages Leonard's aspirations toward it. When Forster seems to speak in his own voice, he sometimes agrees with his narrator and sometimes contradicts her; most often he appears to agree with his main character, Margaret.[10] Although the story itself reveals a nobility about Leonard, the narrator does not much change her attitude as expressed in ch. 6: "He knew that he was poor, and would admit it: he would have died sooner than confess any inferiority to the rich. This may be splendid of him. But he was inferior to most rich people, there is not the least doubt of it. He was not as courteous as the average rich man, nor as intelligent, nor as healthy, nor as lovable." But the rich men in *Howards End* are not very courteous, intelligent, or lovable, though they appear healthy. By denying with his story these authorial remarks of his narrator, Forster takes a more sympathetic position on the qualities of the poor and their eligibility for a place in the novel.

Through intrusions by the author and narrator, as well as through events and statements of the characters, Forster makes judgments not only on the rich and poor but on the drift of civilization of the early twentieth century. Howards End, the place, has often been interpreted as standing for England itself, and the struggle over Howards End is supposed to represent the struggle for England or for its soul. Forster promotes this interpretation by describing the effect of the place upon Margaret. "She recaptured the sense of space," the narrator says of Margaret in ch. 24 as she contemplates Howards End, "which is the basis of all earthly beauty, and, starting from Howards End, she attempted to realize England." London, however, the embodiment of the triumph of commercialism, is encroaching even upon Howards End; and the

Wilcoxes, though they inhabit the suburb, stand for the vices and virtues of London and its active, industrial spirit. In ch. 43, as Margaret congratulates herself on telling her husband of his hypocrisy, the narrator observes of her speech: "It was spoken not only to her husband, but to thousands of men like him — a protest against the inner darkness in high places that comes with a commercial age." Commercial and industrial London is equated with modernism, but not everything modern is bad. Work, energy, and practicality are good. Margaret, in ch. 26, is confident that Henry Wilcox will see his responsibility toward Leonard Bast and give him employment: "Henry would save the Basts, as he had saved Howards End, while Helen and her friends were discussing the ethics of salvation." The energy and achievements of the Wilcoxes are appreciated in the novel, as shown in their contrast with the Schlegels. Margaret herself contends in ch. 13 that work is good for all, even women: "Everyone is the better for some regular work. I believe that in the last century men have developed the desire for work, and they must not starve it. It's a new desire. It goes with a great deal that's bad, but in itself it's good, and I hope that for women, too, 'not to work' will soon become as shocking as 'not to be married' was a hundred years ago."

Modernism thus means energy, work, and their consequences for good or evil. It means also unrest and instability. The narrator implies in ch. 6 that Bast would have been happier — at least more content — in the "brightly colored civilizations" centuries ago, in which "he would have had a definite status, his rank and his income would have corresponded." But nowadays the "angel of Democracy" stirs ambitions that can hardly be realized. At the same time, people become less important and places or possessions more. Helen is optimistic, saying that places are usually "so much nicer" than people. Margaret is pessimistic, thinking, in ch. 15, of the hustle of London: "The more people one knows, the easier it becomes to replace them." The fullest expression of evil in modernism is the motor car, just coming into widespread use among those who could afford it. It already makes too much dirt, which enters the lungs, and goes too fast for the safety of riders and walkers. On a drive Henry points out, in ch. 23, a pretty church to

Margaret, which she misses as they whiz by. The contemporary reader senses the first impact of the automobile's speed: "She looked at the scenery. It heaved and merged like porridge. Presently it congealed. They had arrived." Margaret feels in ch. 31 that London is a "foretaste of this nomadic civilization which is altering human nature so profoundly, and throws upon personal relations a stress greater than they have ever borne before."

In ch. 13 Forster makes much of the imminent decline of London even as it is so pleasurable. Comfortable buildings are torn down needlessly to give way to large ones that constitute the "architecture of hurry." The narrator observes: "Month by month things were stepping livelier, but to what goal? The population still rose, but what was the quality of the men born?" And all the time, as Helen says at the last when the sisters hold Howards End, "London's creeping." Past the meadows, they can see from Howards End the "red rust" in the London air, which is making their place only a "survival": "Logically, they had no right to be alive. One's hope was in the weakness of logic."

This is Forster's ultimate comment on civilization and social class. He is pessimistic, but moderately so, and hopes for a triumph of the broad spirit against narrow logic. He shows the good and bad in human nature and conduct, and in the institutions human beings create. As for the classes into which people divide themselves, they too are mixed. The Wilcoxes are hypocritical and destroy much that is good, but they are energetic and practical and save Howards End. The Schlegels are condescending but idealistic. The Basts live mean lives but show a certain nobility.

The Novel as a Vehicle
for Social Commentary

I went to one of them downtown white workshops
for a couple of months and got all screwed up with
angles of narration, points of view, objectivity,
universality, composition, author-intrusion . . . I
said, to hell with all that! . . . I will intrude, pro-
trude, obtrude or exclude my point of view any
time it suits my disposition. Dig that.
—John Oliver Killens, *The Cotillion*

5.

Fielding, probably the greatest authorial intruder in the history of
the novel, thought that his use of this technique would show his
superiority over mere storytellers. Before and after him, novelists
have favored the practice for the same reason. Seeking acceptance
of the new genre of the novel in the eighteenth century, they defended and promoted it with intrusions placed at the beginning
and end of the story and at many points in between and with explanatory prefaces. Over the centuries, this type of defense has
gradually disappeared. Intrusions nevertheless remain a lively
subject, for they are still shortcuts by which novelists can express
their observations and opinions about human behavior and social
institutions. In these comments novelists usually come closest to
social scientists. Intrusions can be classified by subject, such as
power, social class, economic and legal institutions. From the time
of the greatest intruder himself, authors have used various methods and have developed a particular role for intrusions in the
novel, which connect them to the point of view adopted by the
novelist and hence to questions of authorial omniscience and the
search for verisimilitude. In short, intrusions provide further background for a comparison between the novel and social science.

Fielding's Intrusions

Fielding employed intrusions frequently, placing them both within the narrative and as introductions to major divisions of it. In *Tom Jones* he provides eighteen such introductions, most of them on writing, authorship, the novel in general, and this one in particular. To the four divisions of *Joseph Andrews* he provides three similar but less obtrusive introductions, including one in which he even discusses the division of a story into chapters. Because Fielding had written plays before he turned to novels, it was natural for him, in introducing book 16 of *Tom Jones*, to liken these prefaces to the prologues of plays. In the general spirit of all his prologues, Fielding, in this one, playfully observes that any of them might have been placed anywhere in the novel or in any other novel; in any case, he concludes, the "principal merit of both the prologue and the preface is that they be short." Though for analytical purposes these prefatory digressions may be separated from the novel itself and from shorter digressions within it, the fact remains, as Robert Alter has pointed out, that both the "essayistic and novelistic passages in Fielding's fiction" serve the author's integrated purpose of delineating character and offering commentary on human behavior.[1]

The reasons Fielding gives for his eighteen prefaces to the books of *Tom Jones* are both serious and ironical. In introducing book 2, Fielding remarks that he is, "in reality, the founder of a new province of writing, so I am at liberty to make what laws I please therein." He thus seems to use the prefaces to explain this new genre to the reader. He seeks also, as he notes in book 9, to use them to protect himself against facile imitators who can write a story but lack the "learning and knowledge" to write an essay.

Continuing his slight deprecation of narrative, Fielding asserts in the preface of book 4 that a long story by itself would be boring, so he has chosen to interrupt it with "sundry similes, descriptions, and other kind of poetical embellishments" to keep the reader from falling asleep. For example, he indicates that he shall introduce his heroine, Sophia, with various literary flourishes which the "tragic poets" use.

In several prefaces Fielding gives the reader a sense of partici-
pating in the creation of the story, which fosters the illusion that
the reader is also *in* it to some degree. Fielding sets certain ground
rules in the first chapter of *Tom Jones,* maintaining that since an
author is not dispensing charity, he must consider what the readers
want and tell them in advance what he will offer in his effort to
please. In introducing book 2, however, Fielding describes his
readers as "subjects," but not "slaves," so that although he runs
things, he does so with due regard for their interest and comfort.
Fielding expresses this solicitude in several ways. Early in the novel
he describes Allworthy's house and its setting: "Reader, take care.
I have unadvisedly led thee to the top of as high a hill as Mr. Allworthy's, and how to get thee down without breaking thy neck I do
not well know. However, let us e'en venture to slide down together;
for Miss Bridget rings her bell, and Mr. Allworthy is summoned to
breakfast, where I must attend, and, if you please, shall be glad of
your company" (bk. 1, ch. 4). In the introductory chapter to book
3 he observes that, in order not to waste the readers' time and to
enable them to supply their own conjectures, he will skip "several
large periods of time, in which nothing happened worthy of being
recorded in a chronicle of this kind." For example, since everyone
knows that people like Allworthy mourn their departed friends,
the author does not need to describe his feelings on the death of
Captain Blifil. When Fielding brings Tom to a miserable state, he
takes the readers into his confidence as to how to proceed. He
promises to be faithful to his chosen method of sticking to the
probable, and as he consults his readers, he heightens their interest in what will happen to "this rogue, whom we have unfortunately made our hero" (bk. 17, ch. 1).

Whereas Fielding is a benevolent despot toward his readers, he
does not mitigate his hostility to and dominion over critics. By the
term he generally seems to mean professional literary critics, but
after a few comments directed against them he notes in the preface
to book 8 that by critic he usually refers to "every reader in the
world." He uses his intrusions to declare his independence of critics
and to deny them a place. By the second chapter of the novel he is
already warning the reader that he intends to "digress" whenever

he feels like it, that he is a better judge of this matter than "any pitiful critic," and that critics should "mind their own business," which he never deigns to mention or define. Emboldened by public overestimation of their talent, critics have assumed "dictatorial power" over authors by making firm rules out of the accidental practices of earlier writers, Fielding charges (bk. 5, ch. 1). Moreover, the critic, he explains, has "no other design" but to discover and publicize faults (bk. 11, ch. 1). One of the advantages that Fielding claims for his prefaces is that they give the critic a chance to criticize, for as an author, he has "always taken care to intersperse somewhat of the sour or acid kind, in order to sharpen and stimulate the said spirit of criticism" (bk. 16, ch. 1).

A final reason—perhaps the main one—for Fielding's prefaces and other intrusions is simply the joy he takes in them.[2] Some titles with which he appears to amuse himself as well as the reader are: "Containing Little or Nothing," "Containing Five Pages of Paper," "A Crust for the Critics," and "Too Short To Need a Preface." Fielding admits his prefaces may be the least pleasurable parts of the novel to the reader, yet he himself regards them as "essentially necessary to this kind of writing." He claims not to need to give a reason for his decision, since only critics demand one, and they are not justified in making demands upon writers. But to avoid the dogmatism of critics, Fielding generously agrees to give his reason for the digressions. They are meant to present a contrast. In order to emphasize the interesting quality of the rest of his novel, he inserts these dull prefaces, then invites the reader to skip the rest of them.

Intrusions for Reader Participation

In older novels, intrusions, whatever may have been their authors' intention, usually clarified things for the reader even if they slowed down the narrative. When the author brought the reader into the story, as Fielding did, he made the reader work, but not very hard. Thus the reader's participation is rather easy when Fielding, in *Joseph Andrews*, compares the morning to a "beautiful young lady" whom he calls "Miss ____," adding the footnote, "Whoever the Reader pleases" (bk. 3, ch. 4). Most modern novelists give the reader a harder time when they invite participation. In endowing two different characters with the same name in *The Sound and the Fury* (1929), Faulkner, according to the novelist Nathalie Sarraute, "forces the reader to be constantly on the alert . . . Suddenly the reader is on the inside, exactly where the author is, at a depth where nothing remains of the convenient landmarks with which he constructs the characters."[3] One classification of authorial intrusions is according to their increasing complexity from the reader's point of view. When grouped by method, such intrusions include explanations to clarify a point for the reader; interludes to supplement the narrative; discussions of the novel as a genre and of publishing; comments on the treatment of the characters, involving questions of authorial point of view and omniscience; and novels within novels. The author, in this progression, provides fewer and fewer guideposts to the reader.

The simplest kind of explanatory intrusion is often a translation of a foreign term. Authors frequently resort to this practice in exotic novels to be sure that the reader understands. In *Kim* (1901), for example, Rudyard Kipling parenthetically translates Urdu terms into English in the midst of a dialogue, or has a character use the term in both languages. On another level, he explains in ch. 2 how a character, lying in the grass and looking at a house, is able to do something: "He saw — Indian bungalows are open through and through — the Englishman return to a small dressing-room." A similar technique occurs when an author first tries to convey a mood but then, unsure of success, states the matter in what amounts to an intrusion. Sylvia Plath does so in *The Bell Jar* (1963), adding to her description of a blank, silent scene: "The sound of the cicada only served to underline the enormous silence."[4]

Novelists and playwrights have for centuries resorted to interludes in their narratives similar to Fielding's in *Tom Jones* but for varying purposes. Two recent American novelists, John Dos Passos and John Steinbeck, use this technique to good effect to bring out and emphasize the broader context within which their characters and events find their place. In his *U.S.A.* trilogy (1930, 1932,

1936) Dos Passos employs three kinds of interlude, often in succession. The "newsreel" interlude is a series of unconnected bits of news, headlines, speeches, and popular songs, providing a kaleidoscopic view of the spirit of the time. The "camera eye" interlude is a short, poetic evocation of the author's own personal experience to contrast and harmonize with the social portrait of the newsreel. Finally, Dos Passos inserts biographies of outstanding but typical men and women from various domains: scientists, radicals, politicians, a movie star, industrialists, inventors, a dancer. Steinbeck, in *The Grapes of Wrath* (1939), uses interludes to present generalized, poetic pictures of the specific characters and events in the story. The first interlude in the book describes the creation of the Oklahoma "dust bowl." Later ones show a series of catastrophic experiences in which, as the tenant farmers leave their homes and lands to migrate to California in search of jobs, they become victims of banks, used car salesmen, and merchants along the route. Other interludes show the changing nature of farming caused by mechanization and large-scale ownership, the creation and break-up of overnight migrant communities as they halt the westward push each evening and start again each morning. The final interlude reveals the hopelessness of the journey as unemployment hits the factorylike farms of California in the depression of the 1930s.

The third kind of intrusion was a favorite of many traditional novelists, such as Trollope, whose use of it annoyed Henry James. It often causes the sharpest break in the narrative and is probably the least defensible one. Jane Austen uses it moderately in *Northanger Abbey,* bk. 2, ch. 10, where she refers several times to the novels of Mrs. Radcliffe and then, to carry the story forward, reports that the heroine begins to feel that Gothic tales do not adequately portray the "unequal mixture of good and bad" to be found among the people of central England. Fielding in *Joseph Andrews* intrudes a discussion that bears still less upon his story. He defends the division of novels into books and chapters as the author's way of providing the reader with an "Inn or Resting-Place" and a notice of what is to come (bk. 2, ch. 1). Writing a few years later in the 1760s, Sterne, in *Tristram Shandy,* was already parodying the novel by making sport of the difference between the time it takes to narrate events and the time consumed by the events themselves. He digresses from his story and then discusses his digressions, taking the attitude of Fielding that they offer variety to keep the reader attentive. Again somewhat like Fielding, he invites the reader to supply his own description of a beautiful woman and even provides a blank space for it. Still more playfully, Sterne omits chapters 18 and 19 of volume 6 and places them after chapter 25.[5]

Trollope, the archintruder in this respect, peppers *Barchester Towers* (1857) with talk about the novel itself. Early in the story, in ch. 15, he reveals that Eleanor "is not destined" to marry either of two men she knows. Trollope defends his having given this advance information on the ground that it maintains a "proper confidence between the author and his readers" not to withhold information: "Our doctrine is, that the author and the reader should move along together in full confidence with each other." Approaching the end of the novel, Trollope becomes cuter, doubting he can put everything together in the space which publishing conventions permit him and wishing the publisher, whose name he mentions, could give him more. Just before the end, in ch. 51, he complains that contradictory demands make it difficult for an author to conclude a novel: "When we become dull we offend your intellect; and we must become dull or we should offend your taste." Thackeray, in a similar vein, mentions in *Vanity Fair* that a character's curses are such that even if he wrote them out, the publisher, Bradbury and Evans, could not find a compositor to set the type. In the same novel, ch. 16, Thackeray explains that he excluded a character from a certain scene "in order that this story might be written" at all. In *The Newcomes* Thackeray discusses the economic advantages of the profession of novelist, and an early American author, John Neal, uses his epistolary novel *Randolph* (1823) to assess the arts, publishing and his own work.

Balzac, aspiring to science, acts like a scientist in referring the reader of *Les Paysans* to what the novelist has already established in previous ones. F. Scott Fitzgerald is equally direct in shifting the narrator's point of view. In *Tender Is the Night*, as Rosemary arrives at a party, the author calls attention—needlessly in this case

—to his own action: "To resume Rosemary's point of view it should be said that . . ." (36).

Even in the development of character, novelists find reason to intrude, perhaps in order to give the reader a sense of partnership, as do Thackeray and Trollope, or perhaps as a means of moving the story ahead in a special way. These two novelists often take sides openly for or against a character of their own creation. In *Vanity Fair,* Thackeray writes, ch. 51: "At Levant House Becky met one of the finest gentlemen and greatest Ministers that Europe has produced . . . I declare I swell with pride as these august names are transcribed by my pen; and I think in what brilliant company my dear Becky is moving." In *Barchester Towers,* ch. 8, Trollope takes the other side: "My readers will guess from what I have written that I myself do not like Mr. Slope; but I am constrained to admit that he is a man of parts." Trollope's hint that he as author is in roughly the same position that his readers occupy is made more explicit in his work and that of other novelists. In *The Warden,* ch. 6, he both disclaims omniscience and gives another example of intrusion: "What had passed between Eleanor Harding and Mary Bold need not be told. It is indeed a matter of thankfulness that neither the historian nor the novelist hears all that is said by their heroes or heroines, or how would three volumes or twenty suffice! In the present case so little of this sort have I overheard, that I live in hopes of finishing my work within 300 pages, and of completing that pleasant task—a novel in one volume." Trollope goes so far in the same novel as to have his narrator disagree with his female readers as to Eleanor Harding's character. Further implying a difference between himself as author and an unnamed narrator, Trollope, in *The Way We Live Now,* ch. 19, suggests that no one really can be sure of how things go: "In that moment she all but yielded to him. Had he seized her in his arms and kissed her then, I think she would have yielded." Hawthorne does much the same thing in *The House of the Seven Gables* (1851), ch. 8. He mentions the habitual sound Judge Pyncheon makes in his throat, which some people regarded as the gurgling of blood, according to the curse on his family, and remarks of Phoebe, "when the girl heard this queer and awkward ingurgitation, (which the writer never did hear, and therefore cannot describe,), she, very foolishly, started, and clasped her hands." Around the same time George Eliot used a slight variant of this approach, suggesting in *Adam Bede,* ch. 17, that the narrator did not know of an event when it happened but learned of it much later: "But I gathered from Adam Bede, to whom I talked of these matters in his old age, that few clergymen could be less successful in winning the hearts of their parishioners than Mr. Ryde." Fielding, a century earlier, had already done the same in *Joseph Andrews*, bk. 2, ch. 15. The narrator reports that Joseph and Fanny did not miss Parson Adams: "Indeed, I have been often assured by both, that they spent these Hours in a most delightful Conversation: but, as I never could prevail on either to relate it, so I cannot communicate it to the Reader."

Although in *Adam Bede* and *The Mill on the Floss* George Eliot insists that novelists should deal with the "commonplace," in *Daniel Deronda* (1876) she ironically dismisses a character because he is "low" and probably also because she has no further need of him: "Joel being clearly a low character, it is happily not necessary to say more of him to the refined reader" (ch. 7). A similarly ironical point is made in *Howards End,* ch. 6, when Forster's narrator remarks that the poor are "unthinkable" and not a proper subject for a novel. Thomas Mann, through the narrator of *The Magic Mountain* (1924) also disclaims omniscience, insisting that a certain choice of words is his character's: "But for him and for his relations with Madame Chauchat (we are not responsible for the word relations; it was the word Hans Castorp used, not we), such songs had nothing to do with them" (I, ch. 4). Another example raises a general question of authorial intention regarding such intrusions. In an otherwise omniscient book, *The Grand Parade* (1961) by Julian Mayfield, the narrator says: "Delicately he indicated that Reeves' short stature—he was only five foot four or five —would also be a handicap" (358-359). The uncertainty whether this is an estimate by the character who indicates the man's size, by the narrator, or by the author suggests that this kind of intrusion may not always be a deliberate technique by the novelist; it may be a slip. R. J. Sherrington raises this point concerning several of Flaubert's novels.

There is no doubt, however, about authorial intention in one type of intrusion, the novel within a novel, which is clearly a deliberate technique. Though the novel within a novel is not exactly an intrusion like the others, it is a playful maneuver that can have a similar effect, but on the broad scale of an entire work rather than in a brief excursion here and there. The purpose of this type of intrusion seems to be to heighten the story's verisimilitude and thus to persuade the reader that he is reading and witnessing no mere creation of an author but something real or close to reality.

Cervantes, in *Don Quijote* (1605, 1615), is among the first writers to present something resembling a novel within a novel. Halfway through the story, Sancho Panza tells Don Quijote that the knight's adventures just reported are already the subject of a book with the same title, even though, as the great adventurer reflects, the blood of his enemies is still dripping from his sword. Don Quijote is further assured that twelve thousand copies have been published in several cities and translated into virtually every language. Sancho in his simple way extols the telling of truth in such histories. Don Quijote takes the hero's view, suggesting that actions which reflect poorly on him should be omitted. In the vein of prefaces to other novels of the era, the character who has told of the existence of the book about the knight and his servant agrees up to a point, but adds "it is one thing to write like a poet, and another thing to write like an historian; the poet can relate or sing of things not as they were but as they ought to be, and the historian must write about them not as they ought to be but as they were, without adding or subtracting anything from the truth" (III, 64).

Twentieth century authors have used the technique in their own ways. Thomas Bell, in *The Second Prince* (1935), writes about the adventures of Striker Godown, a character who finally settles down to write a novel. The first sentence he writes is the same as the first sentence of the novel itself. Alberto Moravia's *The Lie* (1965) begins as a diary, in which the writer discusses with himself a novel he plans to write about the events being described in the novel itself. At the end he explains that he is publishing his diary with a few changes and that the novel just read is that diary. In *The Comforters* (1957), Muriel Spark complicates matters by presenting the reader with perhaps three novels. Novel number one is the Spark novel itself. Novel number two is the one that Caroline Rose, a young woman who has religious experiences, thinks is being written about herself and her friends in novel number one. Novel number three is the one Caroline writes during a vacation. Intrusions and varieties of authorial omniscience pervade the three levels. Caroline, while in a hospital, presumably in novel number one, tells a friend that this experience is not part of novel number two being written about her because its author cannot describe a hospital ward. Spark, as the author of novel number one, points out that by such remarks Caroline unwittingly interferes with novel number two. On another occasion, the narrator of novel number one claims to be unable to exclude Caroline when she ought to be excluded; we are also told that Caroline thinks much about the art of the novel, perhaps in connection with novel number three.

Intrusions for Social Commentary

There is a broad, though not consistent, distinction between the kind of intrusion in which the author interrupts the story to talk about it and to make the narrator a part of it, and the kind in which the author interrupts chiefly to offer observations and generalizations about human behavior and social institutions, though these intrusions are usually somehow related to the story itself. It is the second kind of intrusion that brings the novel close to social science. Joseph Warren Beach, a literary historian concerned with the role of the novelist, has shown that George Eliot's *Adam Bede* illustrates three related Victorian tendencies: to edify, to guide the reader's attitude toward the characters, and to explain the characters on the basis of general ideas about human nature. Another historian of intrusions, Irma Sherwood, has related them to philosophical and literary tendencies in the eighteenth century, such as the spirit of criticism and morality, the new genre of the novel borrowing from existing genres, and the novelist's desire to show the importance of his work.[6]

The issue here is not whether intrusions make good or bad novels, or even whether they are necessary devices to enable the novelist to illuminate human behavior and social institutions. The novelist gets across his notions whether by obvious or subtle intrusions, or by keeping himself so far from the story as to satisfy the most ardent opponent of intrusions. The question at issue is what the novelist tells about human behavior and social institutions and how he does so, irrespective of any aesthetic judgment of his method. For the novelist does not need to resort to intrusions; indeed, his views of the individual and society come through to some extent, whether he wants them to or not, by his tone or the actions of his characters, including their speech.[7] Ellen Glasgow, looking back on *The Sheltered Life* (1932), remarks that General Archbold is the "central character . . . and into his lonely spirit I have put much of my ultimate feeling about life." Hardy goes further, asserting that in fiction "characters, however they may differ, express mainly the author, his largeness of heart or otherwise, his culture, his insight, and very little of any other living person."[8] Intrusions make these illuminations more direct and are thus related to the concept of point of view in fiction. As is true of almost any concept in intellectual history, variants of point of view can be traced back almost infinitely. Both the use of the concept and its relation to intrusions, which in turn bring the novel close to social science, can be seen in various eras going back to Plato.

Henry James, drawing attention to point of view in the late nineteenth century in an attack on Trollope for reminding his readers that his narrative is after all only fiction, argued, "It is impossible to imagine what a novelist takes himself to be unless he regard himself as an historian and his narrative is a history." Trollope's technique is a "betrayal of a sacred office," that of the novelist, whose task is the same as the historian's: "to represent and illustrate the past."[9] With only slightly less disapproval, Frank Norris early in this century asserted: "Every novel must do one of three things — it must (1) tell something, (2) show something, or (3) prove something" (21-22). Showing is better than merely telling, and proving is best because it involves both telling and showing. Two decades later Percy Lubbock harked back to James's technique and views, followed by Carl Grabo, who attributed considerable importance to point of view and classified several possibilities:

"chief participant," "composite" and "omniscient author" (33-44). Around the same time Beach summarized the history of the novel: "In a bird's-eye view of the English novel from Fielding to Ford, the one thing that will impress you more than any other is the disappearance of the author" (14-15). Some twenty years later there was another burst of activity, when Norman Friedman made an extensive review of the concept of point of view, as did Richard Stang, systematically analyzing the development of its various meanings. Wayne Booth followed with a defense of "telling" against "showing"; disagreeing with Beach, he insists that the "author's judgment is always present." Though the author "can to some extent choose his disguises, he can never choose to disappear" (20).

Friedman offers eight different points of view in narration, according to the decreasing degree of omniscience as the "guiding intelligence" of the author is withdrawn. The choice of any one of these eight positions depends on the author's purpose. Friedman errs, however, when he asserts: "The characteristic mark, then, of Editorial Omniscience is the presence of authorial intrusions and generalizations about life, manners, and morals, which may or may not be explicitly related to the story at hand" (1171). The connection between omniscience and intrusions is not so strong. Intrusions come just as easily from nonomniscient authors, and the omniscient position hardly requires intrusions. It is nevertheless true that the more an author removes his own voice from the narrative, the less likely he is to intrude directly.

Not all intrusions, moreover, imply omniscience. Thus Fielding in *Amelia* intrudes to disclaim full knowledge at one point and at another he implies omniscience without intruding. Characteristically, Thackeray in *Vanity Fair* often wonders and asks questions about his characters, suggesting less than omniscience, while also intruding to claim "the omniscience of the novelist" (ch. 15). Somerset Maugham's narrator in *Cakes and Ale* (1930), a novel about novelists, abruptly and playfully intrudes into the story to explain why he prefers to write in the first person singular even though the device has drawbacks. He has read about point of view, he notes, in the work of Evelyn Waugh, Percy Lubbock, E. M. Forster, and

Edwin Muir, but found their comments and advice contradictory or useless. Telling a story in the third person implies that the writer knows everything about his characters. As he gets older, the writer sees that life is more complex, feels himself "less and less like God," and is less inclined to "describe more than his own experience has given him." The narrator concludes, "The first person singular is a very useful device for this limited purpose" (215-217).

Several literary historians have also argued that the first-person narrative is more effective in making the reader feel the truth and force of what the novelist is trying to show. This point of view, it is claimed, has greater verisimilitude because the reader knows that no one in real life can command all points of view.[10] Vivienne Mylne, however, has indicated the "paradox" that realism in fiction develops precisely as the author abandons the attempt to show that his story is based on truth or actual events. He can then rely on the reader's recognition that the novel is an art: "An element of masquerade is removed; fiction can be treated for what it is worth" (268). Thus have novelist and reader matured side by side in allowing fiction the widest latitude in its exploration into human behavior and social institutions.

Sociopsychological Insights in the Novel

Fiction will be much the better for standing cheek
by jowl with poetry and philosophy.
— Virginia Woolf, *A Room of One's Own*

6.

Insights into human behavior and social institutions abound in fiction. They are conveyed through the moral implication or lesson of a story, in the dialogue, in intrusions intended to justify a character's specific acts, and in intrusions on any subject a writer chooses.

Looking for a moral implication can be hazardous. Mark Twain introduces *Huckleberry Finn* with the warning that "persons attempting to find a moral in it will be banished." Jane Austen ends *Northanger Abbey* with Henry and Catherine's happy marriage against his father's wishes, adding that his opposition only strengthened their love. As for the moral, Austen does not seem to care much: "I leave it to be settled, by whomsoever it may concern, whether the tendency of this work be altogether to recommend parental tyranny, or reward filial disobedience."

Two other novels by Austen provide balanced moral implications. In *Pride and Prejudice* she shows that pride and a reluctance to display one's feeling may be harmful, leading easily to vanity and prejudice. A minor character, who is more aggressive in courting than are the two sisters who are the main characters, remarks to one of them in ch. 6: "it is sometimes a disadvantage to be so very guarded . . . there are very few of us who have heart

enough to be really in love without encouragement." The story re-
volves around events that help the two proud sisters to express
their feelings more willingly, to temper "complacency" with "sensibility." Austen had already made a connected point in another
novel, *Sense and Sensibility,* whose moral is that easy expressive-
ness needs in turn to be balanced by sense and reason. Marianne,
disappointed in love, intensifies her unhappiness by a self-indulgent display of her feelings. When in ch. 29 her sister suggests the
value of "a reasonable and laudable pride," Marianne rejects the
advice: "No, no, misery such as mine has no pride. I care not who
knows that I am wretched . . . I must feel — I must be wretched — ."
She learns that she must check this tendency.

Dialogue is frequently the vehicle to convey social history in T.
S. Stribling's novel about the American Civil War and Reconstruction periods, *The Forge* (1931). Through a conversation between a Northern general and the head of a committee of former
slaveowners, the author points up the economic and political consequences of the Northern victory. The Northerner freely admits
that he will feed the former slaves so that they can survive and vote
Republican against the interests of the Southern white rulers.
"Why should you gentlemen," he asks the slaveowners, "be surprised that I should try to get the most out of the negroes when
you've been working at the very same thing all your lives? . . . It's
the same thing over and over, gentlemen: in any historic struggle
an oppressed people can usually make shift to ease themselves
somewhat. They offer themselves to the highest bidder in ease-
ments, and at present my bid is much higher than yours . . . And
incidentally, gentlemen, from now henceforth you are going to
have to obtain the products of negro labor by round-about methods, chicane, finesse, and not by simple force. In other words, you
will cease to be gentlemen and become traders, landlords, and
business men" (492-493).

Novelists often intrude to explain the significance to be attached
to a character's specific action. Stribling typically presents a particular action or mood and then indicates its generality. In *Unfinished Cathedral* (1934), he describes a young man's return to a
place: "As Jerry had been away from Florence since his boyhood

days, the shops and stores had the dwindled, shabby look which always surprises a man on such a return." In this way the author indicates that his character was surprised, that shops look shabby when one has not seen them since boyhood, and that one is always surprised at this fact. A few paragraphs later Stribling uses the same technique: "The man hurried on up the long double row of tables with the awkwardness of a laborer among a gathering of middle-class professional business men" (17-18). George Eliot uses a similar method in a less simple way, as in *Middlemarch.* The young intellectual, Will Ladislaw, has expected to leave Middlemarch soon but finds himself lingering there. Eliot explains the reason in ch. 60: "indefinite visions of ambition are weak against the ease of doing what is habitual or beguilingly agreeable; and we all know the difficulty of carrying out a resolve when we secretly long that it may turn out to be unnecessary." Rosamund Lydgate, beautiful and self-centered, has put Will Ladislaw in an embarrassing position. She thinks she can easily overcome his anger but turns out to be wrong. Eliot explains her miscalculation in ch. 78 by generalizing: "Shallow natures dream of an easy sway over the emotions of others, trusting implicitly in their own petty magic."

This type of intrusion and the others that novelists use for general commentary bring the novel close to social science. Insights thus conveyed can be classified according to subject: social class and power; law; economic, cultural, and religious institutions; marriage and the status of women; and interpersonal relations and emotional states, such as the influence of childhood, guilt, and repression. In a somewhat different category are insights in novels regarding social science concepts and procedures. Some of the parallels between the insights in these two genres are so striking as to raise the question of originality. To appreciate fictional insights into social institutions and human behavior is not to suggest that the social sciences have added nothing to them. The social sciences have made valiant efforts to verify such insights and to specify them to the point where they may be useful, for example, in devising policies to alleviate social problems. On the highest level of generalization, however, which is the avowed goal of the leading modern scientific approaches to the study of human behavior, these approaches have not advanced much beyond the formulation to be found in novels.

Social Class and Power

The first category of general psychosociological insights is social class: its basis and distinctions, the power it affords, and certain other concomitants. Balzac was deeply concerned with the basis of class and the relation between economic position and morality in France after the convulsions of the great Revolution. "Since 1789," he observes in *Les Paysans,* pt. 1, ch. 6, "France has been trying to persuade men, against all the evidence, that they are equal." Worried by the continuous social instability inherent in this notion, he takes pains to show the differences between two important classes affected by the Revolution, the peasants and bourgeoisie. The peasant's moral code, as Balzac puts it in pt. 1, ch. 3, is not like the bourgeois code, for "morality" depends on a degree of economic surplus and security. The peasant lives close to nature, "a purely material life" with few of the spiritual luxuries that come with a modicum of wealth. French landowners, he complains, lack the class solidarity of the English. They compete with each other and can manage no form of group solidarity above the family level, though since 1792 they have become dependent on one another as a class.

Other examples in this category touch upon differences in prestige and behavior among the classes. Fielding in *Joseph Andrews* divides people into "high" and "low" according to fashion, or style of dress, from which each class draws more fundamental distinctions to separate themselves physically as well as socially. Somewhat before and ever since Fielding, "manners" in the sense of conduct based on codes have been a staple of fiction. Virginia Woolf shows the overconformity of the social climber in *The Voyage Out* (1927) when describing the personal habits of Mr. Perrot, who "knew that he was . . . not quite a gentleman . . . for he was the son of a grocer in Leeds, had started life with a basket on his back, and now, though practically indistinguishable from a born gentleman, showed his origin to keen eyes in an impeccable neat-ness of dress, lack of freedom in manner, extreme cleanliness of person, and a certain indescribable timidity and precision with his knife and fork which might be the relic of days when meat was rare, and the way of handling it by no means gingerly" (137). An interesting coincidence of such observation in fiction and social science occurs in Thomas Hardy and Thorstein Veblen. In *The Mayor of Casterbridge* (1886), ch. 1, the novelist describes a man's coat as having "the fine polish about the collar, elbows, seams, and shoulder-blades that long-continued friction with grimy surfaces will produce, and which is usually more desired on furniture than on clothes." Around the same time, in *The Theory of the Leisure Class* (1899), ch. 6, Veblen refers to the "confusion" of beauty with expensiveness "best exemplified in articles of dress and of household furniture." With regard to clothing, he observes that "considered simply in their physical juxtaposition with the human form, the high gloss of a gentleman's hat or of a patent-leather shoe has no more of intrinsic beauty than a similarly high gloss on a threadbare sleeve." Yet, Veblen concludes in dead-pan style, "well-bred people regard the gloss on a hat or shoe as beautiful and the gloss on a sleeve as offensive."[1]

The uses and concomitants of class distinctions often appear in authorial commentary. George Eliot expresses the racial aspect of dominance. In *Felix Holt,* ch. 43, she reports that the heroine understands how prejudice based on distinctions of social class corresponds to prejudice "dependent on difference of race and color." In recent years the connection between prejudice and exploitation based on class and on color have been widely explored by sociologists John Dollard, Bernard Barber, and Leonard Broom and Philip Selznick. In *The Mill on the Floss,* bk. 3, ch. 3, Eliot observes concerning the relationship between hostility and intimacy: "People who live at a distance are naturally less faulty than those immediately under our own eyes; and it seems superfluous, when we consider the remote geographical position of the Ethiopians, and how very little the Greeks had to do with them, to inquire further why Homer calls them 'blameless.' "[2]

On the relations between rulers and ruled, or leaders and masses, Thomas Hardy remarks in *The Return of the Native,* bk.

3, ch. 2, concerning Yeobright's aim to bring culture and wisdom to the rural poor: "The rural world was not ripe for him. A man should be only partially before his time: to be completely to the vanward in aspirations is fatal to fame." Hardy extends his observation: "Successful propagandists have succeeded because the doctrine they bring into form is that which their listeners have for some time felt without being able to shape." This point has since been made by many social scientists, such as Dankwart Rustow, who summarizes: "Successful leadership . . . rests on a latent congruence between the psychic needs of the leader and the social needs of the followers" (23). Hawthorne, in *The House of the Seven Gables,* ch. 1, makes the compatible point that leaders are indeed no better than the led. He remarks that Matthew Maule's execution by the town's leaders on the charge of witchcraft shows "that the influential classes, and those who take upon themselves to be leaders of the people, are fully liable to all the passionate error that has ever characterized the maddest mob." George Eliot implies the same point concerning the similarity between the tastes of the upper and lower classes but adds that the former are too busy with their own pleasures to notice that the latter class have their comparable ones. People of high rank, she observes in *Felix Holt,* ch. 7, are like those "antideluvian animals" that are too bulky to see themselves and whose "parasites doubtless had a merry time of it." At the rear of the manor, she continues, the dependents are enjoying a high life not much different from that which the upper-class family enjoys at the front of the manor, and at the expense of the family. From this remark it is but a short step to the politically more significant idea that rulers are often ignorant of the tastes and activities of the ruled. Fielding refines the levels of the social hierarchy by observing that the middle class, being closer to the lower orders, are likely to be more tyrannical than the more distant upper classes. Speaking in *Tom Jones,* bk. 1, ch. 6, of Squire Allworthy's housekeeper, Fielding comments that "it is the nature of such persons as Mrs. Wilkins to insult and tyrannize over little people. This being indeed the means which they use to recompense to themselves their extreme servility and condescension to their superiors; for nothing can be more reasonable than that slaves and flatterers should exact the same taxes on all below them, which they themselves pay to all above them."

With her usual perspicacity, George Eliot also touches on leaders and masses from the bottom upward. Felix Holt is an intelligent worker, a watchmaker, who aims to educate his class to their interests and to remain with them. In refusing help in ch. 5 to obtain "higher" employment, he asserts that he is one worker who does not want to rise above his class either to desert or to lead them: "Why should I want to get into the middle class because I have some learning?" Stating roughly one aspect of what later became known among social scientists as the "iron law of oligarchy," Felix Holt claims: "That's how the working men are left to foolish devices, and keep worsening themselves; the best heads among them forsake their born comrades, and go in for a house with a high door-step and a brass knocker." The higher income leads to "new wants and new motives." He prefers to lead workers while sharing their position. In an early formulation of this aspect of the iron law of oligarchy, Robert Michels has noted that workers who rise to leadership in trade unions and political parties become accustomed to rule and to a higher standard of living which they are reluctant to give up and which increasingly separates them from the rank and file.[3]

Solzhenitsyn has given memorable treatments of the uses of power in extreme situations or closed systems such as prisons and hospitals within broader totalitarian societies. The irony of imprisonment as described in *The First Circle* (1968), ch. 83, is that repression has its degrees. At the end of the novel some of the prisoners are to be transferred out of the best circle of hell, the first, into a worse hell. No matter how much they are repressed, they can still fear more repression. The author generalizes: "Unfortunately for people — and fortunately for their rulers — a human being is so constituted that as long as he lives there is always something that can be taken away from him . . . To avoid these final torments, the prisoner follows obediently the humiliating and hateful prison regime, which slowly kills the human being within him." Solzhenitsyn also describes in ch. 83 the social psychology of prisons, the technique that the rulers of these institutions use to break down the ruled: "The destructive intent of the first few hours of prison is to isolate the new prisoner from his fellows, so that there is no one to offer him any encouragement, so that the weight of the whole elaborate apparatus bears down on him alone." The same process is described by the social scientists Harold Garfinkel and Richard A. Cloward.[4]

Law

Another irony of repression is that it is often carried out, as in prisons, under the color of law. In ch. 86 of *The First Circle* Solzhenitsyn shows how even in prison, with few or no avenues of appeal to legal procedure, the victim can find a way to obtain at least a minor right by means of the law. The power of weakness lies in the resources still available to the exploited, as revealed by the *zek* or prisoner Nerzhin, a mathematician, who extracts his due from the prison security officer, Major Shikin. About to be transferred out of "the first circle" to a worse fate, Nerzhin asks Major Shikin to return a book of poetry the latter had taken from him illegally. The prisoner, whose basic rights are ignored, makes a case for this right by citing prison regulations and Soviet law: "In accordance with item seven of Section B of the prison rules, kindly return the book which was illegally taken from me." Major Shikin feels a mixture of contempt and dislike for this zek, "with his rigid manner and meticulous knowledge of all the laws." Solzhenitsyn observes of Nerzhin: "After five years in prison he had worked out, too, a particularly determined manner of talking with higher-ups —known, in zek language, as the unobjectionable taunt. His words were courteous, but his tone was lofty and ironic — the tone elders adopt when conversing with their juniors." The major gets the book but refuses to return it, whereupon Nerzhin warns: "I hope you haven't forgotten that for two years I demanded from the Ministry of State Security the Polish zlotys which had been taken from me — they'd cut the sum in half maybe twenty times; it was down to kopecs — and I got them back through the Supreme Soviet . . . I will not give up that book to you. I will die in the Kolmya — but from the other side of death I'll tear it away from you! I will fill the mailboxes of all the Central Committee and the Council of Ministers with complaints against you. Give it back without all that unpleasantness." The narrator reports: "And the major of State Security yielded to this doomed, helpless zek, being sent to a slow death."

The role and power of law and legal institutions have been the themes of many novels. Judicial proceedings in particular have been given ironical treatment to show the unjust results of the institutions designed to bring about justice and the way in which the law, the expression of dominant social groups, oppresses the individual. Balzac presents a characteristically realistic and pessimistic view of the very basis of law. The main character in *Le Curé de Village,* ch. 4, asserts that there is a fundamental discrepancy between law, which is a contrivance, and life, which is a fact: "Law, invented for the protection of society, is based upon equality. Society, which is nothing but a collection of facts, is based upon inequality." Legislators, the priest continues, have never decided the issue of whether law should curb or encourage society's tendencies, being content merely to analyze the facts of social life, to label those that seem blameworthy, and to prescribe punishments that have never prevented evil: "Such is the law of humankind." Balzac as author adverts to the subject in *Les Paysans,* pt. 1, ch. 9: "Law, as the legislator contrives it nowadays, does not have all the virtue we imagine it has. It does not affect the entire country equally; it is modified in its application to the point of contradicting its principle." Balzac suggests that the law fails in its effort to impose equality upon social life, for most people do not accept laws they do not like, except those that touch on the most essential affairs of political life, such as taxes, conscription, and serious crime. For the rest, law is generally frustrated when it runs contrary to custom and private interest.[5]

George Eliot and Fielding touch upon law in relation to human nature. Eliot points out in *The Mill on the Floss,* bk. 3, ch. 7, that lives are so intertwined that even justice produces pain among innocent people: "So deeply inherent is it in this life of ours that men have to suffer for each other's sins, so inevitably diffusive is human suffering, that even justice makes its victims and we can conceive no retribution that does not spread beyond its mark in pulsations of unmerited pain." Fielding draws the practical conclusion in *Tom Jones,* bk. 12, ch. 12, that rule by rigid law is still preferable to rule by variable human will: "as the examples of all ages show us that mankind in general desire power only to do harm . . . it will be much wiser to submit to a few inconveniences arising from the dispassionate deafness of laws, than to remedy them by applying to the passionate open ears of a tyrant." The importance of individual variability in the administration of public affairs is pointed out by Disraeli in his novel *Tancred* (1847), bk. 2, ch. 4: "In speculating on the fate of public institutions and the course of public affairs, it is important that we should not permit our attention to be engrossed by the principles on which they are founded and the circumstances which they present, but that we should also remember how much depends upon the character of the individuals who are in a position to superintend or to direct them."

Economics, Culture, and Religion

Novelists offer further insight, through authorial intrusions or dialogue, into the relations between economic and cultural life, the urban institutions accompanying economic development, and religion in modern life. These three institutions are related to one another in the social themes of many novels, just as they are in the social sciences and history.

In T. S. Stribling's novel *The Forge,* set in the South on the eve of the Civil War, two young women doubt that war will come because the industrial North is absorbed in money-making trivia that the agrarian South regards contemptuously. One woman juxtaposes the two ideas: "Who's going to fight us? Why, the North won't fight. Do you know who I met in Washington? A Mr. Breiterman. He was quite wealthy, and guess how he made his money . . . By making shoe pegs! Yes, sir, shoe pegs; the sort our nigger shoemakers whittle out with their pocket knives. Breiterman had a *factory* making 'em!" The two women laugh, presumably at the ridiculous idea that such a society could want a war or win one. The first woman expresses the aristocratic contempt they both feel about Breiterman, his manufacture, and the North: "When I found that out, I simply couldn't be nice to him" (72).

George Eliot and Hardy give authorial comments on the accumulation and spending of capital. In *The Mill on the Floss* bk. 1, ch. 12, Eliot remarks that when money is accumulated slowly, it is spent slowly, and when it is accumulated rapidly, it is spent rapidly: "This inalienable habit of saving, as an end in itself, belonged to the industrious men of business of a former generation, who made their fortunes slowly, almost as the tracking of the fox belongs to the harrier—it constituted them a 'race,' which is nearly lost in these days of rapid money-getting, when lavishness comes close on the back of want." This idea, expressed solemnly by Eliot and by many social scientists, reiterates the casual folk expression: "Easy come, easy go." In *The Return of the Native,* bk. 3, ch. 2, Hardy explains why Yeobright's plan to educate the poor for "wisdom rather than affluence" was a failure: "In passing from the bucolic to the intellectual life the intermediate stages are usually two at least, frequently many more." One such stage is the accumulation of wealth in order to afford luxury. In thinking that the poor could achieve culture before luxury, Yeobright was seeking "to disturb a sequence to which humanity has been long accustomed." In a short story, "The Waiting Supper," Hardy extends this abstraction: "Most great passions, movements, and beliefs—individual and national—burst during their decline into a temporary irradiation, which rivals their original splendor; and then they speedily become extinct."[6] Shepard Clough has reformulated this venerable view: "the peak of civilization in any culture would be expected at the time when economic decline begins" (7). A humorous version is given as one of C. Northcote Parkinson's "laws": an institution receives its perfect architectural home just as it begins to decline. In *Buddenbrooks*, pt. 7, ch. 6, Thomas Mann has the protagonist attribute this observation to an older source: "I have thought of a Turkish proverb; it says, 'When the house is finished, death comes.' . . . I know, from life and history, something you may not have thought of: often, the outward and visible material signs and symbols of happiness and success only show themselves when the process of decline has already set in."

Urbanization is often seen, as in Forster's *Howards End,* to be an undesirable accompaniment of industrialization. In *The Mayor of Casterbridge,* however, Hardy in a curious way emphasizes not urban decay but the rural influence upon the town, even though the novel was published in 1886, decades after the critique against urban institutions had already begun. He describes in ch. 9 the town's "mellow air" bringing in the "feel of imminent autumn almost as distinctly as . . . in the remotest hamlet. Casterbridge was the complement of the rural life around; not its urban opposite." A little later, in ch. 14, the author comments: "Casterbridge, as has been hinted, was a place deposited in the block upon a cornfield. There was no suburb in the modern sense, or transitional intermixture of town and down."

By 1908, H. G. Wells in *Tono-Bungay,* bk. 3, ch. 2, gives a fuller picture of urbanization and its social concomitants: mobility, conspicuous consumption (to use the phrase Thorstein Veblen had recently introduced), and a new morality. Wells's language in the novel suggests that his notions could well have come from the social science of his day. The first-person narrator comments on his newly rich aunt and uncle: "They did a lot of week-ending at hotels . . . We seemed to fall into a vast drifting crowd of social learners. I don't know whether it is due simply to my changed circumstances, but it seems to me there have been immensely disproportionate developments of the hotel-frequenting and restaurant-using population during the last twenty years. It is not only, I think, that there are crowds of people who, like we were, are in the economically ascendant phase, but whole masses of the prosperous section of the population must be altering its habits, giving up high-tea for dinner and taking to evening dress, using the week-end hotels as a practice-ground for these new social arts . . . Curiously mixed was the personal quality of the people one saw . . . And nobody, you knew, was anybody, however expensively they dressed and whatever rooms they took." The narrator reports the new morality of spending: "We became part of what is nowadays quite an important element in the confusion of our world, that multitude of economically ascendant people who are learning how to spend money . . . It is a various multitude having only this in common; they are all moving, and particularly their womenkind are moving, from conditions in which means were insistently finite, things were few and customs simple, towards a limitless expenditure . . . They discover suddenly indulgences their moral code never foresaw and has no provision for . . . With an immense astonished zest they begin *shopping* . . . They plunge into it as one plunges into a career; as a class, they talk, think, and dream possessions. Their literature, their Press, turns all on that; immense illustrated weeklies of unsurpassed magnificence guide them in domestic architecture, in the art of owning a garden, in the achievement of the sumptuous in motor-cars." These ideas, certainly not expressed for the first time in the modern era by Wells, have become a staple of social history and social science, especially since World War II.[7]

The new urban anonymity has been a perverse advantage to the black American, as expressed by the black narrator in Ellison's *Invisible Man* (1952). He finds a rough racial equality in urban life because it erases all forms of individuality: "I hadn't worried too much about whites as people [in the South]. Some were friendly and some were not, and you tried not to offend either. But here [in New York] they all seemed impersonal; and yet when most impersonal they startled me by being polite, by begging my pardon after brushing against me in a crowd. Still I felt that even when they were polite they hardly saw me, that they would have begged the pardon of Jack the Bear, never glancing his way if the bear happened to be walking along minding his own business. It was confusing. I did not know if it was desirable or undesirable" (128-129).

The new morality has been associated with a decline in religion. In *Tess of the d'Urbervilles,* ch. 18, Hardy combines many aspects of this view by referring to "the chronic melancholy which is taking hold of the civilized races with the decline of belief in a beneficent Power." That such belief was not always on an elevated religious plane Hardy also points out in *The Mayor of Casterbridge,* ch. 26, where he describes the feelings of a popular weather-prophet: "He was sometimes astonished that men could profess so little and believe so much at his house, when at church they professed so much and believed so little." A broader social treatment of religion is given by George Eliot in *Adam Bede,* ch. 3, which deals with the new Protestant denomination of Methodism. The novel takes place at the end of the eighteenth century, only a decade after the death of the founder of Methodism, John Wesley. Eliot describes the doctrine of the preacher Dinah Morris, as well as the social context of her thought. Eliot also gives her own view of pristine Methodism: its nonpolitical aim to carry religion to the rural poor, its message of kindness and generosity based on a perhaps overly "literal way of interpreting the Scriptures," and its less attractive changes during the early nineteenth century. She presents these views with the caution: "if I have read religious history aright." Max Weber's interpretation of Methodism is similar to Eliot's at certain points in *The Protestant Ethic.*

Marriage and the Status of Women

"Marriage," admits George Eliot at the end of *Middlemarch,* a novel devoted to many facets of that institution, "has been the bourne of so many narratives." The novel has always been closely related to women as authors, readers, and characters. Novels are filled with discussions of the nature of women, their behavior, their relations with men, and the institutions in which they play a special part. Balzac in an authorial commentary in *Les Employés* enumerates some of the roles and kinds of women in life and art from a male, upper-class, nineteenth-century standpoint: "Of course, there are housekeepers, women meant for pleasure, expensive women, women who are exclusively wives, mothers or mistresses, women entirely spiritual or physical" (11). The themes of the recent women's liberation movement are also relevant to the commentary on women and marriage, though care should be taken not to stretch the examples of the past to fit current attitudes. Because many such themes were expressed long ago in a general way, it is reasonable to adapt these notions to current issues.

Insights into marriage naturally touch upon the status of women. In *Middlemarch,* ch. 75, Eliot writes that Mrs. Lydgate's "discontent in her marriage was due to the conditions of marriage itself, to its demand for self-suppression and tolerance, and not to the nature of her husband." This demand is illustrated amply in the Lydgates' lives as well as in those of others in the novel whose marriages are more satisfying. Despite the author's portrayal of Mrs. Lydgate's weaknesses, there is a suggestion in this comment that the demand is placed mainly on the wives. The requirement of accommodation is mentioned differently but equally convincingly by Virginia Woolf in *The Voyage Out,* where the author observes: "When two people have been married for years they seem to become unconscious of each other's bodily presence so that they move as if alone, speak aloud things which they do not expect to be answered, and in general seem to experience all the comfort of solitude without its loneliness" (195). George Gissing in *The Private Papers of Henry Ryecroft* (1903), Summer, ch. 6, notes that love merely subdues the expression of mutual aggressiveness, and suggesting Woolf's later observation, he asks, "what were the durability of love without the powerful alliance of habit?"

The special features of marriage for women in the middle classes are clearly stated by two women novelists. Ellen Glasgow in pt. 1, ch. 9 of *The Sheltered Life* describes the thoughts of an old Southern gentleman whose daughter wants to marry a carpenter: "After all, class consciousness . . . was not all that it used to be . . . Make Joseph a master builder, he mused idly, put him in the right clothes, and—but, no, it wouldn't do in a woman. It wouldn't do for a girl like Isabella to marry out of her class." Women, marriage studies have shown, are supposed to marry above their class when they go out of it, while men may and more often do marry below. George Eliot in *The Mill on the Floss,* bk. 6, ch. 8, reveals that the basis for this pattern is the restricted freedom of women, which follows from their being symbols of family status as defined mainly by men. Philip tries to persuade his father to agree to his marrying Maggie despite the quarrel between the two fathers, pointing out that she has not been involved in it. "What does that signify?" his father replies. "We don't ask what a woman does—we ask whom she belongs to."

With characteristic bluntness, Thackeray deflates Western soci-

ety's pride in the status of women. In an authorial commentary in
Vanity Fair, ch. 18, he states, introducing a national-religious
stereotype while exposing a sexual one: "We are Turks with the
affections of our women; and have made them subscribe to our
doctrine too. We let their bodies go abroad liberally enough, with
smiles and ringlets and pink bonnets to disguise them instead of
veils and yakmaks. But their souls must be seen by only one man,
and they obey not unwillingly, and consent to remain at home as
our slaves — ministering to us and doing drudgery for us."[8] One
pitfall in such attitudes toward women is indicated by George
Eliot in *Adam Bede,* ch. 15. Concerning Arthur Donnithorne's
attraction to the pretty but kittenish Hetty Sorrel, the author
warns that men may read too much into a pretty face. The relation between beauty and good character is something about which
little is known: "Nature has her language, and she is not unvera-
cious; but we don't know all the intricacies of her syntax just yet."
Behind a beautiful eyelash there may be "depth of soul" but also
"deceit, peculation, and stupidity." With her scientific bent and
interest in heredity in the Darwinian era, *Adam Bede* having been
published in the same year as *The Origin of Species,* Eliot observes: "One begins to suspect at length that there is no direct cor-
relation between eyelashes and morals; or else, that the eyelashes
express the disposition of the fair one's grandmother, which is on
the whole less important to us." As she puts it more earthily, "people who love downy peaches are apt not to think of the stone, and
sometimes jar their teeth terribly against it." Overvaluing beauty
and compliance in women, men may find these qualities, she
warns, to be of doubtful advantage.

In a generally sympathetic portrait of Sue Bridehead in *Jude the
Obscure,* pt. 6, ch. 10, Hardy makes a harsh judgment about the
capacity of women to learn from experience, a judgment difficult
to verify or even to assess on a common-sense level. Jude remarks
that Sue, who once had more liberal views on marriage than he,
had taught him her liberalism and then reverted to traditional
views: "Strange difference of sex, that time and circumstance,
which enlarge the views of most men, narrow the views of women
almost invariably." Hardy too was pessimistic about the value of

education for women. In *The Woodlanders,* ch. 24, he reports of
a woman about to marry a doctor that "she was proud, as a cultivated woman, to be the wife of a cultivated man. It was an opportunity denied very frequently to young women in her position,
nowadays not a few; those in whom parental discovery of the value
of education has implanted tastes which parental circles fail to
gratify." On the same point, Jane Austen draws the obvious conclusion in *Northanger Abbey,* bk. 1, ch. 14. Referring to Catherine's shame over her ignorance of art, the author observes that
ignorance is good if one wants to be liked, which corresponds to
Eliot's remark about marriage's demand for self-suppression. "To
come with a well-informed mind," Austen asserts, "is to come with
an inability of administering to the vanity of others, which a sensi-
ble person would always wish to avoid. A woman, especially, if she
have the misfortune of knowing anything, should conceal it as well
as she can." Madame de Staël made the same point when an offi
cer, sent by Napoleon to arrange her exile from Paris, compli-
mented her on her writing. She told him: "You see, sir, what being
a woman of intellect has brought me to. I pray you, if the occasion
arises, to advise members of your family against it."[9]

Interpersonal Relations and Emotions

Fictional insights touch upon interpersonal relations involving
various emotions, such as love, envy, and hostility; the groups
within which these relations occur, such as the family; and the
stages of life, beginning with childhood. Edith Wharton and E. M.
Forster make broad observations about interpersonal relations
and their emotional basis. In *The Reef* (1912), ch. 4, Wharton
puts this reflection into the mind of a character: "mankind would
never have needed to invent tact if it had not first invented social
complications." Forster, in *Howards End,* ch. 2, distinguishes
between mild emotions such as affection and powerful ones such
as love. Margaret Schlegel's feeling for her sister calls for expression only in the "voiceless language of sympathy," whereas if she
were in love with a man, she "would proclaim it from the house-
tops." In general, Forster maintains: "The affections are more

reticent than the passions, and their expression more subtle."
Forster may mean further than a woman's love for a sister is "affection," but her love for a man is a "passion" in the sense of involving not only stronger feeling but also suffering or pain.

On people's responses to situations, Hardy and Austen make
interesting remarks. In *Far from the Madding Crowd*, ch. 7,
Hardy describes Gabriel Oak's surprise that Bathsheba has so
quickly developed from an "unpractised girl" into a "supervising
and cool woman." The author explains: "But some women only
require an emergency to make them fit for one." In *Sense and
Sensibility*, ch. 36, Austen tells of Mrs. John Dashwood's annoyance at being put into a situation where she must be politely attentive to her husband's two sisters. She could have simply refused,
but knowing that she had this power was not enough to overcome
her annoyance, for as the author explains, "when people are determined on a mode of conduct which they know to be wrong,
they feel injured by the expectation of anything better from them."
On the emotions related to hostility, Trollope, Dostoyevsky, and
D. H. Lawrence make comparable insights. In *The Warden*, ch.
6, Trollope reveals, "It is much less difficult for the sufferer to be
generous than for the oppressor." This remark draws attention to
an oppressor's need to justify his oppression by continuing it. In
The Brothers Karamazov, bk. 2, ch. 8, Dostoyevsky makes the
point more dramatically in describing the father's emotional state:
"He longed to revenge himself on every one for his own unseemli-
ness. He suddenly recalled how he had once in the past been
asked, 'Why do you hate so and so, so much?' And he had answered them, with his shameless impudence, 'I'll tell you. He had
done me no harm. But I played him a dirty trick, and ever since I
have hated him.' " In *Sons and Lovers*, ch. 4, Lawrence describes
how Paul Morel as a small boy accidentally breaks his sister's doll.
He later suggests they "sacrifice" it by burning. "He seemed to
hate the doll so intensely," the author observes, "because he had
broken it."

The effect of intimacy upon hostility has been remarked by
Trollope and Hawthorne. In *Barchester Towers*, ch. 21, Trollope
has a character say: "Wars about trifles are always bitter, espe-

cially among neighbors. When the differences are great, and the partners comparative strangers, men quarrel with courtesy. What combatants are ever so eager as two brothers?" Hawthorne's narrator in *The Blithedale Romance* (1852), ch. 3, finds it odd that he and his companions in the cooperative colony think soon of "getting the advantage" over the "outside barbarians" from whom they have separated themselves. He admits that, "as regarded society at large, we stood in a position of new hostility, rather than new brotherhood." Making a point opposite to Trollope's, Hawthorne's narrator concludes, "Constituting so pitiful a minority as now, we were inevitably estranged from the rest of mankind, in pretty fair proportion with the strictness of our mutual bond among ourselves." Hawthorne draws attention to mankind's hostility to worlds outside the immediate self which impose their forms upon it. In *The House of the Seven Gables,* ch. 12, he has Holgrave attack the past and the dead for their disposition of wealth in the present, for the legal precedents that now bind people, for the dead authors who continue to influence them, for the worship of "the living Deity, according to Dead Men's forms and creeds!" And people today shall do the same to the generations following. Turning to the house itself, Holgrave complains that its "calamity" can be traced to old Colonel Pyncheon's "inordinate desire to plant and endow a family. To plant a family! This is at the bottom of most of the wrong and mischief which men do."

George Eliot vividly shows and cogently analyzes the influence of the family. In *Adam Bede,* ch. 4, she points to the ambivalent power of kinship to make people alike physically and different mentally, indeed to make them interpret in a hostile way the influences that come from those they resemble closely: "Family likeness has often a deep sadness in it. Nature, that great dramatist, knits us together by bone and muscle, and divides us by the subtler web of our brains; blends yearning and repulsion; and ties us by our heart-strings to the beings that jar us at every movement. We hear a voice with the very cadence of our own uttering the thoughts we despise; we see eyes — ah, so like our mother's! — averted from us in cold alienation; and our last darling child startles us with the air and gestures of the sister we parted from in bitterness long years ago. The father to whom we owe our best heritage — the mechanical instinct, the keen sensibility to harmony, the unconscious skill of the modelling hand — galls us, and puts us to shame by his daily errors; the long-lost mother, whose face we begin to see in the glass as our own wrinkles come, once fretted our young souls with her anxious humors and irrational persistence." The special power of the family is experienced in childhood, as Eliot conveys in *The Mill on the Floss,* bk. 1, ch. 7. Though the fears of infancy are not remembered so sharply as are later experiences, "Every one of those keen moments has left its trace, and lives in us still." Childhood, she observes in bk. 2, ch. 1, offers a "sense of ease" like no other because in it "objects became dear to us before we had known the labor of choice." We "accepted and loved" our childhood world "as we accepted our own sense of existence and our own limbs." As people grow older, they strive for better things than they had in childhood, but such ambitions are fortunately controlled by these early affections, which have a "trick of twining round those old inferior things."

Such insights into childhood and family suggest the later more systematic and clinical contributions of Freud. In fact, in at least one observation by Eliot there is more than a suggestion of what was to come in psychoanalysis. In *Middlemarch,* ch. 17, a woman at a gathering furtively puts aside a bit of sugar to give to the children of her poor friends. Helping the needy, the author observes, was "so spontaneous a delight to her that she regarded it much as if it had been a pleasant vice that she was addicted to. Perhaps she was conscious of being tempted to steal from those who had much that she might give to those who had nothing, and carried in her conscience the guilt of that repressed desire." Literature is full of anticipations of the unconscious and other psychoanalytic concepts, as shown by the name given to one concept, the Oedipus complex, after a Greek legend most notably treated by Sophocles. Freud's biographer, Ernest Jones, has remarked that a "certain similarity between his psychological investigations and the divinations of creative writers was often in Freud's mind." As Freud acknowledged in *Studies in Hysteria,* his understanding of this disease was advanced by the insights he found in the "works of imaginative writers," which he supplemented with a "few psychological formulas." Freud not only admired certain writers, according to Jones, but envied the "facility with which they could reach a piece of insight that had cost him much labor to achieve" (III, 418-419).

Social Science Concepts and Procedures

George Eliot's scientific interests brought her, more than any other novelist, to the point of anticipating the notions and even the language of the social sciences. To match her insights to quotations from or references to the social sciences is not to suggest, however, that the latter came directly from novels or that they convey no more than fictional insights. It is simply that some significant and popular approaches in the social sciences are also to be found earlier in novels and in almost the same degree of specificity.

C. Wright Mills, the sociologist, wrote in *The Sociological Imagination* in 1959 that the sociological imagination "enables its possessor to understand the larger historical scene in terms of its meaning for the inner life and the external career of a variety of individuals . . . by means of the sociological imagination . . . men now hope to . . . understand what is happening in themselves as minute points of the intersections of biography and history within society" (5, 7). Trollope a century earlier in *The Warden,* ch. 15, put the matter succinctly when one of his characters ruminates: "What is any public question but a conglomeration of private interests?" George Eliot characteristically comes closer to the contemporary social science formulation. In *Daniel Deronda,* ch. 8, the narrator remarks, ironically rather than pompously: "I like to . . . connect the course of individual lives with the historic stream." Earlier, in *Felix Holt,* ch. 3, she expressed the same idea without irony: "These social changes in Treby parish are comparatively public matters, and this history is chiefly concerned with the private lot of a few men and women; but there is no private life which has not been determined by a wider public life, from the time when the primeval milkmaid had to wander with the wanderings of her clan, because the cow she milked was one of a herd which had made the pastures bare." Eliot also connects private with public morality. In her treatment of the self-righteous banker Bulstrode in *Middlemarch* she shows that his family fidelity and religious piety do not compensate for the harm he does others by his ambition and wealth. In the essay "Moral Swindlers," she explicitly argues that morality goes beyond private virtues. A man should not be called virtuous because "he comes home to dine with his wife and children and cherishes the happiness of his own hearth" if he has spent the day "in an unscrupulous course of public or private action which has every calculable chance of causing widespread injury and misery."[10]

Forster, Turgenev, and Proust all tried to plumb the basic issues involved in understanding human behavior, which have long been discussed in works on scientific method. In *Howards End*, ch. 23, Forster's narrator describes Margaret Schlegel's feelings about her future husband, a practical man, and her sister, an idealist: "The business man who assumes that this life is everything, and the mystic who asserts that it is nothing, fail, on this side and on that, to hit the truth. 'Yes, I see, dear; it's about halfway between,' Aunt Juley had hazarded in earlier years. No; truth, being alive, was not halfway between anything. It was only to be found by continuous excursions into either realm, and though proportion is the final secret, to espouse it at the outset is to insure sterility."[11] Forster is saying that though people know in advance that the extremes are wrong, they cannot in advance act as if the truth lies between them. Rather, they must search both extremes to find exactly where the truth lies, and if they move only between them, their search for truth will yield nothing. Turgenev, in *Fathers and Sons* (1867), ch. 16, puts into the mouth of Bazarov, the young nihilist, some criticisms of the "artistic instinct" that touch upon the question of the representativeness of the individual case. To examine human behavior, Bazarov insists, "the prime requisite . . . is experience of life," in which the "study of detached personalities is scarcely worth the trouble. For all we human beings are alike, in body as in spirit. In each of us there is an identical brain, an identical spleen, an identical heart, an identical pair of lungs, an iden-

tical stock of the so-called moral qualities (trifling variations between which we need not take into account). Therefore from a
single specimen of the human race all the rest may be judged."
This is an explicit argument against art, which seeks variety and
individuality rather than the uniformity that is required for understanding the species. "In fact," Bazarov concludes, "human
beings are like trees in a forest"; the botanist is not interested in
the individual trunk. Proust's narrator also argues that to discover
the essence of the species does not call for studying all its individuals. "People foolishly imagine," the author comments in *The
Guermantes Way* (1921), pt. 2, ch. 1, "that the vast dimensions of
social phenomena afford them an excellent opportunity to pene-
trate farther into the human soul; they ought, on the contrary, to
realize that it is by plumbing the depths of a single personality that
they might have a chance of understanding these phenomena."

"Trees in a forest" and "plumbing the depths of a single personality" are metaphors that do not arouse curiosity when they
appear in novels or poems. Metaphors are also important in the
sciences. Consider such social science terms as "social distance,"
"social pressure" and "social structure." The philosopher Morris R.
Cohen has asserted in *A Preface to Logic* that metaphors pervade
philosophical writing, "play a large part in opening up new fields
of science," suggest the "way in which creative minds perceive
things," and can lead to fallacies when resorted to uncritically (84-
85). George Eliot understood much of this character of metaphorical thinking in intellectual history. In discussing Tom Tulliver's
education in *The Mill on the Floss,* bk. 2, ch. 1, she notes that his
tutor's "favorite metaphor" was that "the classics and geometry
constituted that culture of the mind which prepared it for the re-
ception of any subsequent crop." This theory "turned out as un-
comfortably for Tom Tulliver as if he had been plied with cheese
in order to remedy a gastric weakness which prevented him from
digesting it. It is astonishing what a different result one gets by
changing the metaphor! Once call the brain an intellectual stom-
ach, and one's ingenious conception of the classics and geometry
as ploughs and harrows seems to settle nothing. But then it is open
to someone else to follow great authorities, and call the mind a

sheet of white paper or a mirror, in which case one's knowledge of the digestive process becomes quite irrelevant." Eliot suggests that if Aristotle could see what metaphorical speech had produced since he praised it as an indication of intelligence, he would undoubtedly lament the common tendency to "declare what is . . . by saying it is something else." In *Middlemarch*, ch. 10, Eliot returns to the subject, explaining that Casaubon was wrong in thinking his emotions were a bank from which he could meet "drafts" of affection from the young woman to whom he was engaged, "for we all of us, grave or light, get our thoughts entangled in metaphors, and act fatally on the strength of them." Metaphorical thinking has occupied generations of analysts, undergoing a special revival a few decades ago in the work of the linguist Benjamin Whorf, which influenced the social sciences. Whorf identifies a process called "metaphorical objectifying," by which he means the way in which metaphors guide everyday thinking (163).

Another theme of social science that has preoccupied scholars in recent decades, especially in America, is Max Weber's hypothesis, first published in 1904-1905, that capitalism was aided in its growth by the new religion of Protestantism, more particularly Puritanism, which taught men to regard the pursuit, accumulation, and careful use of wealth not only as a personal advantage but also as a religious duty.[12] In the opening paragraph of *Middlemarch,* published in 1872, George Eliot explains Dorothea Brooke's aversion to "frippery" on the basis of Puritan background, "well-bred economy," and mainly religious feeling. In ch. 51, Eliot describes the banker Bulstrode's religion as reinforcing his desire for wealth. He persuades himself that his motives in any action, including the getting, saving, and spending of money, are to serve his religion. The author asks rhetorically of Bulstrode's self-justifications: "Who would use money and position better than he meant to use them? . . . Also, profitable investments in trade where the power of the prince of this world showed its most active devices, became sanctified by a right application of the profits in the hands of God's servant." Such authorial remarks are not merely evidence of or data for Weber's thesis, which was based on earlier sources, but are analyses of experience like Weber's own.

Eliot anticipated other recent notions in the social sciences. One such influential notion is that of "labeling," which the sociologist Edwin Schur has described as a renewed application of the older notion that crime, juvenile delinquency, and other forms of social deviance are "created" by using these terms to describe certain kinds of behavior (3). In *Middlemarch,* ch. 11, Eliot tells of an argument between brother and sister. Rosamond Vincy claims that brothers are no more entitled than sisters to make themselves disagreeable. Fred replies: "I don't make myself disagreeable; it is you who find me so. Disagreeable is a word that describes your feelings and not my actions." In ch. 23, Eliot puts the same idea more explicitly in an authorial commentary when she explains Fred's attraction to a couple of horse dealers socially beneath him as coming not entirely from his love of horses but also from "that mysterious influence of Naming, which determinates so much of mortal choice." Because what they did was called "pleasure," Fred did not regard it as "monotonous." Such, the author concludes, is "the sustaining power of nomenclature."

The notion of the "unanticipated consequences" of social behavior has received much attention since the publication of an essay by the sociologist Robert K. Merton in 1936. Merton asserted that he was merely trying to give a "systematic, scientific analysis" of this phenomenon, which had been "treated by virtually every substantial contributor to the long history of social thought" (894). Merton later in 1968 used the phrases "unanticipated consequences" and "unintended consequences" interchangeably (115-117). In *Middlemarch,* ch. 57, George Eliot remarks that one of the participants in a conversation sought to check the "unintended consequences" of what she previously said. Treating her own use of this phrase ironically, the author refers to "a rush of unintended consequences" in the play of the children and animals, which upsets the things on a tea-table.

The study of the meaning of the movement of the body and its parts and of the spatial distribution of persons in small groups is of considerable interest in the social sciences. A modern pioneer of the first field, called kinesics, has explained that "body motion is a learned form of communication, which is patterned within a culture and which can be broken down into an ordered system of isolable elements." Two approaches to small-group behavior are sociometry and ethnomethodology.[13] George Eliot, in the description of a small group in *Middlemarch,* ch. 56, anticipated the concerns of these fields. She describes how an employer sympathetic to rural workers approaches a few who are in a sullen mood: "When he advanced towards the laborers they had not gone to work again, but were standing in that form of rural grouping which consists in each turning a shoulder towards the other, at a distance of two or three yards. They looked rather sulkily at Caleb, who walked quickly with one hand in his pocket and the other thrust between the buttons of his waistcoat, and had his every-day mild air when he paused among them."

Other novelists have also anticipated social science concepts. In recent years the notion of personal "identity" and the "identity crisis" has been given wide currency, first in the work of Erik Erikson. Kipling, in *Kim,* ch. 11, describes the main character in solitude, repeating his name to himself, and observes that some whites and many Asians can put themselves into a trance in this way, "letting the mind go free upon speculation as to what is called personal identity." Hawthorne in *The House of the Seven Gables,* ch. 12, remarks that Holgrave, wandering and homeless, "putting off one exterior, and snatching up another, to be soon shifted for a third," never changed his inner character: "amid all these personal vicissitudes, he had never lost his identity."

A social science term that has achieved popular use is the "self-fulfilling prophecy," introduced in 1948 by Merton who nevertheless asserts that the concept itself is not new. He defines it to mean that "public definitions of a situation (prophecies or predictions) become an integral part of the situation and thus affect subsequent developments."[14] Among writers who have used the concept is Forster, in *Howards End,* ch. 7, whose narrator observes of Margaret's fear that even the mention of her sister's unhappy love affair may revive her feeling about it: "The remark would be untrue, but of the kind, which, if stated often enough, may become true; just as the remark, 'England and Germany are bound to fight,' renders war a little more likely each time that it is made." *Howards End* was in fact published in 1910, four years before the outbreak of war between England and Germany. Thomas Mann makes a similar point in *Buddenbrooks*, pt. 8, ch. 5, about a boy who knows he will cry when forced to perform for grownups: "There they stood, and looked at him. They expected, and feared, that he would break down—so how was it possible *not* to?" Forster's anticipation of the notion of the culture of poverty in *Howards End* is reflected later by Chester B. Himes in *If He Hollers Let Him Go*, ch. 10, where the narrator-character is at a gathering of blacks who are discussing the race question. A woman social worker says: "But this isn't just a problem of race. It's a ghetto problem involving a class of people with different cultures and traditions at a different level of education."

Originality of Thought

These parallels suggest that, while social science borrows from the stock of knowledge that human beings have about their own behavior, the novel does so too. Both the novel and social science use familiar notions, rephrase them, and try to add to one's understanding. The contribution each makes is to draw new attention to old truths that illuminate current behavior and events, and to adjust these truths to the specific purpose of the time. They are constantly rediscovering and reapplying general ideas. This may be so even in the physical sciences, though perhaps to a lesser extent, since generalizations in that area are more cumulative than in the study of human behavior. As the physicist Ernst Mach observed in the late nineteenth century, "the majority of the ideas we deal with were conceived by others, often centuries ago" (196). And Merton emphasized that the ideas of "unanticipated consequences" and the "self-fulfilling prophecy" were not new with him, but that he was trying to systematize them and to extend them to new situations. He thus contributed to the understanding of social institutions. Most seekers after new knowledge must understand Goethe's pessimism when he wrote in 1828 that "the world is now so old, so many eminent men have lived and thought for thousands of years, that there is little new to be discovered or expressed." But he adds more optimistically about his theory of colors, "my merit is, that I have found it also, that I have said it again, and that I have striven to bring the truth once more into a confused world" (289-290). Tracing the rediscovery of such general ideas leads to an appreciation for earlier efforts at understanding and helps to extend them to new experiences, even if the general ideas themselves are not really changed or made more scientific. F. B. Kaye, in the introduction to his edition of Bernard Mandeville, put the point convincingly in defending the satirist's skeptical view of human behavior: "sufficient research can make any thought seem stale." If people "rethink" old thoughts, they can, like Mandeville, achieve "that drawing of latent inference from old material, that novel rearrangement of old knowledge, which constitutes the positive side of originality."

There are two important authorial intrusions on the subject of originality. In *Tess of the d'Urbervilles*, ch. 19, Hardy shows an educated man impressed by the milkmaid Tess's ability to express "feelings which might almost have been called those of the age, the ache of modernism. The perception arrested him less when he reflected that what are called advanced ideas are really in great part but the latest fashion in definition—a more accurate expression, by words in *logy* and *ism,* of sensations which men and women have grasped for centuries." George Eliot puts it more simply in *Daniel Deronda,* ch. 64, perhaps unconsciously reflecting Goethe: "Of course all this thinking on Sir Hugo's part was eminently premature . . . But it is the trick of thinking to be either premature or behindhand."

The frequency with which insights appear in fiction has stimulated admirers of some novelists to compile such wisdom and omit the fictional context entirely. Several compilations were made from Balzac's work and one from Dickens'. Samuel Richardson attached considerable importance to such extracts of his novels, by both himself and others, because he feared readers would overlook the lessons in them. George Eliot doubted the value of publishing extracts from her novels, although she cooperated in it, insisting that her books were "not properly separable into 'direct' and 'indirect' teaching."[15]

Despite this denial, "direct" authorial commentary has contributed much to a knowledge of human behavior, although some writers and critics believe that the "indirect" meaning conveyed by the novel as a unit is more satisfying aesthetically. In a skeptical mood, Hawthorne, in his preface to *The House of the Seven Gables* asserts that no matter how artistically effective a novel may be, it cannot add anything to a truth. He is right, but he does not say that the novel cannot contain truth or knowledge. The knowledge contained in authorial commentary is subject to verification by historical and social science methods; indeed, many fictional insights may be stated in the form of propositions or hypotheses about human behavior and social institutions, or of historically limited conclusions about events or social classes, or of moral judgments about the lessons or meaning of human experience. Such insights are convincing and worthy of further investigation for several reasons. First, they ring true; that is, they conform to the readers' general sense of things, to their common sense about themselves as social beings. Frequently they also follow from the events and characters the novelist describes, from the premises in the story, all of which are felt to resemble real experience in some way. Readers thus accept the novelist's conclusion from his premises as applying to social life outside as well as inside the story. Finally, there do exist historical and social-science studies, tested by the evidence according to the best methods that scholars have been able to devise, with which to test in turn the insights found in novels.

Fiction and History

There are authors whose purpose is to tell what
has happened. Mine, if I could attain it, would be
to talk about what can happen.
— Montaigne, *Essays*

7.

Some of the questions involved in comparing fiction and history
were raised in classical antiquity and have emerged again and
again, especially in modern times. In the seventeenth and eighteenth centuries in England and France, novelists and critics debated the merits of fiction (or "poetry") and history (or "philosophy") as methods of describing and moralizing about human
behavior and social institutions. In comparing the writing of fiction and of history, it is necessary to consider the use each genre
makes of the other, verisimilitude, probability, and the help that
readers give to novelists by their "willing suspension of disbelief."

The Connections

That fiction and history are related is inevitable, since art must
have some connection with life, even if only to oppose it. To state
that they are connected but separable is easy. What is more interesting, however, is the nature of the connection, and that cannot
be stated so simply. The two terms, fiction and history, are not obviously comparable. Fiction usually means the story or the novel
itself, a genre of literature, and not the events and characters de-

scribed or analyzed in this genre. History, however, is less clear. It can mean the events and characters in the record of actual social life, as well as the discipline or genre of writing that describes or analyzes these events and characters. Here the term history is used mainly in the latter sense, that is, the writing of history, with which the writing of novels is compared.

Fiction's borrowing from historical events goes back to classical antiquity, so the creators of stories must have presumed that their readers and listeners were attracted by an element of reality in the fiction they enjoyed.[1] The paradox of art is that creators find a way to satisfy the audiences' and the readers' desire for a combination of the recognizable and the unusual. Within the "rules of credibility," argued Fielding in the introduction to book 8 of *Tom Jones,* the more an author can "surprise the reader the more he will engage his attention, and the more he will charm him." He seems to suggest that the novelist must resort to the "marvellous" to heighten interest, but avoid the "incredible" and stick to what is known. Fielding illustrates this method in *Tom Jones,* bk. 1, ch. 3, where he remarks that Squire Allworthy did many things common to people of his class, but if that were all he did, "I should have left him to have recorded his own merit . . . Matters of a much more extraordinary kind are to be the subject of this history, or I should grossly misspend my time in writing so voluminous a work." F. Scott Fitzgerald in *The Crack-Up* puts the same point differently and dramatically: "Reporting the extreme things as if they were the average things will start you on the art of fiction" (178). This is the genius of Dickens—to exaggerate the commonplace and thus to make its essence more memorable—for which contemporary critics accused him of introducing too much romance.[2]

Novelists seeking "truth," even though they define it differently, often make special investigations into social conditions or individual lives that border on scholarly research. George Eliot described her goal in this way: "I undertake to exhibit nothing as it should be . . . The moral effect of the stories of course depends on my power of seeing truly and feeling justly." It is thus not surprising to learn from her biographer, Gordon Haight, that for *Adam Bede* she sought precise information about the appearance of certain flowers, crops, trees, weather, wages, and prices. Nor is it surprising to read this half-facetious comment of the narrator in *Daniel Deronda,* ch. 8: "I like to mark the time, and connect the course of individual lives with the historic stream, for all classes of thinkers. This was the period when the broadening of gauge in crinolines seemed to demand an agitation for the general enlargement of churches, ball-rooms, and vehicles." In *Moby Dick* Melville devoted a chapter to cetology, perhaps to make his novel about whaling more authentic. James Joyce had a prototype for Bloom, to whom he gave traits of other Dubliners as well, including a man he had met only twice. He asked his brother and aunt to tell him all they knew of the man. In naming his main character Bloom, Joyce also drew on his knowledge of Dublin Jewish families with that name. In *Doctor Faustus* Mann discussed fine points of musical theory and history based on his reading and consultation of experts on music.[3]

Of course, Eliot, Joyce, and other novelists made such inquiries not to write history but to create a world and tell a story. The process of writing history is different from that of writing a novel. The novelist, mixing the facts with his imagination, searches for information to learn about a community, a way of life, or an individual, but he nevertheless invents something to change what he learns or add to it.[4]

England in the 1830s and 1840s was a particularly fruitful time for didactic and ameliorative writing in history, the new social science, and the novel because it was a time of social ills and social reform following immediately upon Sir Walter Scott's great popularity as a historical novelist. Major and minor novelists turned for material not only to the social ills themselves but also to the governmental investigations that exposed them. Disraeli, for example, in *Sybil* (1845), describing an imaginary factory town and its workers, bosses, brutality, and disease, drew upon the descriptions of a real town three years earlier by a government inspector. In his preface to the first edition, withdrawn from later ones, he insisted he was not exaggerating but relying on his observations and on "the authentic evidence which has been received by

Royal Commissions and Parliamentary Committees." A French historian of this period of English literature, Louis Cazamian, goes so far as to maintain that the novels of Disraeli, Dickens, and Kingsley were more important than the official reports in informing and arousing public opinion to the evils of the industrial system. William Aydelotte tends to agree, holding that this effect of such novels was more significant than their value as sources of information about the social conditions they described.[5]

Harriet Martineau, one of the most popular writers of the period but hardly known today, made an interesting experiment in didactic fiction in the 1830s in two series of social science novels, one illustrating the principles of the new "science" of political economy, the other the advantages of proposed changes in the poor law. Having written two stories on economic subjects and read Jane Marcet's "Conversations on Political Economy," Martineau felt that the public would welcome a clear explanation of the subject through stories. Contrary to the expectations of several publishers, including her own, her stories were an immediate success, and she became famous. In her twenty-five *Illustrations of Political Economy* (1832-1834), she explains the ideas of Adam Smith, James Mill, and Malthus in a series of tales accompanied by the propositions and lessons stated separately. Martineau clarifies her purpose in a preface to the fourteenth tale, *Berkeley the Banker,* explaining that if the stories do not convey much information, it is because she intends not to offer her views on "temporary questions in political economy" but to give her readers a basis for their own opinions through an understanding of a "few plain, permanent principles."

At this time a Royal Commission was advancing recommendations on the poor law. Favoring these recommendations, the influential Society for the Diffusion of Useful Knowledge asked Martineau to illustrate them for the public. She wrote four tales, *Poor Laws and Paupers Illustrated* (1833-1834), using official reports and her own notions. These tales also attracted much attention but did not sell so well as the other series.[6]

Although she wrote more fiction, Martineau had a low estimate of her capacity in this domain of writing. In a few years she gave it up, despite many requests to continue, "from a simple inability to do it well," as she herself put it in her *Autobiography* (II, 565). That she regarded herself mainly as a publicist is suggested by her testimony that she had great difficulty in inventing a plot, "a task above human faculties." She concluded: "The only thing to be done, therefore, is to derive the plot from actual life, where the work is achieved for us." She insisted that even Shakespeare and Scott could take their "perfect" plots only from "real life" (I, 179-180).

Martineau did think well of her contribution through her fiction to the discussion of social issues — a task she held to be important. She praised Scott for his moral and historical teaching by means of the novel, which she regarded as more effective with the general public than the essays of professional moralists and historians. She was devoted to the social sciences. She believed political economy to be an exact science. In the preface to the nineteenth tale of the *Illustrations,* entitled "Sowers Not Reapers," she asserted her nonpartisanship: "I take my stand upon SCIENCE." She translated a major work of Auguste Comte, a pioneer of modern sociology, describing it as the foundation of a true social science. Her loyalty was thus primarily to public education and social science, seeking to promote them in various ways, including fiction.[7]

George Eliot, a generation after Martineau, also turned to the novel but with much greater artistic success. She thought with characteristic clarity about the relation between the writing of history and fiction. In an unpublished note written around 1880, entitled "Historic Imagination," she pointed out the need for both fidelity to the concrete data of history and the exercise of the imagination. History-writing she found too abstract, but she warned also against "the schemed picturesqueness of ordinary historical fiction."[8]

Sir Walter Scott has long been regarded as one of the authors who best used history as a basis for the incidents, characters, and issues to be transformed into novels. He thereby not only influenced the novel considerably but also the writing of history itself in England and France, at least until history became a scholarly discipline.[9] Recently W.B. Gallie, a philosopher of history, has approached the writing of history as a narrative. "Historical under-standing," he argues, "is the exercise of the capacity to follow a story," to which the historian adds his "explanation" when the story is confusing or hard to believe. Such explanations are "ancil-lary" to the narrative and "are in the nature of intrusions: they are not what we primarily came for—the play, that is the basic thing" (105-107). A good history has a "sequence of incidents and out-comes which are, from the standpoint of reader and audience, acceptable yet unpredictable" (29). Gallie's way of putting the matter brings out the similarity between the writing of history and fiction without making them identical.

In both forms of writing, readers accept the events, even if they are surprising, because they are brought within the readers' com-pass by an explanation. To explain an action by a character, gen-eralizations can be made in the form of intrusions. In *Jude the Obscure*, pt. 2, ch. 5, Hardy has to bring together the schoolmas-ter Phillotson and Susan to develop a sustained relationship, in-cluding marriage. Phillotson hires Susan to fill a sudden vacancy and then recommends she be retained because in a short time he has observed that she is a good teacher. Hardy feels the need to defend or explain Phillotson's action, which the reader may not find convincing at first, so he adds a generalization in the form of a question to the reader: "and what master-tradesman does not wish to keep an apprentice who saves him half his labor?" Thus Hardy accomplishes what he needs for his story and helps the reader to accept his device by explaining it. Eliot follows the same pattern in *Felix Holt,* ch. 33. In a crisis, Felix is concerned mainly with avoiding violence among others without thinking of himself. To help the reader accept such altruism or obtuseness in an intel-ligent man, Eliot offers first a specific and then a general explana-tion. Felix is simply the kind of man who is concerned more with the general interest than with his own; moreover, "Nature never makes men who are at once energetically sympathetic and mi-nutely calculating."

The interaction between historical and fictional writing may be seen in events and in characters—an arbitrary division that breaks the unity of both histories and novels, but is nonetheless useful.

Many novelists have taken real persons and events, famous or not, as the basis for a story. When such persons and events are well known or figure in historical records, such as state papers, wills, newspapers, or letters, that record can be compared, for whatever purpose, with the fictional treatment, bearing in mind that both are limited in various ways. Robert Penn Warren's *All the King's Men* (1946) has been thought to be closely based on the life and public career of Senator Huey Long, who died eleven years before the novel appeared. The author has given an interesting comment on this popular assumption: "For better or for worse, Willie Stark was not Huey Long . . . I do not mean to imply that there was no connection . . . Certainly, it was the career of Long and the atmosphere of Louisiana that suggested the play that was to become the novel. But suggestion does not mean identity." Warren could not make his character a "projection" of Long, because he did not know "what Long was like." Yet he did have "some notions" about what Long represented, and these he tried to express in the novel. One such notion was that democracy may bring a "kind of doom" upon itself. Warren nevertheless denies intending to write a novel about politics: "Politics merely provided the framework story in which the deeper concerns, whatever their final significance, might work themselves out."[10]

Occasionally it is possible to make an even more precise comparison when a work of history and a work of fiction deal with precisely the same broad subject. This occurred in 1966, when two books appeared on the "Beiliss case" in which a Russian Jew was framed in 1911 on a charge of murdering a boy to obtain his blood to make matzos for Passover. The story of this trial for ritual murder is treated historically in Maurice Samuel's *Blood Accusation: The Strange History of the Beiliss Case* and fictionally in Bernard Malamud's *The Fixer*. Though the two authors have overlapping interests, Samuel deals more with the political and social forces leading to the frame-up, whereas Malamud concentrates on the personal agony and ultimate nobility of the victim. Reading the history, one learns early that the plotters will not succeed in all their aims; in the novel, one feels that the plotters' power has doomed the victim. Malamud, using several fictional devices, says

much about life, justice, and at the end even about politics in
Russia. Although Samuel, in contrast, asserts in the preface that
he has "used no fictional devices and invented no conversations,"
he seems to approach such techniques, as when he reports: "Everything about Beiliss turns black, his heart hammers" (248). Samuel
then gives the victim's thoughts in what purport to be the victim's
own words, but he does not cite sources for such information.

Scholarship on the novel has used some techniques of reference
more familiar in history. There are guides to the entire work of
certain novelists. F. B. Pinion's guide to Hardy is given over mainly
to a "dictionary of people and places in Hardy's works," as indicated in the preface, and there are maps of the fictional county of
Wessex including both real and fictional places. Ward Miner has
compared William Faulkner's fictional city, Jefferson, with its presumed model, Oxford, Mississippi. Frank Robbins has studied the
chronology of twelve Barset and political novels of Trollope because doing so "is good fun" and "adds to our knowledge of Trollope's methods" (303). He finds that there are a number of minor
internal discrepancies and that some of the fictional events closely
follow Victorian history. A. O. J. Cockshut, however, shows that
Trollope's characters in the political novels are only remotely related to real people. A connection between fiction and history is illustrated by Pat Rogers, who studied the real Grub Street to height-
en the reader's appreciation of the Grub Street in the satires of
Pope, Swift, and Gay. The usual method is to examine this literature for what it can tell about London life of the period; his own
method is the opposite, "to show how a knowledge of London to-
pography can inform and enrich a reading of the greatest satire"
of the eighteenth century (7).

Since the time of John Dos Passos, to speak only of recent history,
many novelists have used variations of his techniques and some
new techniques to give the flavor of a period or merely to identify
the period in which the novel occurs. In a satiric novel, *Mumbo-
Jumbo* (1972), about white exploitation of blacks and their history, Ishmael Reed tells us much about America and Harlem in
the 1920s, including jazz music and dance, psychoanalysis, President Harding, and the cultural Renaissance among black artists.

He adverts also to Egyptian mythology, occult and voodoo practices, the transfer of African art to American museums, and its recovery for Africa. This novel has footnotes, reprints cartoons and photographs, and lists a "Partial Bibliography" of 104 items, many of them works of scholarship and at least a few spurious ones in the spirit of the novel itself.

Novelists have various purposes for introducing historical characters into their stories: to mark the time, to heighten interest or credibility, or simply to interpret a character, process, or era. Thackeray is typically formal in introducing Napoleon as *Vanity Fair,* ch. 18, approaches the wars bearing his name: "Our surprised story now finds itself for a moment among very famous events and personages, and hanging on to the skirts of history." Trollope, who enjoyed discussing his characters in his *Autobiography,* remarks that he could not "kill" Kate Woodward of *The Three Clerks* (93-94). But he notes later that he did "kill" Mrs. Proudie of *The Last Chronicle of Barset* merely because, while writing this novel, he overheard two clergymen at the Athenaeum Club complaining that he had introduced the same characters in several novels (230-231). In this way Trollope pursued his goal, outside his novels, of making real and historical some of the characters inside them. George Eliot playfully does something similar at the end of *Felix Holt*: "As to the town in which Felix Holt now resides, I will keep that a secret, lest he should be troubled by any visitor having the insufferable motive of curiosity." So does an African author of modern times, Chinua Achebe, when he reports in *No Longer at Ease* (1960), ch. 5, that his main character is interviewed for a job by four members of the Public Service Commission of Nigeria. One member, representing one of the country's three regions, is asleep during these proceedings. Moving between the fictional and the real world, the narrator comments parenthetically: "In the interests of Nigerian unity the region shall remain nameless." In *The Man Who Cried I Am* (1967), a novel seeking to record recent history, John A. Williams prefers not to give dates but to set a mood and establish a chronology by referring to events and processes likely to be remembered by most readers. Thus 1940 is suggested by references to the peacetime draft, swing bands, the Japanese in China, the assassination of Leon Trotsky, and the Nazi offensive. Williams includes historical characters as well as historical matters, such as the Negro units in the United States army, the forthcoming independence of African states, and the election campaign of 1948.

The Question of Superiority

The argument as to whether history or fiction is the superior genre cannot be settled unless one asks: superior for what purpose? The case for the superiority of fiction goes back at least to Aristotle and has not changed much since then. Aristotle in ch. 9 of the *Poetics* follows, extends, and disputes Plato on the representation of nature by art. "Poetry" is superior to history, he asserts, in the sense that it tells "what might happen," whereas history only tells "what has happened." He concludes: "For this reason poetry is something more philosophical and more worthy of serious attention than history; for while poetry is concerned with universal truths, history treats of particular facts." Despite changing concepts of both genres, especially in the last two or three hundred years, this concept has been widely held: fiction seeks a broader and more enduring truth than history. A corollary has been equally popular: that fiction allows the writer greater freedom to draw a moral, to make judgments. "Lessons for moral development," noted Madame de Staël, "based upon the rewards of virtue, do not always emerge from a reading of history." The novel is better suited to this task, she claimed. Following de Staël, Balzac argued in the *Comédie,* I, ch. 33, that as a novelist, free to invent, he has done "better than the historian" in punishing the wicked. Fiction, according to Hardy, in his essay "The Profitable Reading of Fiction," "is more true, so to put it, than history or nature can be," because the novelist can ignore the "monstrosities of human action and character" which occur in history and cannot be explained. The French philosopher M. Guyau asserted that the novel is history purified of its accidents and irrationalities and hence unites the essences of poetry, drama, psychology, and social science. E. M. Forster took the same position: the novel can go beyond the evidence to make human character better understood. The historian Herbert Butterfield felt that history's fidelity to the facts makes it as "true to life" as the novel "but farther away from the heart of things" (18). Norman Mailer, in *The Armies of the Night* (1968), subtitled *History as a Novel. The Novel as History,* appears to believe that the novelist can correct the historian by bringing finer instruments to the observation of human affairs.[11]

Francis Bacon in *The Advancement of Learning,* bk. 2, ch. 13, took the foregoing position but with a notable difference. Poetry, being a result of the imagination, is unrestrained by the real world. It can give what history denies by "feigning" historical actions, thus satisfying man's desire for more virtue and greatness than is found in history itself. "Poetry" is thus both a substitute — a "shadow" rather than the "substance" — for reality and a perfection of it.

The superiority of history has no such staunch advocates as the opposite position, except that it is regarded by most analysts as better for its own goals. H. G. Wells held that the novel is trivial unless it deals with great social issues, but the same may be said of history. Despite the popular belief in fiction's superiority, the novel has had to rely on history as a record and as a genre. The earliest modern novelists sought to give the status of truth and historicity to their stories. Then French novelists of the seventeenth and eighteenth centuries "solved" the problem of the attractiveness of both genres by devising the notion of "verisimilitude."

French Eighteenth-Century Novel

There are three excellent studies of the French eighteenth-century novel, by Vivienne Mylne, Philip Stewart, and English Showalter, building upon a earlier one by Raymond Alden. Mylne gives several reasons why the novel claimed "some of the credit and privileges of history" in this early period. First, the novel, as a new form with a low reputation, naturally sought the prestige of the "prosperous and relatively important genre." Second, the novel was not itself rigorously defined and could therefore approach related literary forms. Third, historians of the time aspired to write well, making the difference between history and literature less clear than now (20-21).

The way in which the French novel of the eighteenth century used history shows how the question of the relation between history and fiction was first worked out in modern times. Mylne reveals that the early novel's defense against the various charges of its detractors established the basis for its later defenses, including contemporary ones. The novel's advocates were concerned mainly with the charges of immorality, deceit, and untruth, against which they justified the new genre as worthy in itself, as improving upon historical writing, and as being truth rather than fiction. The period seemed to be obsessed with credibility while craving also contemporaneity. Showalter points out that by the mid-seventeenth century, the "novelist could not admit to having invented his story, as the poet could; consequently he began to pose as a historian." He did so by introducing specific elements of chronology and geography, personal names, money, and a narrator who could attest to the truth of the story. The novelist could thus not write in the third person, as if he knew everything; he had to write from a limited point of view. "The contract between readers and novelists," concludes Showalter, "allowed for no art; the novelist had to account for all his information" (175-176).

Stewart shows that the very word "histoire" was ambiguous, referring both to history and to story. It was believed that what was invented was not true, therefore false and corrupt. The novelists, according to Stewart and Mylne, felt they must deceive the reader. Stewart argues that "illusion was the salvation of fiction" by putting a premium on certain fictional techniques to make the illusion convincing (26). These techniques produced "vraisemblance," or verisimilitude. Mylne recalls that this term meant in the seventeenth century not so much truth as "true-seeming" or "calculated to give an impression of truth" (13).

The significance of these early techniques and arguments for later fiction and social science is considerable. Both Mylne and Stewart point out that the eighteenth-century first-person novels ultimately won an important right for the great fictional age of the nineteenth century: to drop the pose of truth and to practice the novel as a form of art. In seeking to portray real life in order to gain acceptance, the eighteenth century novel, Mylne explains, touched upon three domains: the "external world," that is, "the realm of nature, either in its original state or shaped by man's activities"; "the human society in which the individual lives"; and "the individual man or woman whose actions, thoughts and feelings" are the subjects and plot of the novel (264). These three categories — nature, society, and the individual — are also the ones introduced in eighteenth-century social thought. They still constitute the large domains of the social sciences today.

Early in the twentieth century Alden pointed out that the notions of verisimilitude advanced two centuries earlier in France were intended to restrict novelists, to make them adhere to the truth. In response, they modified verisimilitude, resemblance to truth, in the effort to escape the worst features of the requirement to stick to the factual. Aristotle had raised the question in order to liberate the writer from such a strict adherence to the facts, to permit a portrayal of experience based on the imagination, to bring together the imitative and the ideal, and to use the truths of history as a basis for transcending it. Not long before Alden was making his point about Aristotle, Leslie Stephen was discussing the same broad question in relation to Hawthorne, who "gave one solution of the problem, what elements of romance are discoverable amongst the harsh prose of this prosaic age." Because the novelist is required by the genre to "come into the closest possible contact with the facts," he then has the problem of how "to introduce the ideal element which must, in some degree, be present in all genuine art" (230).

The same technique is interpreted differently from time to time. The intruding author is now widely held to make the entire relationship between author and reader less credible, yet at the beginning of the novel such "interruptions" of the narrative were thought to enhance credibility by suggesting that the author could personally attest to the truth of his story. In the nineteenth century the novelist could drop the pose of personal knowledge and enjoy the liberty of art, the avowed invention of a story as a commentary upon life. De Tocqueville in *Democracy in America*, II, ch. 25, connected the demand for verisimilitude in literature with the popularity of drama and attention to the facts of life that develop as a nation is "lapsing" into democracy. Equality and democracy, he wrote in 1835, during the height of romanticism in Europe, divert men from the contemplation of "ideal beauty." Competition and the desire for success rivet their attention upon what is before and around them, rather than upon an ideal that is not present and exists perhaps only in the mind. "The imagination is not extinct" in a democracy, "but its chief function is to devise what may be useful, and to represent what is real." Although he was speaking of the drama, which he regarded as "democratic" because it was direct in its appeal, did not call for preparation to enjoy it, and was hence "so much within the reach of the multitude" — these remarks may be taken to refer to the general spirit of literature.

Shortly after the triumph of verisimilitude — perhaps even before it became so widely accepted — observers questioned whether such precise fidelity to life was the best way to portray or comment upon it. "Photographic realism" has always been a somewhat pejorative term, suggesting that what it offers in fidelity to detail it loses in broad meaning. Especially with the insights into human behavior introduced by modern psychology and Freudian approaches, it has become customary to view the "absurd" as more "realistic" than the traditional faithfulness to detail and to approach earlier literature in this spirit. Thus Frederick Crews has remarked that "Hawthorne appears less arbitrary, more 'true to life,' in some of his fantastic plots if we happen to be familiar with modern case-histories" (261). To recent generations, Kafka's novels reveal more about the effect of bureaucracy than do more "realistic" novels like those of Balzac or Trollope, or the studies of social scientists. Such critiques of photographic realism go back many years. Dostoyevsky wrote in a letter of 1868: "What most people regard as fantastic and lacking in universality, *I* hold to be the inmost essence of truth. Arid observation of everyday trivialities I have long ceased to regard as realism — it is quite the reverse." Hardy, writing on "The Profitable Reading of Fiction," called attention to the need for distinguishing "temporary" from "eternal" truths. Temporary truths are found in novels faithful to the "garniture" of life — clothing and "phrases of the season" — rather than to life itself; but there is little left after "our first sense of its photographic curiousness." To Proust in *The Past Recaptured*, "An hour is not merely an hour. It is a vase filled with perfumes, sounds, plans and climates. What we call reality is a certain relationship between these sensations and the memories which surround us at the same time (a relationship that is destroyed by a bare cinematographic presentation, which gets further away from the truth the more closely it claims to adhere to it)" (271). Ellen Glasgow, writing new prefaces to a special edition of her novels long after their first appearance, described how she gave up "external verisimilitude" for the "more valid evidence of the imagination." Of *The Voice of the People* (1900) she remarked: "Every house that I mentioned was then standing, every tree, every stone, every brick." But in her later books she abandoned "accurate geography" as less important than "sound psychology." She sought the "distilled essence of all Virginia cities rather than the speaking likeness of one."[12]

Verisimilitude and Probability

Verisimilitude and probability went together in the prefaces to hundreds of novels in the eighteenth and nineteenth centuries in England and France, in which the authors claimed a factual basis for their stories. Closeness to the truth — verisimilitude — was one way of putting the matter, while probability — the likelihood that an event or a character could be found in real life — was another.

Aristotle had long ago raised the general question in the *Poetics*, ch. 9. The historian tells things that have happened; the poet tells things that "might happen, that is, that could happen because they are, in the circumstance, either probable or necessary." To emphasize probability, Aristotle also expressed his position paradoxically, in ch. 24: "Probable impossibilities are to be preferred to improbable possibilities." Note the restriction of his point to what is probable (likely) or necessary (required) in the circumstances (the situation the author has created). Whether something is likely or required thus depends on the persuasion of the novelist. Locke, in another context and following Plato, developed this point when he insisted that the "faculty" used to examine whether propositions are certain or only probable "is that which we call reason."[13] Thus the "reason" sets up an opposition to the improbable, a hurdle that the novelist overcomes by some form of explanation. Either he has prepared the reader for the "hurdle," or he must help the reader past it with an intrusion. Several major novelists have been bothered by this requirement, noting that the historian has an easier time of it because when he sets down an event that taxes credulity, he is believed because he can prove it really occurred. The fiction-writer, however, cannot prove the occurrence of an event readers sense to be improbable, so he must be more careful, as Fielding noted in the introduction to bk. 8 of *Tom Jones*, "to keep within the limits not only of possibility, but of probability too," for "what it is not possible for man to perform, it is scarce possible for man to believe he did perform." Balzac, in the course of explanations that he feared the reader might find tedious, interrupted *Les Paysans* in pt. 1, ch. 9 to remark of the novelist: "the historian of manners is subject to harsher laws than those which govern the historian of facts; he must make everything appear probable, even the truth itself, whereas in the domain of history proper the impossible is proved because it occurred." Dickens had difficulty on this point throughout his career, having to defend his portrayal of conditions as true even if hard to believe. In his preface to *Nicholas Nickleby* (1839), he exasperatedly complained that people who are willing to believe in the extremes of character in real life somehow become unwilling to do so when they read a novel.

Poets and novelists have for centuries followed Aristotle's distinction between history—or what has happened—and credible fiction—or what might have happened. Montaigne was interested in possible events even if they never actually occurred, so long as they revealed "some human potentiality." Pope distinguished the "probable fable" as including actions that might happen "in the common course of Nature." In a typical effort to differentiate the novel from the romance, Clara Reeve in the late eighteenth century stated the issue of probability in a way that summarized earlier statements and apparently inspired later ones. To unite the merits of the romance and the novel, "there is required a sufficient degree of the marvellous to excite attention; enough of the manners of real life to give an air of probability to the work; and enough of the pathetic to engage the heart on its behalf." Scott spoke of the novel's events as "accommodated to the ordinary train of human events, and the modern state of society." Trollope followed with the prescription: "A novel should give a picture of common life enlivened by humor and sweetened by pathos." Balzac wrote of the need to justify events in *Les Paysans* before the "tribunal of probability." To Hardy, the "writer's problem" was how to "balance" the "uncommon" (to lend interest) and the "ordinary" (to keep to reality). A contemporary American novelist, Herbert Gold, in explaining his apparently autobiographical novel, *Fathers* (1967), echoed the eighteenth century: "It did not happen like this, but it might have."[14]

Hardy gave one answer to the problem which plagued Dickens, that is, the reader's unwillingness to accept in fiction the extreme characters he accepts in life itself. Hardy suggested in *The Life* that in creating a balance between the "uncommon" and the "ordinary," the novelist should never make a character incredible: "The uncommonness must be in the events, not in the characters" (150). It is doubtful that Dickens could have been spared his frustration by this device, yet it offers the novelist a guideline. Indeed, more authorial intrusions seem to be directed toward helping the reader past the hurdle of an improbable character than an improbable event — where the two can be easily distinguished, as is not always the case. It would be interesting to test this hypothesis systematically. Intrusions from Fielding and George Eliot illustrate both the novelist's concern with probability in general and his tendency to try to explain extreme characters rather than extreme events.

In *Joseph Andrews*, bk. 1, ch. 4, Fielding reports Lady Tattle's remark, upon seeing Lady Booby walking arm in arm with her footman Joseph, that this should surprise no one, for the couple's intimacy has been common gossip for months. The author then

reports that Lady Tattle spreads the news the same day. An attentive reader might wonder why a gossip would be so diligent in
spreading "old business." Fielding provides a footnote, to preserve
the consistency or rationality of his character: "It may seem an
Absurdity that *Tattle* should visit, as she actually did, to spread a
known Scandal: but the Reader may reconcile this, by supposing
with me, that, notwithstanding what she says, this was her first
Acquaintance with it." Thus Fielding, while accomplishing his
purpose of keeping Lady Tattle consistent, accomplishes another
purpose of suggesting her claim to a knowledge of all gossip. Later, in bk. 2, ch. 13, Fielding states that Mrs. Slipslop affects not
to recognize Fanny. Again with a double purpose, the author observes: "It will doubtless seem extremely odd to many readers, that
Mrs. Slipslop, who had lived several years in the same house with
Fanny, should, in a short separation, utterly forget her." The fact
is, Fielding continues, Mrs. Slipslop remembered Fanny very well.
In order to "satisfy the most curious reader that Mrs. Slipslop did
not in the least deviate from the common road," Fielding then
launches a long digression about "high people" and "low people"
and their different roles in different places. When Mrs. Slipslop
ignored Fanny, she was maintaining her social position according
to these complicated and sometimes puzzling rules. Thus once
again Fielding uses the occasion of preserving the consistency of a
character's actions to accomplish another purpose as well, in this
case to describe differences in the attitudes and behavior of social
classes.

Several examples from George Eliot are equally instructive as to
the novelist's special desire to avoid violating the reader's expectation of human nature. In each case, she bases her appeal on ex-
ceptions to that expectation or to "human nature" itself. In *Daniel
Deronda,* ch. 9, she anticipates that readers may object that her
characters are not acting in accordance with human nature.
"But," Eliot notes, "let it be observed, nothing is here narrated
of human nature generally: the history in its present stage concerns
only a few people in a corner of Wessex." In *The Mill on the Floss,*
bk. 6, ch. 3, the narrator addresses the reader: "If it appears to
you at all incredible that young ladies should be led on to talk con-

fidentially in a situation of this kind, I will beg you to remember that human life furnishes many exceptional cases." In *Middlemarch,* ch. 62, she again appeals to special conditions: "Unwonted circumstances may make us all rather unlike ourselves."

Despite its vaunted freedom from rules and its amorphousness, the novel began with, and has retained, at least one important convention in the combination of verisimilitude and probability. Kenneth Burke has spoken of "conventional form" in literature, which involves an "expectancy" in the reader even before he experiences a poem or novel (159-160). The reader assumes that a novel will have a certain fidelity to reality even if it disdains photographic realism. He expects certain kinds of behavior in people in accordance with their age, sex, nationality, occupation, social position, marital status, or physical qualities. These are the basic attributes with which novelists and social scientists work. The novelist constructs his characters to conform to such expectations to a degree credible to the reader. Fictional conventions involve two social conventions that the novelist must attend to: the expectations which the reader brings to a novel from his own life and experience — that is, the writer must understand his audience; and the expectations which the reader acquires from the novel itself — that is, the writer must persuade the reader that a given character is constructed so consistently that the reader can believe in him as both a type (doctor, plumber, dressmaker) and an individual. These conventions and understandings often make it possible for readers to predict what will happen in a story. Moreover, verisimilitude and probability can sometimes make the novel itself a prediction of real life. The capacity or intention to predict is something the novel has in common with social science, which in recent decades has considered prediction an important aspect of a science.

Willing Suspension of Disbelief

In making its way against the venerable forms of literature that preceded it, the novel stressed its chief virtues, that it dealt with ordinary people and true-to-life events. Because the early public and critics held the novel to this fidelity to life, novelists had also to seek a little room for imaginative maneuver, for invention, so they developed the concept and practice of verisimilitude, the invention of characters and events to look like real ones. Readers were implicitly asked by novelists — they had been asked by poets — to make an imaginative foray together, to accept as in a sense true something that both knew was not actual fact. Readers, so to speak, granted this right or privilege to novelists in the course of the nineteenth century; and for their part novelists, so to speak, earned by their talent this right or privilege to drop the pose of verisimilitude and to create art openly. Thus novelists could write in the third person as "omniscient" narrators. This new conventional form meant that readers began to grant to the novelist what they had long granted the poet, their "willing suspension of disbelief" to the extent of accepting the status of an author claiming to know everything about a story from an impossible number of viewpoints.

This useful concept of the willing suspension of disbelief has a distinguished history. Its origin, at least in the form in which it has come to be used in modern times, is usually attributed to Coleridge. In his *Biographia Literaria,* Coleridge describes how he and Wordsworth discussed "the two cardinal points of poetry, the power of exciting the sympathy of the reader by a faithful adherence to the truth of nature, and the power of giving the interest of novelty by the modifying colors of imagination." They conceived the idea of combining these powers, which led them to the *Lyrical Ballads.* Their plan was to compose two kinds of poem. Coleridge would compose the first type, in which "the incidents and agents were to be, in part at least, supernatural," and to which the reader would be aroused to react as if they were real. Wordsworth was to compose the second type, in which "subjects were to be chosen from ordinary life" but treated with such freshness that the reader would be aroused to "a feeling analogous to the supernatural" in appreciating the "loveliness and the wonders of the world before us." In his poems, Coleridge hoped that his treatment of supernatural subjects would have a "human interest and a semblance of truth sufficient to procure for these shadows of imagination that willing suspension of disbelief for the moment, which constitutes poetic faith" (II, 5-6). By a slight alteration of this wording, many advocates have characterized all poetry—not just "poetic faith"—as requiring the willing suspension of disbelief.

Fielding anticipated Coleridge in this concept and phrase by three-quarters of a century. In his introduction to book 8 of *Tom Jones,* he explains that he will give his characters no superhuman or supernatural powers. He speaks of readers who have "so little historic or poetic faith" that they believe nothing possible or probable unless they have seen it. Poetic faith to Fielding is what it is to Coleridge: the reader's willingness to accept as true what is close to the truth but is not confirmed by experience. Poetic faith is thus the reader's willingness to allow the author to go a little distance beyond experience in order to create something that fits in with his artistic purpose. Fielding points out that the historian can justify the "incredible" by proving it happened, whereas the writer of fiction, whose invented characters and events do not find documentary support, must be more careful not to exceed the limits of credibility because he has no way of proving the truth of what he recites. But Fielding argues that this limitation need not condemn the novelist to banality. He can still present characters and events beyond the reader's experience and knowledge, for if the writer stays within the bounds of credibility, he has done his duty and may rely on the reader to go along with him. The novelist has "discharged his part; and is then entitled to some faith from his reader, who is indeed guilty of critical infidelity if he disbelieves him."

In *Joseph Andrews,* bk. 4, ch. 13, Fielding used another portion of Coleridge's later phrase, "that willing suspension of disbelief for the moment, which constitutes poetic faith." Fielding introduces the notion that the lovers Fanny and Joseph are really brother and sister and hence cannot marry. People take opposing positions on the truth of the report, in accordance with their hopes. Mr. Booby says judiciously that they must await the arrival of Joseph's supposed parents to inquire into the matter. As the narrator puts it, "Mr. *Booby* now desired them all to suspend their Curiosity and absolute Belief or Disbelief, till the next Morning, when he expected old Mr. *Andrews* and his Wife." The phrase and the advice

—to suspend belief or disbelief for a while—are the same as Coleridge's, but the context is different. In Fielding, the characters are asked to withhold judgment as to the truth of a claim until it can be tested. In Coleridge, the readers are presumed willing to believe something to be true even when they know it not to be true, in order to be delighted by the poet.

Although the concept may antedate Fielding too, Coleridge's popular formulation of it owes much to Fielding.[15] Poetic faith is slightly different from the point that novelists frequently made in prefaces both in Fielding's time and well before it. The idea was that the author must persuade the reader to accept as true something the author knew was not true. In Clara Reeve's formulation in the preface to her *The Progress of Romance* (1785), the perfect novel made each scene "appear so probable, as to deceive us into a persuasion (at least while we are reading) that all is real."[16]

The notion of a suspension of judgment is suggested by Plato's view, in *The Republic*, of the place of art in the ideal republic. He claims that it is with the lower part of the soul—the emotions—that a person responds to art. As with other illusions, one must apply a higher faculty—reason—to correct the representations of art. In enjoying poetry, Plato says, reason "has relaxed its watch over these querulous feelings," the emotions (X. 605). These ideas contain a hint that a person momentarily suspends his reason to allow himself some pleasure in art. The notion or the term is used by Austen, Hardy, Henry James, and Forster.

In Austen's *Sense and Sensibility*, ch. 29, Marianne Dashwood, believing that others have turned the man she loves against her, remarks to her sister: "Whatever he might have heard against me—ought he not to have suspended his belief? ought he not to have told me of it, to have given me the power of clearing myself?" In an essay of 1888, "The Profitable Reading of Fiction," Hardy comes closer to the Fielding-Coleridge idea. The reader seeking relaxation in a novel, Hardy advises, should "be not too critical." The reader should believe in the author "slavishly, implicitly," despite "his coincidences, his marvellous juxtapositions, his catastrophes, his conversions of bad people into good people at a stroke, and *vice versa.*" Harking back to the language of eighteenth century verisimilitude, Henry James in a preface to *The American* explains that the novelist seeking to deal with "experience liberated" from the requirement of realism must keep the reader under the "illusion" that there has been no departure from the restraints of his "general sense of 'the way things happen.' " Stressing the writer's art rather than the reader's willingness to go along with the illusion, James notes that when the novelist "successfully palms off on us" his romantic view, then "the way things don't happen" is "artfully made to pass for the way things do."[17] E. M. Forster in *Aspects of the Novel* asserts that novelists find it congenial to end a story with love and marriage, knowing the reader tends to regard both as permanent: "we do not object because we lend them [the authors] our dreams" (87).

More recently psychological analyses have been advanced concerning the audience's response to art, using the notion of the suspension of belief. Early in the twentieth century a British psychologist, Edward Bullough, suggested that one needs a modicum of "distance" from a work of art in order to appreciate it. If one's personal life is too closely involved, as in the case of a man jealous of his wife watching *Othello,* one may become too anxious to take the play as art. Bullough implied that a "predisposition" to disbelieve in the relevance of the work of art to one's own self is needed; that is, in a sense one must be able to suspend the capacity to identify with what is seen or read (398). Hawthorne alluded to the same necessity in *The House of the Seven Gables,* ch. 10, describing Clifford's inability to appreciate the stories Phoebe read to him because they were untrue and hence failed to arouse his interest or because they affected Phoebe so much that he took them to be real calamities. Simon Lesser, taking a directly Freudian approach, interprets the willing suspension of belief to refer to the reader's relaxation, despite the anxieties Bullough emphasized, to the point where he can accept a novel's special world. Reminiscent of Plato, he also holds that the reader thus relaxes "the vigilance usually exercised by the ego" (192).

Social science has not considered the process of the suspension of disbelief, perhaps because it primarily involves mechanisms of individual reaction. This process is, however, analogous to one in scientific method, the posing of hypotheses. The artistic and the scientific functions call upon people to accept a condition or a statement for the moment, to suspend their judgment rather than reject at once what is put before them. The rationale, however, is different. In science, they are asked to suspend judgment only until the evidence is adduced, whereas in art they are asked to suspend disbelief indefinitely in order to allow themselves pleasure and instruction.

Literature and Life

Reporting the extreme things as if they were the
average things will start you on the art of fiction.
—F. Scott Fitzgerald, *The Crack-Up*

8.

Many discussions of the relation between art and life set forth extreme positions: art reflects life, art distorts life, art influences life, life determines art. Unfortunately these positions are usually imprecise as well as extreme. Unclear themselves, these pronouncements refuse to recognize any value in other approaches. Though such ardor has been harmless in ordinary discourse on art and life, it has blocked reasoned analysis of the relations between them, which may require compromise and nuance. The position that art —in this case the novel—merely reflects society is only a vague starting point that too often becomes a conclusion closing off further inquiry. The position that literature is after all not the same as life is easy to accept, but it does not encourage inquiry into the connections between them. Different implications accompany the proposition that literature is not the same as life. Ultrarealists and avant-garde theorists argue that the gap between art and life must be eliminated, whereas radical aesthetes insist that the connections between art and life must be eliminated.

Fiction does reflect society in that it has provided a record of what certain people did—how they loved and married, grouped themselves into social classes, conducted various enterprises, and set up homes. Fiction has also revealed how people have thought about themselves and other matters, such as God, the family, politics, and race. Fiction has further affected people's lives by helping them to form their own attitudes and values toward what has existed and what should exist. But all of these "reflections" have been produced through the eyes and minds of individual novelists, who have differed in what they saw and how they chose to describe it, even though resembling one another in important respects. Fiction has also sought to be more than a picture of life. Novelists have wanted to point a moral directly or indirectly and so to offer a critique as well as a portrait. Novelists claiming to offer a "pure" portrait have necessarily limited points of view and goals, which limit their portraits correspondingly. When they offer critiques, however, they consciously select aspects of life that they want to comment on, such as poverty, hypocrisy, and the capacity for love or hatred. They deliberately emphasize these aspects at the expense of others. Thus, while revealing much of value concerning those elements of life that interest them, novelists necessarily ignore other elements that may interest their readers or other novelists. Fiction becomes a compendium of what writers thought it important or even profitable to bring to the attention of prospective readers. As such, it shows what the authors take life to be and what they want their audience to take it to be. This conclusion may complicate matters for those who seek simple connections or gaps between literature and life, but it is supported by the evidence. It also points up the need for further inquiry and indicates the lines along which such inquiry should proceed in order to understand the actual relation between the novel and social life. This moderate conclusion, therefore, is more stimulating than either extreme position, because it fosters inquiry instead of halting it with programmatic approaches that have become platitudes in their own right.

Fictional Treatment of Social Relations

Any examination of the relation between novels and social life is handicapped by the paucity of data on both sides. There are few summaries of fictional themes, and these few have seldom been systematically compared with social behavior or institutions based on independent historical or social science inquiry. Both tasks are difficult, one reason being that the fictional portraits or stereotypes themselves have frequently helped to shape the attitudes — if not the evidence as well — with which a person approaches the empirical study of social life. The existing comparisons of the novel and social life, though they have reached different conclusions, nevertheless offer more reliable answers to the question of the degree to which fiction resembles social life than do the hasty impressions that are so abundant. Such comparisons run the gamut from French medieval romances dealing with crime to American fictional treatments of artists, women, the Southern plantation, strikes, homicide, and violence.

Frederick Riedel compares about twenty French medieval romances involving crime with the law of the time in order to see if there is a relation between morality and legal norms. His aim is to help the scholar and general reader better to understand these romances through understanding their relation to the legal situation of the day. Riedel assumes that the narrative poems reflected general attitudes toward crime; indeed, the "chief principle" behind his selection of them is their "fidelity" both to social life and to the criminal law (3). Not surprisingly, therefore, he finds that even though the writers of the narratives were "under no compulsion to make them legally accurate," they stayed "remarkably close to contemporary law" (8). His study, though suggestive, is limited by its selection of narratives precisely for their "realism" and by its comparison of fiction with law, which is itself mainly a prescription for behavior rather than an indication of it. At times Riedel compares the romances to law and at times to behavior, without adequate distinction. But his work reveals the method that such comparisons must follow: to test literature against other sources of knowledge.

As part of a study of "the artist in American society," Neil Harris considers the fictional treatment of the artist in the 1840s and 1850s. He finds that "the fictional artist began to diverge significantly from his genuine counterpart; indeed, mythic images stimulated imitation and further confused the artist's status" (218). Mixing fictional sources with journalism and biography, Harris sees a change from the conception of the artist as a sensitive, spiritual, extravagant romantic to one that emphasized his absorption into a professional status more consonant with the "success ethic" of the country after the Civil War (251). This study is likewise useful for pointing up difficult tasks hardly yet attempted.

Closer to the kind of study needed is Dorothy Deegan's *The Stereotype of the Single Woman in American Novels.* Assuming that "literature is a sensitive medium which both creates and reflects attitudes of society," she analyzes 125 novels about the United States that were highly regarded at their time of writing and which deal mainly with white people in a realistic style (ix). Among the novels analyzed are such well-known ones as Hawthorne's *The House of the Seven Gables,* Howells' *The Rise of Silas Lapham,* and Wharton's *Ethan Frome,* as well as such lesser-known ones as John Fox's *Heart of the Hills* and Joseph C. Lincoln's *Doctor Nye.* Included, for example, are two novels by Hawthorne, eleven by Ellen Glasgow, three by Sherwood Anderson, one by Sinclair Lewis, and two by Mary Roberts Rinehart. The earliest novel was published in 1851, the latest in 1935; nineteen are from the nineteenth century, seventy-one from the period 1900-1919, and the remaining thirty-five from 1920-1935.

Deegan reports that single women at least thirty years old do not appear in 40 novels by 12 authors, while there are 150 such women in the remaining 85 novels by 52 authors. Of these 150 single women, only seven are major characters. Deegan's assessment is that these novels reveal an "inconsistency" in their portrayal: single women are shown to be respected for their goodness yet are often interested in gossip, physically unattractive, engaged in humble employment if at all, unambitious, and exercising little "wholesome influence" in their communities (111-112). Comparing this portrait to the reality shown in psychological and social analyses of single women, Deegan finds that "few novelists have probed the inner reaches of personality on a psychosexual level," nor have most appreciated the degree to which single women had become economically independent and were supporting others. Not one of the 150 characters "could be called truly representative of the thousands of single women who have won 'eminence' " or achieved "success," and none of these fictional women have "even a commendable achievement." Deegan concludes that although "social thinking is generally found to be in advance of social fact," in this case the reverse is true: "the actual status and achievement of the single woman is found to be in advance of the fictional picture" (120-125).

What Deegan thus finds is that novels follow popular attitudes toward the single woman rather than her actual or evolving status in social life. Two less systematic studies reach a similar conclusion. Ernest Earnest compares the treatment of women in American novels from the Revolution to World War One with their roles as emerging from historical sources, concluding that there is a vast gap between the two sets of portraits. In a study of Victorian women in fiction and in society, Françoise Basch discovers that the novel reflects the ideal or the stereotype more than the reality. David Davis, in a 1957 study of homicide in nineteenth-century American fiction, offers one hypothesis about the stereotypic treatment of women. He accepts the changing status of women as they took to employment in a growing industrial and urban society. The consequent anxiety of men about their own status, he suggests, combined with a growing fear of the debilitating effect of the increasing freedom of the sexes, produced in fiction an unattainable feminine ideal which also associated sex with death. Such a fictional stereotype along with the male anxieties could have also formed a basis for the fictional stereotype of the unattractive and ineffective single woman reported by Deegan.

Francis Gaines, examining the fiction of the slave plantation in the American South in relation to the facts, finds a fictional "tradition" that describes an "irresponsible lordly class" of aristocratic whites and a class of obsequious black slaves who are "cheerful in acceptance of a humble lot, unambitious, ignorant, superstitious, fantastically funny" (3). The tradition is inaccurate about both classes, representing "a dramatization of the lurid, the volatile, the sensational, of plantation life" (187). Gaines explains the "sweep of the plantation legend" on three grounds. It alone appealed to the "innate American love of feudalism" or the "craving for a system of caste." It portrayed the black slave as simple, rustic, humorous, credulous, spontaneous, and "gifted in song and dance," thereby providing a venerable character type "proverbially dear to the masses." It revealed the plantation, which was in fact recent, as from "a long and rosy perspective," suggesting a "different and a more resplendent age" and constituting "our chief social idyl of the past" (2-4). To these grounds for the plantation legend may be added a fourth: the myth justified or exonerated the system of exploitation that it concealed or glorified. Jay Hubbell, like Gaines, mentions two kinds of novel about the South, one emphasizing the virtues of the plantation system, the other its evils. They have made the region "subject to greater misrepresentation in fiction than any other section" (27). He points out that many of these novels have been written by Northern and English writers, and been published and bought outside the South. Even Southern writers have been tempted to distort life in the region to satisfy this market. Such analyses indicate that the plantation novel, like the novel about single women, portrays not the social reality it ostensibly touches but a different reality of social attitudes, stereotypes, and ideological needs. The "tradition" Gaines analyzes portrays not the reality of plantation life but that of white expectations, preferences, and stereotypes. These realities inspire such novels rather than being portrayed in them. A recent socioeconomic analysis of the plantation system by Robert Fogel and Stanley Engerman holds that leading social science studies have been hardly less stereotypical than the fiction.

Fay Blake, examining the fictional treatment of strikes, finds that strikes were already occurring in American industrial life before novelists turned to them as a subject. When novelists did advert to industrial life, it was "in an almost prurient obsession with urban degradation," to shock the reader and to show poverty as a "punishment" rather than to consider the new social environment seriously (15-16). How novelists treated strikes depended not only on their own "insight and skill" but also "on how contemporary society regarded" industrial conflict. When great strikes affected public opinion, novelists responded by writing about strikes; when there were fewer strikes, the number in novels declined. To this extent, fiction reflected social life. Before 1900, however, Blake reports, most actual strikes were peaceful and successful, while all fictional strikes were violent and in vain. Novelists seemed uninterested in the facts of social life, needing for literary purposes "a violent clash between two contending forces." After 1900, then after World War One, and again following the depression of the 1930s, novelists turned increasingly and more skillfully to strike stories. In these novels the strikes showed the breakdown of society and heralded a new order (1-3). Here again the novel appeared to be responding more to public opinion and to the writers' own vision of the evils of the social order than to the desire to portray an institution directly and for its own sake.

Davis in his study of homicide in American fiction, like Riedel on the French medieval romances, is interested in the relation between moral ideas about homicide expressed in fiction and those expressed in other sources, such as philosophy, theology, psychology, and law. From among the American novels written on his theme between 1798 and 1869, he selects a number that are representative of the period, the regions, and the various cultural influences, so as to compare the fictional "murder trials and legal decisions" to actual ones, especially with respect to attitudes toward insanity and moral responsibility (xvi). Davis concludes that where the legal and fictional treatments are comparable, the legal ones deal with insanity "in terms of abstract faculties, as if the individual could be isolated from the social forces of his environment," while the novelists "were free to explore emotional associations and social relationships" even if often stereotypically (86-87). Washington Irving's "The Story of the Young Italian" in *Tales of a Traveler* (1824) foreshadowed "a theme which was to be repeated countless times in American magazines and popular romances before the Civil War." Like the moral philosophers, Irving in this tale combines "a theory of environmental causation with a belief in individual guilt and responsibility," modified by a subtle and sympathetic treatment (34-35).

Both David Davis and Kenneth Lynn have made observations on the place of violence in American fiction. Davis in a 1966 article warns against exaggerating its significance while claiming that it stems from an artistic tradition, the presence of some violence since the Revolution, and a need to portray violence whatever may be its actual incidence. Lynn, surveying violence in American literature and folklore for the National Commission on the Causes and Prevention of Violence, appointed by President Lyndon B. Johnson in 1968, also warns against assuming that literature is "a mirror image of life," while asserting that its "recurring themes of violence" do "bear witness to the continuing violence of American life" (226-227).

These comparisons of fiction and life reveal mainly that novelists usually write about issues which agitate public opinion and generally use contemporary conflicts such as strikes, or contemporary stereotypes such as the classes on the slave plantation, to supply the elements needed to appeal to readers. Thus the connection between literature and life may not be the one a novel ostensibly sets forth, may be easily exaggerated, and often is more circuitous than simple propositions have implied.

A curious effort by a British moralist, published in 1871, which appealed to the prurient interest of Victorian readers while criticizing similar interests in the previous century, is William Forsyth's *The Novels and Novelists of the Eighteenth Century, in Illustration of the Manners and Morals of the Age.* His object was to use the novels, most of which he found dull, as "unconscious" and therefore reliable "hints" of "manners and customs" (11). Although he describes his own time as superior in science, social policy, and sexual morality, he warns that novels do not necessarily describe all people accurately. Thus one should not think that "all ladies spent their time in frivolous amusements or intrigues of gallantry," as the eighteenth century novelists "too often represent them," nor that the nineteenth century has absolutely "nothing to be ashamed of in our morals and conduct," even though "we are much more refined than our ancestors of a hundred or a hundred and fifty years ago" (42, 50-51). Forsyth then extracts the details of life from the novels of the eighteenth century, involving dress, parties, street life, crime, prison, drinking, gambling, and classes. In an odd change of emphasis, he criticizes the early women novelists, Richardson, Fielding, Smollett, and later writers as immoral, but gives so many details of their coarseness and indecency as to suggest that he wants mainly to titillate his readers by this familiar method of plunging them into what he purports to abjure — a method that he in turn attacks when used by others.

Art as Reflecting Life

Besides the studies seeking connections between specific kinds of fiction and specific eras, efforts have been made at a more abstract level to find relations between the arts and life in general. A recent sociological work by Joan Rockwell, entitled *Fact in Fiction: The Use of Literature in the Systematic Study of Society,* asserts that "the patterned connection between society and fiction is so discernible and so reliable that literature ought to be added to the regular tools of social investigation." Literature can be shown to be "a product of society," she insists, rather than "simply entertainment" or the "result of private fantasy." Fiction is "not only a representation of social reality" but also an agency of "social control," for it is important in the "socialization of infants, in the expression of official norms such as law and religion, in the conduct of politics," and it provides "symbols" in the domain of norms and values (3-4). Her effort to illustrate these relations between fiction and life, however, fails to show the general pattern.

Pitirim Sorokin gives much attention to the place of the arts in civilization. In *Social and Cultural Dynamics* (I, 369-370) he warns that the work of the few "top artists" is probably less representative and more fluctuating than that of the "mediocre" and less talented majority. However, in his later summing up, *The Crisis of Our Age,* he calls the fine arts in particular, "one of the most sensitive mirrors of the society . . . What the society and culture are, such will their fine arts be." He tries to demonstrate that the fine arts of "contemporary Western culture," including its literature, exhibit the same form of "disintegration" to be found in the broad culture itself, though he confuses the relationship by using the crisis in the arts as one of the elements making up the crisis in the entire culture (30). Although he maintains that "contemporary art is primarily a museum of social and cultural pathology," he cautions that, if it is "a faithful representation of human society, then man and his culture must certainly forfeit our respect and admiration" (67).

Well before Sorokin spoke of "disintegration" in art and society, Leslie Stephen had already doubted the "tempting" inference in *English Literature and Society*. If art or literature decays, he observes, it does not prove that society decays. Characteristically, he hesitates to consider "these large problems" but does not accept "such sweeping conclusions." Stephen takes his place alongside those who see a connection between art and life: "That there is a close relation between the literature and the general social condition of a nation is my own contention." The relation varies, however, and is far from simple. In the end, he is too cautious and eclectic to see a fixed pattern: "To say the truth, literature seems to me to be a kind of by-product. It occupies far too small a part in the whole activity of a nation, even of its intellectual activity, to serve as a complete indication of the many forces which are at work, or as an adequate moral barometer of the general moral state" (21-22).

Some advocates of the connection between literature and life, unable to be as frank as Stephen about the failure to establish a general relationship, seem to think their position is strengthened by arguing that the artist unconsciously reflects or portrays the life of his time. Forsyth argues in this way, and so does Herbert Read, to whom the artist "is gifted with the most direct perception of natural form." This perception is not necessarily conscious. Indeed, artists "are to a considerable degree automata . . . they unwittingly transmit in their works a sense of scale, proportion, symmetry, balance and other abstract qualities which they have acquired through their purely visual and therefore physical response to their natural environment" (11). Hans Sedlmayr, like Sorokin, sees art as the evidence of a general cultural crisis and therefore urges that an abnormality or excess "illuminates the deeper and more hidden" aspects of an era. This approach leads to the "zone of the unconscious, for the actual meaning of such forms is hidden from their creators," who cannot explain what they do (4). Unfortunately, calling the artist an unconscious transmitter of signals and signs brings one no closer to discovering the pattern or general relationship between art and society.

Elmer Stoll, a Shakespeare scholar, is one of the most implacable critics of the notion that art and life reflect each other. He takes a position close to that of the social scientist in at least one respect in *From Shakespeare to Joyce*: "The evidence in art and literature is only corroborative, and can be used only when there is external evidence of the same tenor already" (21). He concedes that the novel is closer to life than are drama and poetry, and that inferior literature is closer still than great literature. On the whole, he nevertheless argues, the view that art and life are closely connected has limitations. Artists often reject the spirit of their times. Thus, many artists take up "primitive" themes and treat them in "primitive" styles. Others adopt an "open interest in sex" and reject traditional concepts of beauty in favor of forms regarded as beautiful by "primitive" cultures. Such approaches, "a product of the subtle modern imagination, are not the image of our life" (10-11). Furthermore, he maintained in *Shakespeare Studies,* English Victorian life has been thought to be sober, while its great poetry and fiction were "highly romantic" and "inspired by a spirit of protest and revolt" (65-66).

To show the uncertainty of moving from art to life, Stoll criticizes the view that a change in Elizabethan society is reflected in the change from Shakespeare's loose relations among the classes to Ben Jonson's more fixed relations among them. He cannot believe that Jonson, only nine years younger, reflects such changes by 1600, when in 1590 Shakespeare, presumably also reflecting society, saw rather different class relations. He also denies that in medieval times women enjoyed liberty because in certain farces they get the better of men. The point of the comedy is precisely that the "weaker should get the better of the stronger" (9). Confounding the relation of art to life, Stoll borrows from Oscar Wilde by giving examples of the upper classes imitating the behavior they have found in literature. His point is that literature "reflects the taste of the time rather than the time itself, and often the two are widely different." The times change only slowly, and popular taste, "always romantic," may change no more quickly (39-40). Neither

English Restoration drama nor French drama of the same period, the one passionate and violent, the other serene and almost prudish, reflect—or reverse—what is thought of as English and French society. "What we have," Stoll insists, "is only the reflection of what the French on the one hand and the English on the other delighted in at the theatre." The French brought "all their virtues" there, the British left theirs at home (55-56).

Complaints that literature distorts life come through in all ages. In 1971 Mary Mebane, a black teacher in the American South, observed: "When I read reviews of current fiction by and about black Americans . . . I wonder how I'll ever be able to become a member of the black community." Black lives are not so predominantly given over to drugs and crime: "Where are we residents of Durham County? Rural, black farmers and factory workers, domestic workers, common laborers all . . . Are we not worthy of being celebrated in song and story?" A literary historian, Jay Hubbell, criticized American novelists of the 1920s and 1930s for not having "the high regard for the actual fact that seems basic to the scientist and the historian." While defending the novelist's right to "depict and condemn the ugly aspects of American life," he argues that their works have provided propaganda for totalitarian forces in the world and that American fiction and films have produced "anti-American sentiment" among European intellectuals with no other experience of American life (23-24). Bernard De Voto made the same point during World War Two, arguing that the American literary penchant for self-criticism was misleading not only people at home but also totalitarian theorists in Europe seeking out American and democratic weaknesses. He describes as a "literary fallacy" the notion that a society may be judged by its literature. The fiction of the 1920s portrayed Americans as cheerless and uniform when they were cheerful, energetic, and variegated. Still earlier C.F.G. Masterman, writing about a complacent England on the eve of World War One, held that great literature gives no more accurate a picture of life than do newspapers filled with reports of "violence and madness" (3-4). Literature in fact "has no tolerance for the existence of comfort and security which to so many people seems the last word of human welfare" (7).

Defoe and Fielding, in the early years of the modern novel,

hinted at distortions in it. In his preface to *Moll Flanders*, Defoe says that the story of this woman's wicked, though repented, life requires as much realism as possible, which will make it more interesting to the reader than the "penitent part." He implies that a certain distortion is inevitable, given the popular taste and an author's natural inclination to satisfy it. Fielding, in the introduction to book 8 of *Tom Jones,* reveals that the novelist must stay within the probable, especially when portraying moral behavior, whereas he can go beyond it in portraying "knavery and folly" because in such themes he can rely more on his readers' credulity.

Although life does not so much affect literature, literature may perhaps influence life. There are advocates on both sides of this question too, yet the precise influence of literature on life is elusive; at least, there are few reliable studies of it and no definitive judgments about the general nature and direction of the influence.

Rockwell affirms a point made for centuries by social thinkers and moralists: "The universal existence of censorship tells us that there is a common opinion among the rulers of humankind that literature has some effect on people besides providing them with entertainment" (29-30). Fiction thus may have a corrupting or an ennobling effect — "the power to mobilize public opinion, change the accepted values and norms, and force a change in social relations themselves" (40). Lovers of literature usually speak of its good effects. Charles Dudley Warner, essayist, novelist, and Mark Twain's collaborator, believed not only that "enduring literature is the outcome of the time that produces it" but that it is, from an "ethical and not from a religious point of view, the most potent and lasting influence for a civilization that is worth anything" (3, 19). Madame de Staël's first sentence of *De la Littérature* (1800) declares: "My purpose is to examine the influence of religion, custom, and law upon literature, and the influence of literature upon religion, custom, and law." Regarding fiction specifically, she had already written in 1795 that it amused, "but when it moves the heart, it can have a great influence upon all human conceptions." The ability to create such fiction, therefore, "is perhaps the most powerful means of guidance or enlightenment."[1] Since at least the seventeenth century, the novel in France and England was regarded as dangerous to morality and hence influential. Such views of the novel were even worked into the novel itself. As late as 1891, Hardy in *Tess of the d'Urbervilles,* ch. 12, included a testimony to the novel's good influence. Tess is told by her mother that she should have been careful in her relations with Alec d'Urberville. "How could I be expected to know?" she cries. "Why didn't you warn me? Ladies know what to fend hands against, because they read novels that tell them of these tricks; but I never had the chance o' learning in that way, and you did not help me!"

Despite the faith that some authors have in the influence of fiction upon life, it has been very difficult to demonstrate it systematically. A hypothesis by Irving Leonard, in *Books of the Brave,* illustrates the problems involved in such inquiries. His thesis is that the romantic fiction which arose in fifteenth century Spain and spread rapidly to France, England, and the Americas influenced the conquistadors to undertake their journeys and make their conquests in the New World. "Fictional writings," he asserts in the preface, "are not only the subjective records of human experience, but sometimes the unconscious instigators of the actions of men by conditioning their attitudes and responses." Leonard follows other historians in suggesting that it may sometimes be the inferior works that are the more influential, such as *Uncle Tom's Cabin* and the tales of Horatio Alger and Frank Merriwell. The Spanish adventurer's "matchless courage and driving force did not spring from brawn and endurance alone; his febrile fancy had much to do in spurring him relentlessly on to unprecedented exploits. Some of the visionary passion that animated him had its inspiration in the imagined utopias, adventures, and riches alluringly depicted in the song and story of his time." Leonard is aware that this influence cannot be directly shown. All that he claims is that the conquistadors had such visions and that these early romances were actually shipped from Spain to the New World.

Relation Between Art and Life

The relaxation of legal and customary restrictions in the United States on the frankness with which sex and violence could be portrayed in literature and the mass media made a public issue of their effects in the late 1960s and early 1970s. Special concern revolved around the effects of television, which occupies by far the greatest attention of audiences, especially the young, and which displays much violence. Two national commissions and one scientific advisory committee were established to inquire into these effects, and two major scholarly reviews of the evidence appeared. Although they hardly touch upon the novel, these surveys do have some bearing on it.

The United States Commission on Obscenity and Pornography, reporting in 1970, found "no reliable evidence to date that exposure to explicit sexual materials plays a significant role in the causation of delinquent or criminal sexual behavior among youth or adults" (169). The report adds, however, that the data cannot be said "absolutely to disprove such a connection" (286). It concludes, apparently on this basis, "that greater latitude can safely be given to adults in deciding for themselves what they will or will not read and view" (171). The report deals mainly with the mass media, and it does not say that these media have no effect, only that they have no harmful effect. Sexual materials, it was found, do arouse desire and lead to increased sexual activity, but mainly in patterns to which people are accustomed. A few months before, in late 1969, the United States National Commission on the Causes and Prevention of Violence went further, reporting that "we are deeply troubled by the television's constant portrayal of violence" (188). Although the commission found "little that is proven beyond a reasonable doubt about the full social impact of the mass media," it concluded: "The preponderance of the available research evidence strongly suggests, however, that violence in television programs can and does have adverse effects upon audiences—particularly child audiences" (195). Early in 1972 the United States Surgeon General's Scientific Advisory Committee on Television and Social Behavior presented its report, *Television and Growing Up*. Cautious, ambivalent, and unclear, the report nevertheless states: "While the data are by no means wholly consistent or conclusive, there is evidence that a modest relationship does exist between the viewing of violence and aggressive behavior" (183). As the report frames the question, the committee tried to determine what changes in television would significantly reduce the tendency to aggression in the audience. But the committee decided that the state of knowledge did not permit a "confident" answer (9).

Other scholarly reviews of the evidence were made around the same time as these three reports. It began to appear that one's position on the effect of pornography and violence in literature and the mass media depended on one's attitude toward censorship. Those favoring full freedom of expression tended to find little or no evidence of harmful effects, thereby concluding that restrictions were unnecessary or harmful. Advocates of good literature began to find themselves in the somewhat uncomfortable position of holding that "good" literature had good effects but "bad" literature had little or no effect.[2] Scholarly studies supported the position that the mass media could not be shown to have harmful effects. A review by Walter Weiss in *The Handbook of Social Psychology* stated that the charge of harmful effects and the defense against it both "have been based on tenuous grounds" (124). An article by Joseph Klapper in the *International Encyclopedia of the Social Sciences* summarized: "It has been repeatedly demonstrated that by far the most common effect of mass communication is to reinforce its audience's pre-existing interests, attitudes, and behavior and that the least common effect is to convert audience attitudes and behavior" (III, 82b).

Some novelists shed light on these points concerning the effects of literature and the relation between literature and life. Sir Walter Scott, introducing a novel by Smollett in his *Lives of the Novelists,* anticipates the social science conclusion that literature usually supports the readers' predispositions: "To a reader of a good disposition and well-regulated mind, the picture of moral depravity presented in the character of Count Fathom is a disgusting pollution of the imagination. To those, on the other hand, who hesitate on the brink of meditated iniquity, it is not safe to detail the arts by which the ingenuity of villainy has triumphed in former instances" (83).

On the position of women in life and fiction, Virginia Woolf makes some persuasive remarks in *A Room of One's Own:* "Indeed, if woman had no existence save in the fiction written by men, one would imagine her a person of the utmost importance; very various; heroic and mean; splendid and sordid; infinitely beautiful and hideous in the extreme; as great as a man, some think even greater. But this is woman in fiction. In fact . . . she was locked up, beaten and flung about the room." Or: "She pervades poetry from cover to cover; she is all but absent from history" (74-75).

While the connection between literature and life is not clear even though known to exist, certain extreme views as to what the connection ought to be confuse it further. There are two avant-gardes. One, largely aesthetic, wants to eliminate any connection between art and life. The other, more political, wants to eliminate any gap between art and life.

The extreme aesthetic position was cogently stated by Oscar Wilde in his essay-dialogue "The Decay of Lying," first published in 1889 and again, considerably revised, in 1891. Some of these ideas were suggested in James Whistler's "Ten O'Clock" lecture in 1885, which Wilde both criticized and used.[3] Wilde summarizes the "new aesthetics" in three points. First: "Art never expresses anything but itself . . . So far from being the creation of its time, it is usually in direct opposition to it . . . To pass from the art of a time to the time itself is the great mistake that all historians commit." Second: "All bad art comes from returning to Life and Nature, and elevating them into ideals. Life and Nature may sometimes be used as part of Art's rough material, but before they are of any real service to art they must be translated into artistic conventions." Third: "Life imitates Art far more than Art imitates Life . . . It follows . . . that external Nature also imitates Art. The only effects that she can show us are effects that we have already seen through poetry, or in paintings." Wilde's "final revelation is that Lying, the telling of beautiful untrue things, is the proper aim of Art."

Wilde's purpose is to establish the superiority of the creative human imagination. "Where, if not from the Impressionists," he asks, echoing Whistler, "do we get those wonderful brown fogs that come creeping down our streets, blurring the gas-lamps and changing the houses into monstrous shadows? . . . The extraordinary change that has taken place in the climate of London during the last ten years in entirely due to this particular school of Art." Nature is "our creation," and how we see it "depends on the Arts that have influenced us." Nature, moreover, is repetitive, while art creates something "incomparable and unique." The literature of his time, Wilde complains, is "commonplace" because it tries to imitate life and facts instead of "lying" through the imagination of the writers. The "decay of lying" thus means the decay of art.

Relentless in his attack upon realism, Wilde denies that "Art expresses the temper of its age" or its "moral and social conditions," although he cannot maintain this position consistently. He holds that the past is seen "entirely through the medium of Art," yet "Art, very fortunately, has never once told us the truth." He offers the example of Greek sculpture's false portrayal of women, in contrast to "an authority, like Aristophanes," whose picture is different and more reliable. Here he accepts the notion that there is a reality to be found in nature, and that the plays of Aristophanes are a better guide to it than sculpture. He also weakens his point that art and life are separate by admitting that good art sometimes uses nature as "rough material" to be "translated into artistic conventions." So Wilde does not conceal that he is exaggerating to make a point. "The nineteenth century, as we know it, is largely an invention of Balzac"; there is no nineteenth century, he implies, except as the creative imagination has shown it to us. In the same kind of exaltation of human creativity, he holds in "The Critic as Artist" that "criticism is more creative than creation, and that the highest criticism is that which reveals in the work of Art what the artist had not put there" (407). Nothing is objective to Wilde; everything is what the imagination makes it. Nature is made by art, art by criticism, and so on in an endless spiral leading away from "reality" to "imagination." In his criticism of Whistler's "Ten O'Clock" lecture, Wilde again momentarily relates art to something in life: "An artist is not an isolated fact, he is the resultant of a certain milieu and a certain entourage." But this milieu is not exactly social, for an artist "can no more be born of a nation that is devoid of any sense of beauty than a fig can grow from a thorn."

The more political avant-garde often sees beauty in precisely the reality that Wilde abjures, and in, paradoxically, the attempts to change that politically unacceptable reality. The anti-art position in its modern form developed in Europe after World War One and enjoyed popularity in the United States in the 1950s and 1960s. All of its advocates were political radicals of a sort, but the avowed Marxists among them constituted a more politically disciplined group. Anti-art is an attack upon the "artificiality" of art, its consecration in museums and conventional theaters, and its traditional association with the middle and upper classes of education, wealth, and commercialism. It aims to strip art of its presumed bias in favor of "bourgeois values" and its role in entertaining bourgeois audiences. Art is to be made at once more natural, less differentiated from life, and instrumental in changing the distribution of power in society.[4]

Wilde opposed the ugliness of realism, seeking to preserve beauty in life through art. He feared that if we do not change "our monstrous worship of facts, Art will become sterile, and Beauty will pass away from the land" (294-295). The anti-art advocates, however, see beauty elsewhere, in struggle, in magnifying the ugliness of a technological society, and in trying to use art to change the world instead of amusing or pleasing it.

Difficulty Relating Art to Life

It is easy, and justified, to reject the extreme positions that art should avoid life or that it should become indistinguishable from life. These positions not only mark the limits of the relation between art and life but also emphasize the difficulties in establishing what is, rather than what ought to be, the connection between them. The question of this connection is raised largely in modern times, when art has sought not so much to serve divine purposes or to create beauty as to show the nature of social life and to offer a critique of it. George Boas has drawn attention to the problems of dealing with self-consciously modern movements in art since the French Revolution, involving such factors as borrowings from the past, efforts to be different from the past, conflicting or at least varying interpretations of the present, and reliance on a more distant past to separate oneself from a recent one. Such difficulties are illustrated by the alternation of fictional styles over long periods, as between Cervantes and Fielding; by differences in the fictional treatment of sex, which put their significance in question; by the ambiguity of the relation between fiction and life, as suggested by Hawthorne; and by the fact that novelists create their own world which both they and their readers take to be a real world of some sort, whatever its relation to the changing world of the readers in different periods.

Borrowings and alternations of style complicate the effort to relate literature to the life of a particular time. In the early seventeenth century in Spain, Cervantes wrote *The Adventures of Don Quijote,* which parodies the romances written a century and more earlier, and injects some realism into those stories by making the hero a comic figure. More than a century after *Don Quijote,* Fielding in England tried the opposite tack in *The History of the Adventures of Joseph Andrews,* imitating the title of the Spanish work and adding the plain subtitle: *Written in Imitation of the Manner of Cervantes, Author of* Don Quixote. Fielding harked back to Cervantes in order to add romantic adventures to an essentially realistic novel. How close Fielding came to Cervantes is shown by his description of Parson Adams saving a woman from attack and then announcing to her: "Be of good cheer, damsel, you are no longer in danger of your ravisher, who, I am terribly afraid, lies dead at my feet; but God forgive me what I have done in defense of innocence."

Changes in the fictional treatment of sex may indicate changes in morality and sexual behavior, or they may only indicate changes in what is regarded as appropriate to express in literature. Such variations also complicate the effort to relate literature to life. Consider this similarity in two widely different authors, cultures, and eras. In ch. 34 of *Tess of the d'Urbervilles,* a novel of rural England published in 1891, Hardy describes Tess and Clare, husband and wife, eating: "he found it interesting to use the same bread-and-butter plate as herself, and to brush crumbs from her lips with his own." In *Mountolive,* a novel taking place just before

World War Two in Alexandria and published in 1959, Lawrence Durrell describes in ch. 1 the leading character, an Englishman, with his Egyptian mistress lying on the sand: " 'Wait,' she said suddenly. 'There is a crumb on your lip.' And leaning forward she took it softly upon her own tongue."

G. Legman pointed out the essential problem in 1949 when he contrasted the toleration of violence and the proscription of sex in American popular arts and fiction: "In life, however, the situation is the reverse. So that we are faced in our culture by the insurmountable schizophrenic contradiction that sex, which is legal in fact, is a crime on paper, while murder—a crime in fact— is, on paper, the best seller of all time" (19). Since Legman wrote, the treatment of sex has become fully explicit, yet this change has not affected the use of violence and has probably become merely another element in it. Nor can it be certain that the greater freedom to describe sexual relations has brought literature closer to life, for novelists had already managed to convey sex even when the freedom to do so was severely limited. Alongside the cautious treatment of sex in Victorian fiction, for example, there was much pornography that achieved its effect without resorting to obscene or proscribed words, as Steven Marcus has demonstrated. Anticipating a change in estimation of the Victorian era, Bernard Shaw in 1929 held it to be an "exceedingly immoral age" because of its sexual exhibitionism. Far from reducing sexual interest, the fact that the Victorians "upholstered" rather than "dressed" women made them "a masterpiece of sex appeal." The appeal was enhanced by covering the body extensively while "making a little revelation of some kind."[5] E. E. Kellett attributed "the (largely imaginary) Victorian prudery and reticence" to the habit of family reading, which necessarily excluded overt sexual themes in the presence of children (48). He pointed out that much Victorian literature was created for the family and the household.

In the light of the current freedom to treat sex explicitly, of the existence of Victorian pornography having affinities to the great literature of the same era, and of the recent widespread reissue of Victorian pornography, it is interesting to consider how George Eliot and Edith Wharton, for example, described sexual scenes.

In *The Mill on the Floss,* bk. 6, ch. 10, Eliot indicates that Stephen is aroused by the shape and position of Maggie's arm. "Who has not felt the beauty of a woman's arm? — the unspeakable suggestions of tenderness that lie in the dimpled elbow, and all the varied gently-lessening curves down to the delicate wrist, with its tiniest, almost imperceptible nicks in the firm softness." This loving description suggests or symbolizes more intimate parts of the female anatomy and may be as sexually arousing as a contemporary treatment of such parts. Clearly, therefore, the prohibition against explicitness did not greatly hamper earlier novelists. Even if fictional men's and women's sex lives were not depicted fully, it does not mean that they had none or that novelists ignored this part of their character's lives. Edith Wharton could indicate sexual feeling by a mere hint, as in *The Reef:* "The hand nearest him still lay on the railing of the balcony, and he covered it for a moment with his. As he did so he saw the color rise and tremble in her cheek" (59). Nowadays a woman, at least in a novel, would surely have to experience a much more intimate contact to be convincingly said to be aroused. Yet this does not constitute a real difference. Wharton by her gentle hint gives the reader as much as a more explicit description might give today.

If it is the emotion, and not the stimulus, that counts, the descriptions of Wharton and Eliot suffice. Readers of *The Reef* today do not find the incident unclear or any more quaint than a reference to a gas light instead of an electric bulb. Wharton's method does not mean that her characters are less capable of experiencing sex, or experience it any the less, than characters in the most recent novel filled with sex. Indeed, her two characters, Darrow and Sophy, go on to have a week-long affair in a hotel, though Wharton waits to mention it openly. As for being "modern," that is a trait to be found in many eras, especially since the French Revolution. In Wharton's story, Sophy speaks to Darrow in a contemporary vein while they are having their affair: "I'm not so sure that I believe in marriage. You see I'm all for self-development and the chance to live one's own life. I'm awfully modern, you know" (62).[6] The language may sound stilted, yet the sentiment, the situation, and Sophy's slight irony are all perfectly in tune with contemporary fiction of the most emancipated sort. The problem is to interpret such similarities from era to era when trying to relate sex in fiction to sex in life. Albert Guerard revealed the full extent of the difficulty when he remarked in 1949 that readers "are now willing to go back to Hardy for the qualities which in 1920 seemed so old-fashioned" (431). Thus readers only need wait for a "modern" era to find virtues in a remoter period which a more recent one rejects.

Contemporary novelists in any era usually find it an advantage to deal with the present because readers are interested in their own time and contemporaneity relieves the novelist of the heavy burden of competing with the past. Hawthorne, however, saw the need for the writer to enjoy a relief from realism and relevance to actual life. In the preface to *The Blithedale Romance* he laments that the novelist does not have enough "license" to stray from the "real world." In contrast, in the "old countries" long familiar with fiction the "romancer" is granted the "privilege" that "his work is not put exactly side by side with nature." In the preface to *The House of the Seven Gables* Hawthorne had already asked his readers not to connect his tale too closely with the "realities," and in ch. 10 he describes Clifford's discomfort because he is unable to distinguish the stories Phoebe reads him from the realities of life. The narrator approves Clifford's refusal to listen to fictional calamity: "Is not the world sad enough, in genuine earnest, without making a pastime of mock-sorrows?"

World Order in the Novel

The freedom that Hawthorne sought, to stray from life while portraying it, has been granted to novelists since his time. Novelists both before and after him have used this freedom to impose their own order upon what they see in and borrow from life, creating also their own worlds that are not exactly life, yet something like it, which their readers can inhabit for a while. Readers and writers alike know that this world of the novel is not real and yet may be treated as real even outside itself.

In a perennial argument concerning art and life, some insist that art must come as close to life as possible. Since life does not show itself in neat patterns, the novel should not seek perfect plots but should reproduce the planless events of life, deal with character, and present objects as they appear in life. This position unites such otherwise different writers as Trollope, Dreiser, and the French "new" novelists. The other extreme does not deny that art should somehow represent life but emphasizes that since art is not and cannot be life, it must take advantage of the fact that it is after all artifice. The novelist should therefore consciously impose his own form and supply, as do Hardy, Henry James, and Forster, the coherence and significance that life itself lacks. Neither view prevails in its extreme form, but the latter view more correctly and more often describes what novels do. In Forster's words in *Aspects of the Novel,* novels "suggest a more comprehensible and thus a more manageable human race, they give us the illusion of perspicacity and of power" (99). Explaining the prominence of love in fiction, he observes that the novelist endows his characters with his own constant preoccupation with the relations among them, with the result that they are more sensitive to one another than are persons in real life. At the same time, however, fictional characters often know less about each other than do people in real life, and perhaps as a corollary, the real-life reader often knows more about fictional characters than they know about one another. All this, Forster reveals in an intrusion in *A Room with a View* (1908), ch. 14, has more to do with the mechanics of novel-writing than with the realities of life. Noting that Lucy, though engaged to Cecil, is "nervous" about George Emerson, the narrator explains: "It is obvious enough for the reader to conclude, 'She loves young Emerson.' A reader in Lucy's place would not find it obvious. Life is easy to chronicle, but bewildering to practice, and we welcome 'nerves' or any other shibboleth that will cloak our personal desire. She loved Cecil; George made her nervous; will the reader explain to her that the phrases should have been reversed?" Those in the audience, whether of novels, plays, or films, often experience this feeling, easily recognizing that a character is wrongly hostile or sympathetic to another, and they are impatient for him to learn the truth as the author has permitted them to learn it.

In a short story, "The Real Thing" (1893), Henry James has amusingly dramatized the idea that the fake can be more "real" than the real, as it is in Hollywood, where American actors are more often preferred in Chinese roles than are real Chinese. The narrator, a magazine illustrator, finds his servants, a Cockney girl and an Italian immigrant, better models of English people than are an English lady and gentleman who want to work for him because they have no means of support. His servants thus become his models, and the proper but impoverished English couple become his servants. Of the lady, the narrator remarks: "She was the real thing, but always the same thing." Of the English couple, he observes that they became victims of the "perverse and cruel law in virtue of which the real thing could be so much less precious than the unreal."

In the course of imposing his own order on life, the novelist creates a special world. Hints of his Godlike creativity are not lacking in novels. Paul Hunter, dealing with early English fiction, suggests that Puritan novelists brought in God to avert disaster, but that with Fielding it was the writer who was avowedly and clearly in control; he did not need God to save Tom Jones now and again. Thackeray in the preface of *Vanity Fair* calls himself the "Manager of the Performance" and his characters the "puppets." Flaubert writes to a correspondent on March 18, 1857, that he has invented everything in his work outside himself, for one of his "principles" is that the "artist must be in his work as is God in the creation, invisible and all-powerful." In modern times, Alain Robbe-Grillet in *For a New Novel* carries on the tradition by equating the creation of a novel with the invention of man.

The world of fiction, moreover, takes on real aspects for the community of authors, critics, and readers. Writing about *Fontamara,* Silone remarks: "I invented a village, using my bitter memories and my imagination, until I myself began to live in it."[7] André Maurois adds: "This world of Balzac's creation became more real to him than the world he lived in. He gives news of it in passing, like gossip from the real world: 'Now let us talk of serious matters. Who is to marry Eugénie Grandet?' "[8] In a note to his translation of *The Book of a Thousand Nights and a Night*

(1886), Richard Burton recounts: "Some years ago I was asked by my old landlady if ever in the course of my travels I had come across Captain Gulliver" (113). Novelists can treat their invented stories and characters as real in the same or other novels. Hermann Broch, in his trilogy *The Sleepwalkers* (1932), discusses ideological developments since the Renaissance, drawing not only upon history but also upon incidents in the novel itself. Two characters in Forster's *Howards End,* ch. 13, discuss Cecil Vyse, but the author does not indicate he is only a character in his earlier *A Room with a View,* ch. 8. In *Elmer Gantry* (1927), chs. 26 and 28, Sinclair Lewis refers to the leading character of *Babbitt* (1922) and to his own *Main Street* (1920). Even better known is Mark Twain's opening of *Huckleberry Finn* (1884) with a reference to his own *Tom Sawyer* (1876). A contemporary literary historian, David Goldknopf, invokes Moll Flanders in a discussion of current attitudes toward sex: "Moll, by the way, would have been astounded by this development" (57).

Treating Fictional World as Real

The main issue is how to find a patterned, systematic connection between art and life. The search is complicated by the tendency of intellectuals to exaggerate differences and to perceive change. In the modern era, for example, to compare the pace of change with that in previous times forces one to rely on earlier observers who were equally impressed with the pace of change in their time. In the attempt to chart and measure change "objectively," therefore, these earlier assessments are both objects of study and guides at the same time. Even if it could be objectively asserted that social change today is greater than it was a hundred or so years ago, it would have to be recognized that the effect of change upon human attitudes and behavior then was probably as pervasive as the effect of change today. Indeed, the effect might have been greater then because people have lately become more accustomed to rapid change.

In 1825 a critic complained, as many do today, of "this fickleness of tastes, in habits and customs, which makes everything pass before our eyes with the speed of light, not leaving the spirit or the heart time to become attached to anything."[9] A few years later George Eliot began *Felix Holt* with a lament that the recent displacement of horse-drawn coaches by the railroad had made travel less interesting and less suitable for telling stories. Since World War Two, a similar lament has often been heard about the railroad's displacement by the airplane. Writing in 1902, William Dean Howells pointed out that travel-writing had declined partly because travel itself "has become so universal that everybody, in a manner, has been everywhere, and the foreign scene has no longer the charm of strangeness" (26). People today do not think of 1902 in this way, yet Howells wrote of that time as people do of this time. Jane Austen, in an "Advertisement" to *Northanger Abbey*, explained in 1816 that because she had completed the novel in 1803 and had begun it even earlier, it was then "obsolete" in parts. People today do not think of the first fifteen years of the nineteenth century as a period of great change, yet Austen observed that "during that period, places, manners, books, and opinions have undergone considerable changes." This combination of relativity and similarity poses a serious difficulty for a sociology of literature. Today some observers think obscenity or freedom in the arts is excessive and that it must have been much more restricted a couple of generations ago, yet in the 1920s Upton Sinclair complained that the Broadway theater portrayed "every conceivable crime" and sexual relationship "except the rarer and more obscure forms of abnormality" (21).

The separate worlds of fiction and reality have points of similarity and contact in the mind of the novelist, in the analysis of literary critics and historians, and in the less systematic responses of readers. Literary critics and historians treat the fictional world in a way analogous to that in which social scientists and historians treat the real world: analyzing, comparing, tracing influences, and posing hypotheses to understand events, actions, and motives. From time to time there are new approaches to individual authors, genres, or periods, just as in history and social science there are new approaches to individual statesmen, social processes, and historical eras. The world of fiction is created by the novelist, the real world by the people in it. Despite the analogies, however, the differences remain important. In view of these difficulties, it becomes clear that the study of the relations between the fictional and real worlds, in whatever period of time, is only in its infancy. The sociology of literature has its chief task before it: to make more precise, in face of the formidable barriers, the connections between fiction and history, literature and life.

Literature as
a Social Science

There is a long-standing quarrel between
poetry and philosophy.
— Plato, *The Republic*

9.

The novel and social science are so obviously different in goal and method that it is useful to consider some of their similarities. The novel usually tells an imagined story. Social science, however, aspiring since the growth of positivism to be a genuine science, tries to set forth a series of related propositions, with the evidence for them, about what it regards as the real world. One of the greatest perils in comparing these two realms of thought is the variety which each displays, so that almost any generalization can be contradicted by an example. There are different approaches to social science and different kinds of novel. This analysis is itself an act of generalization and abstraction subject to all the limitations and difficulties of these methods of inquiry. The similarities and differences between the novel and social science are so intertwined that they must be considered together.

Method of the Novel

Of the two main ways in which the novel tells about human behavior and social institutions, the first method is the general meaning contained in a novel, the "lesson" or moral conveyed by the totality of its impact and the special world it creates. For example, Franz Kafka's *The Trial* (1925) pictures the helpless individual facing the power of impersonal bureaucracies. This is a universal theme, which different readers and generations may interpret in their own ways while remaining within a broad span of common meaning. Fictional themes on this level deal with recurring human issues, such as the relation of the individual to society, love, and other passions. The novel has the special merit of dramatizing these broad themes to show how they work out in individual cases. Thus, in *Bread and Wine* Silone shows how the individual faces certain political groups and moral codes rather than discussing such confrontations solely in general and abstract terms. In *Lord of the Flies* Golding reveals how individuals try to cooperate and fail; the lesson is much more effective than a summary statement of the same general principle in a textbook of anthropology or sociology. In many such novels, there is another level of meaning, the particular setting. The details of era and locale explain other aspects of human behavior and social institutions, such as noble or base characters, social classes or professions, and modes of life such as rural-agrarian or urban-industrial. In addition to their universal themes, novels such as those of Jane Austen, George Eliot, Dickens, and Hardy contain more specific social lessons of this sort.[1]

The second method of the novel is the direct statement by a character, as often occurs in Mann's *The Magic Mountain,* or by the author or narrator himself. Such statements, closer to social science, have a broad range. The same ideas can be found in both novels and social treatises or histories. Indeed, a writer may express the same idea in both a story and an essay. Hardy, for example, makes these same two points, using the same words, in his essay "The Dorsetshire Laborer" (1883) and his novel *Tess of the d'Urbervilles* (1891): when one knows many individuals of a class, one's stereotypes fade; and mobility and urbanization are exemplified in the annual migrations of farm laborers.

Two other similarities appeared early in the development of the novel and social science as corollaries to their aim of illuminating social life. Both sought to explain life on the basis of institutions created by men and women rather than by appealing to immutable absolutes and divine powers. Both also widened the scope of inquiry to include social classes and processes formerly ignored or seldom given major consideration in poetry and drama or in history and philosophy. Partly because of these interests and partly because of their status as newcomers challenging older genres, the novel and social science had low status among the learned and the defenders of intellectual tradition but were nevertheless popular among the lower and middle classes and the advocates of a broadening economic and political system. The novel's connection with women was a special feature that for some time kept it in low regard.

Although the two modes of social commentary showed such similarities, the relationship must not be pushed too far. The failure of such an effort has been revealed in several recent attempts to derive the meaning of novels from contemporary or traditional philosophic systems. George Swann, for example, posits vague connections between Defoe and Aristotle, Richardson and Kant, Fielding and Hume, Dickens and J. S. Mill, Meredith and Hegel, and Hardy and Eduard von Hartmann. Gilbert Ryle is so cautious in stating the presumed connection between Austen and Shaftesbury that it can be easily accepted, as can equally tenuous connections to other philosophers. S. P. Rosenbaum, the editor of a collection of essays of this sort, including Ryle's, properly warns: "The usefulness of seeing connections between literature and philosophy can be lost if their fundamental differences are forgotten" (1).

The connections between the novel and social science, however, are much closer and more demonstrable. Nor does the influence always go from social science to fiction. The novel anticipated social science, especially in the stories and intrusions of George Eliot, who was much interested in scholarship and science. Though she became a great novelist, she was at first hostile to the genre and did not turn to it until she was thirty-seven years old. In 1839, at age nineteen she wrote in a letter to a former teacher that novels and romances had had a "pernicious" influence on her (II, 22-23). She believed that anything beneficial to mental discipline could be obtained from history and that one did not need romance for relaxation because truth is stranger than fiction and more reliable for the drawing of "inferences" about human nature. She had nevertheless always had a "vague dream" of writing a novel, perhaps in part to show how it ought to be done, and started one in 1856. Her interest in social inquiry did not flag; it was the subject of many of her essays and fictional intrusions.

A note on "Historic Imagination," apparently written by Eliot in 1880, the year of her death, anticipates and parallels the methodological approach of a prominent social scientist, R. M. MacIver, who was born in Britain two years later, received a classical education, and spent his most active years as a social scientist in the United States. His study of *Social Causation* (1942) shows that a modern, professional social scientist with an appreciation of art as a mode of understanding had affinities to Eliot, a Victorian novelist with an appreciation of the value of systematic social inquiry. Eliot called for the "exercise of a veracious imagination in historical picturing," by which she meant an approach to opinions, institutions, and inventions that would avoid the limitations of plot and picturesqueness in the novel and the limitations of excessive abstraction in the writing of history. She pointed to the need to concentrate on detail and evidence, and where the evidence is scanty, she suggested "supplying deficiencies by careful analogical creation" (*Essays*, 446). MacIver also insisted upon appropriate comparisons of specific situations to determine cause. He too stressed evidence and the need to make an "imaginative reconstruction" where the evidence is inadequate (264). He too called this process a "sympathetic reconstruction" designed to supply coherence to the data, to be carried out by sociologists "not as outsiders but as in some degree ourselves participants" (391-392). The similarity in ideas and language is striking.

Systematic Inquiry

The similarities and analogies between the novel and social science go beyond the coincidence of approach in Eliot and MacIver and are found by comparing fictional goals and methods with those of more systematic social inquiry. There are convergences and distinctions between the two genres with respect to the following elements of scientific procedure: abstraction, hypothesis, evidence and experiment, cumulative coverage, and prediction. The differences between poetic and scientific truth may then be considered.

The novel and social science differ widely in goal. Fiction creates its own world, only partly and to varying degrees based on actual human behavior and social institutions; it includes characters, descriptions of imagined events in a pattern, and evaluations or critiques of its subjects. Social science seeks systematic inquiry into the real world on the basis of canons of evidence, theories, hypotheses, deductions, and experiments. The two approaches are therefore subject to differing criteria for evaluation and appreciation. In practice, however, they are closer than this gap would suggest, because the novel often states or conveys generalizations, while social science so often fails in its goal of generalizing on the basis of rigorous scientific method that this is perhaps its chief shortcoming as a science. Generalizations emerging from the totality of a fictional world or simply stated in intrusions add little to the readers' stock of knowledge, for the novel's virtue is rather that it makes broad conclusions clearer by presenting concrete detail and arousing sympathy for the characters. The novel can make people better appreciate that men cheat, or that love can be painful, but it does not discover such general statements, nor does it attempt to tie them together or base them on argument and evidence in the way that a social science treatise would. A novel's dramatic effect may thus reinforce a social truth, as Hawthorne states in his preface to *The House of the Seven Gables:* "the truth, namely, that the wrong-doing of one generation lives into the successive ones, and . . . becomes a pure and uncontrollable mischief." He does not deceive himself, however, that expressing the truth or a moral in artistic terms makes it more valid or true. As he notes, "A high truth, indeed, fairly, finely, and skillfully wrought out . . . may add an artistic glory, but is never any truer, and seldom any more evident, at the last page than at the first."

George Eliot, too, considered generalization in the novel. In *The Mill on the Floss* (bk. 4, ch. 1), where she lovingly dwells on the details of family life, she concedes, perhaps ironically, that she shares the "sense of oppressive narrowness" that may weigh upon her readers "in watching this old-fashioned family life on the banks of the Floss." She adds, however, that these lives must be seen truly and in detail "if we care to understand" the effect of such narrow circumstances upon people who live in them, especially the young. Every "historical advance of mankind," Eliot continues, is accompanied by the suffering to be found in the "obscure hearths" she describes. Comparing the novel to science, again perhaps ironically, she assures us that "we need not shrink from this comparison of small things with great; for does not science tell us that its highest striving is after the ascertainment of a unity which shall bind the smallest things with the greatest?" The answer, on a general level, is that science does proceed in this way, but its binding of small things with great is not the sort that the novel attempts, as George Eliot knew.

The novel's binding of the small and great usually has to do, as in *The Mill on the Floss,* with moral categories. In contrast, social science usually seeks to encompass many types of events in broad, connected propositions which deal with variables, such as age, education, income, and occupation, as they relate to each other, for example, or as they affect   and may be affected by—variables involving attitudes, predispositions, and social changes. The subjects of novels and social science thus often converge but never fully coincide. Henry James, as Dorothea Krook has shown, was interested in money and the people who possess a great deal of it because he saw money as the "supreme instrument of power" in our society and wanted to understand the moral issue of the effect of its possession on the "quality and conduct of life." He was not, however, "concerned with power as a function of the ownership of the means of production or of the distribution of parties and pressure-groups or of the status-seeking propensities of modern man" (11-12). These are the subjects of the social sciences. The nature of money, international exchange, income distribution, and bank-note circulation all touch moral issues at some points but are not themselves moral issues in a strict sense. The goal of understanding moral and other questions remains the same for the novel and social science, but the questions usually differ, and the methods too. The fictional world is more an artifact than the real world and is hence more satisfying to man's hunger for meaning, understanding, and the vindication of moral ideas. The social sciences also create a special world to some extent, but usually not for these purposes or with these results. The two types of world are based on different criteria and are subject to different canons of judgment.

Selection, or abstraction, is common to the novel and social science. As Trollope comments in *The Warden* (ch. 6): "It is indeed a matter of thankfulness that neither the historian nor the novelist hears all that is said by their heroes and heroines." Since both must select, it is important to reject the facile distinction that the novel is concrete and specific, while social science is general and abstract. Social science of course abstracts. The student of revolution, for example, seeking its general character, takes the common features from a variety of specific revolutions and combines them into a "model" that is not any one of the revolutions he has examined. The novelist abstracts, but in a different way. He selects and emphasizes to reveal a portrait of a special world that is self-contained while resembling the real world in varying degrees. He may exaggerate certain human traits—fidelity or duplicity, perhaps—that are in essence abstractions from the less clear contexts in which they are found in the real world. His story may emphasize irony or the unfortunate pressure exerted upon the individual by a job or calling, a political party, economic hardship, or even wealth, thus imposing an order in which some things are included at the expense of others left out. He takes the large world, or the many worlds, of reality, plays upon them imaginatively, and presents to the reader a smaller, more specialized world. As Guyau pointed out nearly a century ago, when Balzac concentrates many passions into one that dominates a character, he is simplifying by abstraction.[2]

In abstracting, the novel and social science gain in breadth of reference or dramatic effect but lose in concrete detail. Writers in both genres, therefore, are concerned about the degree to which their "samples" reflect the reality from which they are selected. Novelists, however, are only implicitly concerned with this point, except for the rare statement of Thomas Mann in *The Magic Mountain* (II, 552). The narrator, discussing a visit by Hans Castorp's uncle to the sanitarium, describes only one incident of the visit. "We give this," the narrator explains, "merely as an example of the sort of experience the four or five days supplied him." If too much detail is lost the abstraction creates a mere stereotype, as George Eliot often remarked. In 1856, when she turned to fiction, she published an essay on "The Natural History of German Life," in which she pointed out that abstractions are generalized knowledge suitable for science but not so useful when seeking concrete truths of life and behavior as means of arousing sympathy, stimulating social reform, or linking the social classes in a common humanity. She found the "social novels" of her time wanting: they "profess to represent the people as they are, and the unreality of their representations is a great evil." She regarded these portraits as unsympathetic, romantic stereotypes and called for a "natural history of our social classes," unlike the falsification by social theory or by painting, "which looks for its subjects into literature instead of life." These approaches did not show the working classes truly and revealed the peasants as joyous although "no one who is well acquainted with the English peasantry can pronounce them merry." A century earlier Fielding, in the introduction to book 9 of *Tom Jones,* had already criticized the writer who "takes his lines not from nature, but from books," producing characters who are "only the faint copy of a copy." At the time that Eliot's essay appeared, she also began to write fiction. In "The Sad Fortunes of the Rev. Amos Barton," published in her *Scenes of Clerical Life,* Eliot made the same points in both the story and an intrusion. In her second work of fiction, *Adam Bede* (ch. 17), she returned to the theme, calling for the "faithful representing of commonplace things." On a more general level, Eliot's essay drew attention to the different "images that are habitually associated with abstract or collective terms — what may be called the picture-writing of the mind." In 1922 Walter Lippmann impressed the American intellectual community by his distinction between "the world outside" and "the pictures in our heads" (3, 81), the latter phrase resembling Eliot's. Dorothy Van Ghent has remarked that fiction's "value lies less in confirming and interpreting the known than in forcing us to the supposition that *something else might be the case.*" This remark points up the comparison between fiction and history, literature and life. The novel, to be a "source of insight," as Van Ghent phrases it, need not be a true, demonstrable representation of something that happened in real life. "Like a science," she asserts, "the novel proceeds by hypothesis." The novel's hypotheses are the "conditions" it "takes from life" and creatively arranges; that is, the novel creates "a series of hypothetical events" from which the characters and events follow logically (3-4). This type of hypothesis, however, is not the main one used in social science. Social science deals in real not hypothetical or imagined events, and it proposes hypotheses, or conjectural statements, as possible explanations of observed facts. The explanatory conjectures are thus imagined in social science, whereas it is the "facts" or the characters and events that are imagined in the novel. Though he regarded novels as unreliable portraits of real life, Fitzjames Stephen in 1855 pointed out their value as "hypothetical 'guesses at the truth' " and suggested that novels, "perhaps, offer a greater number of such hypotheses than are to be derived from any other source; and though they give them in a very confused, indefinite manner, they gain in liveliness and variety what they want in precision" (153).[3]

The hypothesis in the novel, as in social science, enables it to withstand error. Trollope, aware that some of his assumptions about legal matters were wrong, reported in *Doctor Thorne* (1858), ch. 45, a suggestion that novelists should have a barrister to set them straight. "But," he explained reasonably, "as this suggestion has not yet been carried out . . . I can only plead for mercy if I be wrong in allotting all Sir Roger's vast possessions in perpetuity to Miss Thorne, alleging also, in excuse, that the course of my narrative absolutely demands that she shall be ultimately recognized as Sir Roger's undoubted heiress." The logic of the story and the moral cannot be seriously affected by the novelist's errors in the details, for example, of musical theory in Mann's *Doctor Faustus* or of whaling in *Moby Dick.*

Nirad Chaudhuri has complained that Forster's *A Passage to*

India is false in the sense that it "presents all the Indians in it either as perverted, clownish, or queer characters." The book is therefore "insultingly condescending to self-respecting Indians, Muslim and Hindu" (93). If Chaudhuri is right, Forster's novel should perhaps not be taken as a guide to the real India, but this caution does not mean that the novel's moral meaning and even its characters are not valuable. In the same way, an hypothesis in social science may be proved false by the evidence, yet it may be valuable in directing attention to important questions and data about social institutions and even to other hypotheses that may be confirmed by the evidence. On a larger scale, a real event like the Sacco-Vanzetti case in Massachusetts in the 1920s may be first regarded as a miscarriage of justice and then reinterpreted to consider the victims guilty, without affecting the aesthetic value of the many works of art created in the belief that the two men were innocent.[4] Finally, in art the idea of the "willing suspension of disbelief" implies that there is value in accepting as true what is doubtful or even known to be untrue; the value lies in apprehending something beautiful or instructive. In science, a hypothesis may be accepted even if doubtful because it directs attention to the evidence or, even if not confirmed, because it helps to explain what is accepted as true.

The approach to evidence and proof is different in the novel and social science. In a sense, the "evidence" in fiction is infinite because the novelist may offer as much or as little as he wants to or can create, or thinks the reader needs. Moreover, if the novelist tells something about a character or describes an event, readers cannot very well challenge its veracity. The sources in the social sciences must be treated with much more caution and skepticism. A novelist can count on readers to accept it if he tells them that a character is selfish, and he can show the character to be exclusively so. In real life or in the record of it, a character is not usually found to be so consistent; it is therefore not safe to assume that everything he does is motivated by selfishness. Consider what Balzac remarks in "The Young Conscript" in *Domestic Peace*. A noblewoman, Madame de Dey, hopes to avoid the Reign of Terror by going to her large estate in Normandy. There she manages to cultivate the citizens and to remain on good terms with the aristocracy. Her "exquisite tact," the narrator remarks, "allowed her to hold her course along the narrow way within which alone she could meet the requirements of this mixed society, without humiliating the touchy self-esteem of the *parvenus* on the one hand, or shocking the pride of her former friends on the other" (74). Unless Balzac chooses to give incidents in which her tact failed, readers must accept his word that it succeeded. In the social sciences the inquirer cannot accept without inquiry such a judgment in the sources. Balzac also assumes, and readers do not argue the point, both that parvenus are touchy and that the aristocracy would be shocked by one of their own cultivating the middle class even in such a dangerous time. Though there is much evidence to support this assumption about attitudes of social classes, social science would test its degree of accuracy, which is one reason that social science often seems so obvious. Often, however, the novelist gives a contradictory or varied portrait of a character or an event, and within this latitude literary critics may offer a new interpretation. Frederick Crews, for example, has explained Coverdale's relation to Zenobia, Hollingworth, and Priscilla in *The Blithedale Romance* in psychological terms not exactly available to Hawthorne a century earlier. The world of the novel in this sense may offer some scope for experiment analogous to experiment in science.

Social science has a responsibility to seek completeness of coverage of social behavior and institutions and to offer studies, hypotheses, and theories that build upon one another. Completeness in this sense means to cover what are regarded, according to the approach taken, as the most influential institutions; and the building of explanations and evidence means that they are cumulative, each related to and dependent on the previous accomplishments, all leading to statements of both wider import and greater scientific rigor. Although social science falls far short of this standard, it is generally directed toward it. The novel has no such stated or even implied goal or standard, nor any means of approaching it. Occasionally, a critic or historian will applaud the novel's coverage of certain kinds of behavior or lament its failures. Gilbert Highet, for example, by implication has laid down a program for the novel by listing the aspects of American life it deals with poorly or otherwise inadequately, including organized amusement, certain professions, and the psychology of groups such as teams or crowds. He also lists those aspects that the novel covers well, such as social history and some regional differences. Bernard Bergonzi, who has noted an increasing connection between contemporary and older novels, does not suggest that this connection implies any form of cumulation in the sense found in science. The fact that Tournier's *Friday* (1967) revises Defoe's *Robinson Crusoe* (1719), or that Golding's *Lord of the Flies* (1954) picks up a theme from Ballantyne's *The Coral Island* (1858), in no way implies that the later version is the better one except aesthetically to those readers who prefer it.

Science in general, if not social science in particular, reveals progress in two senses. First, more is reliably known about the properties of things and their relations. Second, hypotheses, laws, and theories have an increasing capacity to explain facts already known.[5] If there is progress in the arts, it is not of this sort. To determine whether the greatest art of every age is better than that of any previous age would require identification of the greatest art in various ages, a task that seems insurmountable if objective, measurable criteria are to be used, as in science. Several decades ago Lascelles Abercrombie found a kind of "progress" in poetry, yet he cautioned that there is not "a constant and uniform movement in art" and that whatever progress he found "carries with it no suggestion of improvement" (43-44, 53). More recently Arthur Koestler has found a limited kind of cumulation in art but is equally cautious in not claiming too much for it.[6] The opposite view on progress has been more often held. Madame de Staël argued in *Literature Considered in Its Relation to Social Insitutions* that the "very first creations of the imagination . . . are far more brilliant than even their happiest successors." In the poetic imitation of nature, for example, freshness is the controlling element, so that "with the very first impetus it can reach a certain kind of beauty that cannot be surpassed." She concludes: "Whereas in the cumulative sciences the latest stage is the most wonderful of all, the power of the imagination is the keener as its exercise is fresher."[7]

As for the novel's value in the systematic coverage of social history, Alexander Gerschenkron has offered some persuasive remarks concerning the Soviet novel touching upon economic institutions. He argues that the economic historian should be interested in these novels, even though they are written "in the service of the economic policies of the Soviet government," because they offer "fragments of information" useful either in supporting conclusions reached from direct study of economic data or in supplying "impulses and viewpoints" to the economic historian that may direct his inquiries into useful channels. Such fiction may also enable the scholar to acquire "some sense of the everyday atmosphere of Soviet economic life," which is essential to a full understanding of it (300, 317). But Gerschenkron also asserts that Soviet novels, no less than those of other countries' economic experience, may be misleading. Their special value lies in the fact that other sources on Soviet economic life are so scanty. In this special case, then, the novel takes on increased value in its coverage of a certain kind of institution in a certain place and time.

Social science, to the extent that it aims to emulate physical science, seeks to predict. A hypothesis is a form of prediction, and so is an experiment, whether it occurs in a laboratory under fully controlled conditions or is based on quantitative or other data, some of whose variables are held constant to determine the effect of other variables and thus to isolate influences or causes. The prediction of real events such as economic conditions, revolutions, and social movements is not often achieved in social science. When predictions are accurate, they are seldom based on scientific method except when they use probability theory. The mathematics of probability captivated some eighteenth century thinkers, who optimistically tried to apply it to social life. The Marquis de Condorcet thought that the French Revolution, which victimized him, had inaugurated an era that would lead to mankind's perfection. "If," he demanded, "man can predict with almost complete certainty the phenomena whose laws he understands, and even if when these laws are unknown to him he can predict future events with great probability on the basis of the past, why should it be regarded as a chimerical undertaking to delineate, with some de-

gree of truth, the future of mankind from the results of its past?"
(VI, 236). The early novelists of the late seventeenth and eighteenth centuries wrote many prefaces explaining that their stories
were true or probable. In her "Essay on Fiction" (1795) Madame
de Staël found such stories and characters "so believable . . . that
one is easily convinced" they could have happened "just that way."
Since the novel has already "happened," it can "happen" again.
As she put it, "A novel is not a story of the past but often seems to
be one of the future."[8]

A fictional analogue of prediction in the sciences is foreshadowing, a form of prediction within the framework of the story itself.
Foreshadowing prepares the reader for things to come. The writer
may foreshadow several events and actually bring about only some
of them; or he may prefer a very gentle foreshadowing in order not
to reduce suspense. Trollope professed in *Barchester Towers,* ch.
15, not to mind giving away some of his plot, believing that "the
author and the reader should move along together in full confidence of each other." George Eliot was more cautious, at least in
her intrusions. As Will Ladislaw is about to leave Middlemarch, in
ch. 10, Eliot proposes: "Let him start for the Continent, then,
without our pronouncing on his future. Among all forms of mistake, prophecy is the most gratuitous." In *The Mill on the Floss,*
bk. 6, ch. 6, Eliot, describing Maggie as passionate and ambitious,
adds that her fate cannot be predicted from her character, since
external events also have their effect: "Maggie's destiny, then, is at
present hidden, and we must wait for it to reveal itself." Eliot in-
dulged in foreshadowing, however, and on at least one occasion,
in *Adam Bede,* ch. 48, called attention to it, giving it both a quality of prediction and inevitability. After Hetty is saved from death
but condemned to deportation, the author tells of two men approaching the place where Adam had seen Hetty and Arthur embracing. In this much sadder time, the two men are drawn "by a
common memory" to the old scene. The narrator does not name
the men but tells the reader: "you know who the men were." Harriet Martineau expressed a curious position in her *Autobiography*
on the relationship between events in a novel. Acknowledging her
own limitations in this respect, she regards the mental capacity to

devise fictional plots as "evidently the same power as that of prophecy." She believes that plot calls for a thorough comprehension of connected events leading to an inevitable conclusion, a process akin to prophecy and hence beyond human ability. For this reason, "every perfect plot in fiction is taken bodily from real life" (I, 179-180).

Fictional foreshadowing, inevitability, and prediction go together within the story, but there is also a form of prediction that extends outside the story. This is the sort of prediction that Picasso made when someone told him that his portrait of Gertrude Stein did not really look like her. "Don't worry," he is said to have replied, "it will."[9] This suggests an inscrutable vision of the artist. Dostoyevsky, criticizing the realists, contended that "our idealists have actually *predicted* many of the actual facts" of the last decade of Russian "spiritual development." Recently some observers have found in Joseph Heller's *Catch 22* (1961), a story of World War Two, "predictions" about the conduct of the war in Vietnam by the United States in the 1960s, including the flight of deserters to Sweden.[10] The implication is that this novel influenced as well as predicted behavior. In *The Quiet American* (1955), Graham Greene's description of advisers in South Vietnam in the early 1950s constitutes a prediction of the American approach and failure a decade and more later. Antiutopian novels such as Aldous Huxley's *Brave New World* (1932) and Orwell's *Nineteen Eighty-four* (1949) try more deliberately to predict, or at least to warn about, the direction of social life. More than a quarter-century after *Brave New World* Huxley wrote an essay, *Brave New World Revisited* (1958), in which he observed that his prophecies were being realized sooner than he had expected. Comparing his own prophecies with Orwell's, he thought that the world was more likely to resemble the portrait in *Brave New World* than in *Nineteen Eighty-four*.

The novel sets up so many hypothetical, imagined situations resembling real ones that it is not surprising to see some of them realized. Pat Rogers argues that Pope so well understood social disorder that the Gordon Riots of 1780 may be seen as one of the "implied predictions" of *The Dunciad* (1728, 1742). Prediction in both the novel and social science nevertheless does not meet the strict criteria of science, though it does suggest their broad interest in the past as a guide to understanding the present and discerning some aspects of the future.

Hawthorne's point that the aesthetically fine demonstration of a truth does not add to the validity of that truth emphasizes the difference between poetic truth and scientific truth. Poetic truth is unlimited in scope, usually applies to all experience in all eras, and is not confined historically. It is also a moral truth, embodying wisdom rather than an empirical uniformity based on hypothesis and evidence, and hence is not limited by them. Finally, poetic truth is expressed in aesthetically pleasing language, a feature that is an important element of its capacity to persuade. Such a truth is expressed in Pope's couplet, in *An Essay on Criticism:* "Words are like leaves; and where they most abound,/Much fruit of sense beneath is rarely found" (309-310). In contrast, historical truth involves a wide band of human experience, such as revolution, poverty, or prejudice, and is based so directly on evidence that it can and must be modified as new facts are discovered. Its purpose is also to summarize experience, yet within narrower confines and without the aesthetic goal of poetic truth. Scientific truth aims at an even broader spectrum of experience and is thus more like poetic than historical truth, except that science seeks to connect its truths into a system. As Ernest Nagel points out, scientific truth is precise, testable, expressed often in magnitudes, and therefore subject to frequent modification. Poetic truth, not subject to these rigorous criteria, may, like Pope's couplet, be accepted unchanged for perhaps as long as human beings contemplate themselves. Historical and scientific truths are self-corrective. This is not to say that art cannot be so; indeed, it often is so in at least one sense. Some novels seek to correct the excesses of previous ones, as *Don Quixote* criticizes the novel of chivalry, *Northanger Abbey* the Gothic novel, and *Madame Bovary* the circulating-library romantic novel. These corrections again show how similar — yet different — are the novel and social science.

Critiques of Society

As descriptions of human behavior and institutions, the novel and social science early became critiques of society as well. Each, moreover, has alerted its readers to aspects, often regarded as evils, that might be missed in their complacency or their absorption in life itself. Thus Hardy wrote in his notebooks in 1885: "The business of the poet and novelist is to show the sorriness underlying the grandest things, and the grandeur underlying the sorriest things."[11] Hawthorne earlier made the same point in an intrusion in *The House of the Seven Gables,* ch. 2, where he remarked that poetic insight is the capacity to see "the beauty and the majesty" in things that appear sordid. Social science has likewise tended to deal with similarities and differences, to find and to alert people to relationships that might not normally be seen. Montaigne observed: "Resemblance does not make things so much alike as difference makes them unlike" (815-816). Madame de Staël, in *De l'Allemagne,* characteristically borrowed this notion, improved upon it, and then attributed it to Montesquieu: "Understanding consists in recognizing the similarity among different things and the differences among similar things" (IV, 203-204). George Eliot held a similar view in *Impressions of Theophrastus Such:* "To discern likeness amidst diversity, it is well known, does not require so fine a mental edge as the discerning of diversity amidst general sameness" (145-146). Novelists and social scientists often make people look at what they would prefer to avoid. Novelists show men's petty ambitions and hypocrisies, social scientists dwell on their weaknesses and problems, and both like to reveal the gap between men's professed values and the realities they create.

From its beginnings the novel in France and England sought to criticize society and guide its readers. In the dedication to *Amelia* Fielding remarks that this novel is "sincerely designed to promote the cause of virtue, and to expose some of the most glaring evils, as well public as private, which at present infest this country." Among these evils are certain laws, a lack of physical security, corrupt magistrates, and unjust prison systems. Fielding makes bold to suggest in bk. 1, ch. 1 that there is a "science" that produces perfect "models" in various domains, and that novels are the

"models of Human Life" from which to learn "the Art of Life."
This attitude of the novelist was especially well represented in Victorian fiction, leading James Russell Lowell to complain by 1847
that "the propagandist of every philosophical soup-and-bread society assumes the disguise of a poet" and that literature assaults
the reader with the "balance of trade" and "merciless statistics"
(106).[12] American novels took the same path. A.N. Kaul, for example, has shown that the great novelists of the nineteenth cen
tury not only explored social reality but offered a critique of it by
picturing an "ideal" community or "conception of social relationships" (4). Xole Sills has identified a genre of Western "social
science fiction" which, since antiquity, has created "imaginary
worlds for the purpose of exploring the potential development of
society" (473).

The critique of society has probably always been an aspect of
art but seems to have grown in importance in the eighteenth century, especially on the eve of the French Revolution. It is connected with the emergence of the artist from the status of crafts-
man to greater personal and ideological independence in Europe
in the sixteenth and seventeenth centuries as well as with the new
philosophic thought of those eras and the ideological and socioeconomic changes emerging more clearly in the eighteenth century. James Leith has described the views of the French philosophes
and encyclopedists who held that art should be used as a means of
elevating morality. Seeing an ordered universe as described in the
new physical science and aware of the social ills pointed out by
the new social science, they sought the means to impose a greater
order on society. The idea that art could be one of these means
reached a high point under Jacobin rule following the Revolution.
These developments gave a great impetus to art as a critique of society. Many scholars date the modern outlook from that era. This
modern outlook, Lionel Trilling has explained, holds that "a primary function of art and thought is to liberate the individual from
the tyranny of his culture" (xiii). This "idea of the adversary culture" has gained adherents in recent years and has often come to
be taken for granted. David Daiches also describes this kind of re-
bellious art which opposes tradition, glorifies alienation, and then
becomes part of the "official culture." As he puts it, "Society ex-

pects its culture heroes to be alienated, and often rewards them for it." Another critic, Morse Peckham, calling his work *Man's Rage for Chaos,* holds that man seeks order and that the function of art is to frustrate this desire by providing a fictional disorder. Opposition to the chic avant-garde approach to art, however, did not wait for the 1960s. George Eliot, because she believed in the power of art, had complained in *Impressions of Theophrastus Such* that "our delicious sense of the ludicrous" was given such free play that it "makes every passion preposterous or obscene, and turns the hard-won order of life into a second chaos" (87).

Yet Eliot herself played the role of the artist as critic and dissenter with respect to other aspects of social life. Although the tendency now is to identify the critical novelists with radical political thought, their dissent is often more general and less political. The artist's desire to stir the public is not necessarily motivated by political views. Coleridge admitted that he and Wordsworth in the *Lyrical Ballads* sought to stimulate the reader to see the supernatural as human and to see the novelty of the ordinary.[13] So politically conservative a novelist as Ellen Glasgow criticized in *A Certain Measure* the "artificial glow of the past American idealism" and appreciated the "liberty not to believe, and . . . not to be glad" (118). As C.F.G. Masterman has observed of English literature early in this century, which is not regarded as especially radical, "Literature has no tolerance for the existence of comfort and security which to so many people seems the last word of human welfare" (7). Edith Wharton drew attention to this notion in an early short story, "Expiation" (1904) in *The Descent of Man,* in which one woman writer who specializes in "colloquial ornithology" envies another whose fashionable and superficial novel enjoys success because it shocks the public. The first writer admits that there is a "ravenous call for attacks on social institutions — especially by those inside the institutions!" (206-207). H. G. Wells regarded the novel as a powerful means of educating the public, concerning abuses by government officials, for example. He called it "the social mediator" between the classes.[14] The philosopher T. H. Green had in 1862 described it similarly as "the great reformer and leveller of our time" (41). So prevalent was this view of fiction in Europe that when in 1895 Theodore Herzl wanted to arouse public opinion to the needs of the Jews, the French novelist Alphonse Daudet advised him to write a novel instead of a tract. "A novel reaches farther," Daudet said to the founder of Zionism, reminding him of *Uncle Tom's Cabin*.[15] When the Persian writer Muhammad Jamalzadeh sought early in the twentieth century to advance the novel in a culture still loyal to traditional literary forms, he pointed to its educational value in providing useful information about various kinds of people, social classes, and occupations.

Though social science seeks objectivity, it is like the novel in its critique of society. Historians have always judged, to some extent, the events, personalities, and groups they describe. Modern social science began as an effort to find the bases of social stability, then became an arm of social reform. Recently, objectivity has been attacked as little more than a support for the status quo, and some social scientists have reverted to the advocacy of reform or revolution, but more openly and consciously than in earlier times.[16] Persons studying social institutions and human behavior have sought to influence them in one direction or another, in accordance with their own sympathies. Their abilities have been useful both to ruling groups and to those challenging them. Generally, the critique of social scientists has, like that of novelists, been sympathetic to the liberal ideals developed in the eighteenth century and has directly or by implication argued in favor of exploited groups, for international cooperation, and for government action to promote social welfare. Above all, much of social science is also devoted to bringing the public's attention to social problems with at least the implicit aim of reform.

Just as social scientists share this interest in social reform with novelists, so some novelists have occasionally expressed their "objectivity" in the manner of the scientist. Often such expressions by novelists are only innocent ironies arising out of disappointment at public indifference. This ironic pose, less often adopted in social science, is the hallmark of Thorstein Veblen. In his last book, *Absentee Ownership* (1923), he culminated a lifetime of criticizing capitalism and the business ethic with still another claim to objectivity or indifference. Although he admits that a "description

. . . will sometimes look like fault-finding," he denies any "presumptuous aspiration to reprove, amend, hinder, improve, or otherwise interfere" with the "appointed task of the constituted authorities" (37-38).[17] Hawthorne, in his preface to *The House of the Seven Gables,* admits that "the author has provided himself with a moral," that he would be gratified if it would save mankind, "or, indeed, any one man," from error, but he does not "flatter himself with the slightest hope of this kind." Hawthorne seems also to anticipate Veblen's mood in the preface to *The Blithedale Romance,* where he admits that he had Brook Farm "in his mind" but hastens to add that he does not "put forward the slightest pretensions to illustrate a theory, or elicit a conclusion, favorable or otherwise, in respect to socialism." Hardy expresses a similar modesty in *Jude the Obscure* (pt. 5, ch. 5): "The purpose of a chronicler of moods and deeds does not require him to express his personal views upon the grave controversy above given." Of course, he already had. In his notebooks Hardy remarks concerning reviews of *Jude* that an author may be accused of impiety or subversion even when he is challenging neither the "universe" nor "human institutions."[18] Jane Austen too in *Northanger Abbey,* after much moralizing, concludes the novel by leaving to "whomsoever it may concern" the judgment as to the moral of the story.

Ironical as they may be, such attitudes on the part of novelists probably limit their interest in furthering social critique and reform through their works. Artists generally have been suspicious of organized radical movements, which usually seek to enlist them in a cause at the same time that they consider artists too individualistic. As Alain Robbe-Grillet has indicated in *For a New Novel,* the "Socialist Revolution is suspicious of Revolutionary Art," and justifiably so. The artist "puts nothing above his work," which "cannot be reduced to the status of a means in the service of a cause which transcends it," even if he is a sincere revolutionary (36-37). The more specific the novel's critique of society, in fact, the more limited is the novel's scope and applicability. Thus Hawthorne's *The Blithedale Romance* is valuable and enduring more as a critique of absolute idealism than of Brook Farm or even of the utopian community in general. Corrupted idealism is still an important part of social life, but the utopian communities of the present are somewhat different from those of Hawthorne's time.[19] Dickens's *Hard Times* (1854) fits the mood today because it criticizes a conception of life based only on "facts," materialism, and minute calculation while ignoring imagination and play. Likewise, Hardy's *Jude the Obscure* (1895) deals not merely with specific marriage regulations but also with the individual's desire for spontaneous relations with others and with human adaptation to the changing, "uprising times" in which so many generations of men and women find themselves.

The novel's extraordinary capaciousness — its inclusion of great detail and moral breadth — makes it instructive even considered against social science. The more optimistic advocates of social science, such as George Lundberg, while recognizing the value of literature "as a sort of social science," insist that it is to social science one must turn in order to validate literature (101). Lewis Coser asserts the same relationship between the two approaches. In an ideal sense, they are right, but the trouble is that they compare the achievement of the novel with the unfulfilled promise of social science. If the achievements of both are compared, the gap considerably narrows. The promise of social science is based on a faith in its future that is no more justified, scientifically, than is the opposed notion that social science can never be a rigorous set of interrelated propositions, laws, and theories explaining observed, acknowledged facts about human behavior and social institutions.

The Challenge of
Science to Literature

It is possible to set a limit to the progress of the
arts, but not to the discoveries of the intellect.
— Madame de Staël, *De la Littérature*

10.

The intermingling of the world of the novel and the world of reality has led to the blurring of distinctions between literature and
science, especially by the partisans of literature. When modern
physical science arose in the seventeenth century, the defenders of
literature mistakenly tried to show its superiority over the new
form of knowledge. Centuries later they had to give up, but then
the advent of the contemporary social sciences presented a new
challenge and a new target. Fifty years ago the philosopher De
Witt Parker argued that there is "more to be learned of the human mind in its living reality from the study of any branch of art
than from most of the books of the psychologists and sociologists"
(178-179). This could have been true at the time for many people,
and it may be true even now, but the easily drawn implication —
that art is somehow superior to science — is not true. Art provides
knowledge even if it is not science. For centuries the extremists on
both sides have used the common goal of art and science, including social science, to create a false rivalry between two different
modes of seeking knowledge. The arguments and the drama of
confrontation, however, have been more exciting than an early
acceptance of the separate spheres of the two approaches would

have been. The unreasoned competition may have also taught something of value.

Vindication of Literature as Knowledge

Novels have much to tell about the real world of human behavior and social institutions. Though this idea has been widely accepted as a common-sense proposition, it has been denied by some philosophers. Margaret Macdonald, for example, who admits that fiction refers to real persons and events, insists nevertheless that the statements about them in a story are neither true nor false. Such statements are not "informative assertions" about reality but are no different in their "function" from the "purely fictional elements, with which they are always mingled in a story" (181). Margolis holds that verisimilitude may persuade one to regard fictional statements as referring to a real world and may even heighten the appreciation of a story; but the story itself, as a story, cannot be said to refer to the real world.[1] This view is excessively mechanical and logical, as well as untrue to experience. Norman Campbell, a scientist, does not hesitate to claim that science may have value even when it violates logic, and the same attitude may be taken toward literature.

Other philosophers have argued both that literature makes statements which may be judged true or false (truth-claims) and that many of these statements are actually true. John Hospers maintains that such truths, though incidental to the work of art and undocumented, may increase its value. He introduces the notion that these statements may be direct and explicit, in which case they can be clearly judged to be true or false, or they may be "implied" and not necessarily intended by the author, in which case they can nevertheless tell truths about the world outside the work of art itself. Morris Weitz vindicates literature as a form of knowledge by resorting to a similar concept, that of the implicit meaning "exhibited through . . . plot, character, and dialogue," which he exemplifies in various fictional works (9). Other critics and philosophers have also taken the broader position recognizing literature as a form or source of knowledge.[2]

Science and art thus have the goal of understanding, which they pursue in different ways. Newton or any great scientist of an earlier time would be a great scientist today, but he would know much more than he or anyone knew then, because science is cumulative. Yet Shakespeare or Dickens would not necessarily be greater today because of the great plays or novels created since their times. They might be greater simply because today there is more experience of human behavior and even more knowledge of it, but if that is the case, it has resulted from the illumination provided by both science and art. Despite this difference in cumulative quality, there are similarities between science and art. It is no longer so widely accepted, for example, that the artist is entirely "emotional" and the scientist "intellectual." John Dewey pointed out several decades ago that scientists, like artists, grope and "press forward toward some end dimly and imprecisely prefigured," and that artists, like scientists, necessarily go beyond inspiration to transform and organize the material of experience and imagination (73). Both require intellectual boldness, as Morris Cohen has suggested in *The Meaning of Human History*. Campbell remarks that science, especially in the creation of theories, involves imaginative and personal knowledge comparable to that in art. Thackeray in *The Newcomes* (II, ch. 47) suggested the similarity of thought in the artist and scientist. Speaking of a couple in love, the narrator refers to two famous contemporary zoologists: "How can I tell the feelings of a young lady's mind; the thoughts in a young gentleman's bosom? — As Professor Owen or Professor Agassiz takes a fragment of a bone, and builds an enormous forgotten monster out of it . . . so the novelist puts this and that together . . . and thus, in his humble way a physiologist too, depicts the habits, size, appearance of the beings whereof he has to treat."

Influence of Science on the Novel

Pursuing the biological analogy, Zola developed the idea of the novelist as scientist. M. Guyau, a philosopher and contemporary of Zola, criticized such exaggerations and held that though the novelist is not a scientist and need not try to act like one, he does have to take into account what science has discovered and thus avoid basing his conceptions of the world on false assumptions. Literature has taken science into account. The social impact of various sciences — and their derivative, technology — has been so pervasive for several centuries that it has influenced all thinking persons whether they welcome or detest it. Novelists and poets have sought to understand science, to assess its effects upon society, to portray its processes and the people who engage in them. This effort has been appropriate, illuminating, and salutary. When, however, novelists have sought to emulate science closely or to displace it, they have drifted from their moral function and dissipated their energies in useless forays, usually into regions they have not understood.

Since the rise of modern science, literature has somehow responded to it. In the seventeenth and eighteenth centuries, it was chiefly astronomy and physics that absorbed novelists and even more so poets, affecting their ideas of the place of man and earth in the physical world. Many were able to reconcile science with moral and religious ideas, especially since prominent scientists, such as Newton, saw their discoveries as further evidence of divine artistry, and their main effect was to loosen the hold of classical and medieval thought.[3] Poets were inspired in language and imagery. When scientific ideas became too complicated for the nonspecialist to understand, literary men began to criticize them as alien and materialistic.

In the middle of the nineteenth century, evolution theory further disturbed many novelists, bringing other sciences, mainly biology, to bear upon literature. Novelists began to be concerned with the place of man in the world of animal nature, and the impact of science upon traditional moral and religious ideas was increased. The earlier impact was fairly optimistic; the new one much less so. The focus of interest was upon Darwinian thought, although evolutionary ideas had already had an impact upon literature before the publication of *The Origin of Species* in 1859. In a study of novels published from 1860 to 1910, Leo Henkin has found that many of them dealt with the Darwinian loosening of Christian faith and that many others used evolutionary ideas in a blend of science and fiction associated with the work of Jules Verne. Ellen Glasgow, who began writing toward the end of the nineteenth century, was among the novelists who welcomed Darwin's influence. *The Origin of Species,* she notes in *A Certain Measure,* was the book that most influenced her youth, "and it was in response to this benign and powerful inspiration that I conceived my first novels" (58).[4]

Twentieth-century physical science has had an almost entirely baleful influence upon the novel.[5] With the accumulation of earlier impacts, the full effect of technology — including war, bureaucracy, and the deteriorating environment — has led to a questioning of the value of science itself, perhaps as often in treatises as in literature. Jerry Bryant has found a correspondence between modern physics and the mood of the contemporary American novel. He claims that the fictional themes of the "individual versus authority, of self-knowledge and self-ignorance, of rebellion against forces (natural or human) that would violate the integrity of the subject" are produced by the special nature of modern physics, as well as by social science and philosophy (23). Such broad characteristics, however, are found in all eras of the novel, as Bryant admits after still another vain effort to derive fiction from philosophy.

The trouble with these attempts is that the large themes they define are found in the novels of almost any era as responses to impulses that are just as constant in science and social thought. Novelists today do not understand science any more than literary men did in the early nineteenth century, when they began to attack it. Literature reacts to science not directly but indirectly by contemplating the results of science and technology that are experienced in social relations. Right now, for example, society is beginning to react to discoveries and their applications in genetics, the physiology and chemistry of sex, and the aging of body and mind. As these themes are felt in social life — themes such as are implied in the greater control over birth, sex, and death — novelists will react to them more and more. This reaction will not be directed to science itself but to the effects of science upon human affairs. Novelists will probably react as they have in earlier eras to the impact of the sciences; that is, novelists will have their fictional characters discuss the recent discoveries and their effects, the moral choices they offer or deny. Such influences of science upon literature will be easy to discern. It will be more difficult, perhaps impossible, to trace convincingly the direct effect science will have upon the deeper themes of fiction. Perhaps the main effect of science is to interdict certain conceptions to novels by making them no longer acceptable, rather than to impose specific, identifiable attitudes and themes not already found in fiction.

Effort To Emulate Science

Difficult as fictional efforts to respond to science are to trace, they have been appropriate and sometimes illuminating. The novel's claim to supplant science, however, has been inappropriate, characterized by little more than bravado. This claim has been peculiarly though not exclusively French. Around the middle of the nineteenth century Balzac and Flaubert adopted it, using, as did the social sciences of their time, biology and natural history as models. Several decades later Zola made similar claims and spoke of the novel as an experiment. Three-quarters of a century later, French practitioners of the "new novel," such as Alain Robbe-Grillet, were still at it, some continuing to use biological analogies, such as Nathalie Sarraute, and a larger number preferring to follow more directly the phenomenological approach in philosophy popularized by Sartre, the philosopher and belle-lettrist.

In 1842 Balzac gave the title "The Human Comedy" to a number of his stories, to which he related others he was still to write. He also wrote a preface to the first volume based on and extending earlier remarks of Félix Davin, a young novelist who admired him, in which he set forth objectively the intention, origin, and plan of this long work. Its idea originated in a "comparison between humanity and animality." God created a "single model" of the animal; the different species emerged from differences in environment. Even before the debates among the scientists on this point, Balzac asserted, he had already noted that "society resembled nature," in that society molds mankind into many different types in accordance with their environment. Thus, "there have always been and always will be social species just as there are animal species." Balzac defined his task as describing these social species — their vices and virtues, passions and traits, and the main events of their interaction. By uniting similar characteristics, he, like a scientist, would create types and thus write the neglected history of manners and customs: "French society would be the historian, I should be only the recorder."

A decade or so later Flaubert expressed even greater ambitions for the novel. It was time, he announced in a letter of March 18, 1857, to endow the novel, through an unrelentingly systematic method, with the predictive capacity of the physical sciences. He had earlier implied in a letter of January 16, 1852, that art ought to become more abstract by emptying itself of material content and thus freeing itself increasingly of subjects until style alone — pure art — should remain. A generation later Zola specified Balzac's biological approach by speaking of chemistry and physiology and joined to it Flaubert's emphasis on method. Following what he understood to be the experimental medicine of Claude Bernard, who rejected the notion of literature as science, he hailed the age of the "experimental" or scientific novel. Zola described the novelist as both an observer and an "experimenter" who "sets his characters going in a particular story designed to show that the succession of events will be such as determined by the phenomena under study" (16). The experiment goes beyond sheer description; the novelist "must modify nature without departing from it" (18). At times Zola wrote as if the novelist had already experimented, or ought to experiment, or would one day experiment when physiology as the science of mankind had achieved the certainty of physics and chemistry. In any case, he believed that the progress of the novel toward science had at least begun and was irreversible. Though all human phenomena were absolutely determined, Zola admitted that he and the "science of man" could not yet "formulate laws" (23). The physiologist could already explain the nature of individual man's physical and chemical makeup acting under the influence of heredity and environment. The novelist then took the "isolated man from the hands of the physiologist" to explain man in that society which man himself created (25). Understanding would lead to control, Zola held, apparently looking to the future: "When the times will have advanced, when we know the laws, we shall merely have to act upon the individuals and their surroundings if we want to arrive at the best social condition" (28).

Such ideas today belong only to the history of literary thought. Soon after they were offered, their idealistic exaggerations had already been exposed.[6] Zola's own novels do not bear them out, even though they do reveal, as A. E. Carter shows, his medical interest in diseases and in physical and mental degeneration.

Objectivity in the New Novel

The penchant of "advanced" novelists or critics to speak in terms of science dies hard or rather just lives on. Three-quarters of a century after Zola's romantic embracing of physiology and objectivity, the "new novelists" in France returned to and adapted such ideas in response to popularizations of phenomenology and existentialism. Still pursuing biological analogues, the novelist Sarraute regards human impulses, sensations, and movements as analogous to tropisms, which is the title of one of her books. In another, *The Age of Suspicion,* she sees suspicion as "one of the morbid reactions by which an organism defends itself and seeks another equilibrium" (74). Susan Sontag, a critic, sees the "new sensibility" expressed in a "new non-literary culture" whose arts "draw profusely, naturally, and without embarrassment, upon science and technology." This idea leads her back to old exaggerations and obscurities or clichés, such as that "there can be no divorce between science and technology, on the one hand, and art, on the other," or that "Today's art, with its insistence on coolness, its refusal of what it considers to be sentimentality, its spirit of exactness, its sense of 'research' and 'problems,' is closer to the spirit of science than of art in the old-fashioned sense" (297-299). The quest goes on.

The contemporary quest of the novel to emulate science has taken the form of objectivity. True to its tradition, the French new novel, emerging in the early 1940s but not christened until the late

1950s, has in its various and even conflicting forms sought to respond to science by becoming like it in some ways, that is, by removing from fiction as much contrivance as novelists can dispense with. Joseph Warren Beach in the early 1930s pointed to the "disappearance of the author" since Henry James. The French novelist and critic Robbe-Grillet in *For a New Novel* then signaled the disappearance of plot and character. According to the more extreme wing of the new novel, fiction should appear as documentary for the reader to interpret without direction by the author, much as a scientific report sets forth all the evidence from all points of view, even if the scientist does favor one hypothesis over the others.

Some simple examples may illustrate the change in the role of the novelist. In *The Mill on the Floss* (bk. 1, ch. 3), George Eliot not only describes a gesture but tells its meaning: "Mr. Tulliver took a draught, swallowed it slowly, and shook his head in a melancholy manner." In *Lawd Today*, published posthumously in 1963, Richard Wright often guides the reader in the same way but prefers to describe gestures and leave it to the reader to interpret their meaning from the context. When Jake is impatiently waiting for his friends, the author describes his actions: "He crossed his legs, uncrossed them, sat up straight for above five seconds, leaned over a second, then sat up straight again" (66). When two friends are playing the "dozens" and insulting each other, two others observe and are convulsed with laughter, which Wright describes neutrally in physical terms such as: "Slim and Bob rolled on the sofa and held their stomachs"; "Slim and Bob groaned and stomped their feet"; "Slim and Bob beat the floor with their fists" (80-81). Even less information is provided the reader by Robbe-Grillet in *Jealousy* (1957). Much of the action is obscure until one considers the title as a clue and accepts the aid of the book-jacket of the original French edition, which indicates the novel is about a jealous husband who suspiciously observes his wife from various angles of the house. At the beginning, Robbe-Grillet presents a plan of the house on the land. He makes the reader sense an observing character, the husband, by explaining that the wife "seems" to do certain things or is "probably" doing this or that, since the husband, looking from a distance, cannot be certain. In addition to the floor plan of the house, Robbe-Grillet gives precise details of the plantation around it: thirty-two banana trees here, twenty-three there, sixteen in another place, and the numbers in the rows. Such details are also to be found in many older novels, such as Hawthorne's *The House of the Seven Gables,* ch. 1, where he describes the building and land in similar terms though not such quantitative ones. The difference is that Hawthorne is less neutral, describing the surrounding houses as "typical of the most plodding uniformity of common life" and the main house as having a "meditative look" and a "beauty" lent by an old elm — terms such as Robbe-Grillet eschews.

Modern novelists are like the earliest ones in wanting to come closer to life; but they choose different means, which usually downgrade plot and seek to reduce the obvious role of the author. In two letters of January 16, 1852, and March 18, 1857, Flaubert had already put forth such ideas. In the earlier letter he revealed that he would like to write a book "about nothing, a book with no exterior connection, which would stand by itself by the internal power of its style, as the earth stands in space without support, a book which would have hardly any subject or at least a practically invisible one, if that were possible." In the second letter he warned that the writer must not put himself into his novel. Accordingly, he had invented everything in *Madame Bovary,* for the power of the writer, like that of God, must be felt but not seen. Even Trollope, who understood the importance of plot to the reader, called it in his *Autobiography,* "the most insignificant part of a tale," and insisted on the primacy of character (106). James Joyce, in the same vein as Flaubert, has the hero of *A Portrait of the Artist as a Young Man,* ch. 5, describe artistic creation as a process in which the artist starts out at the center of the work but ends up outside it: "The personality of the artist . . . finally refines itself out of existence . . . The artist, like the God of the creation, remains within or behind or beyond or above his handiwork, invisible." E. M. Forster, taking his usual common-sense view in *Aspects of the Novel,* examined the "tyranny" of plot and characters, sympathized with the modern authors who wanted to do away with prearrangments and contrivances distant from real life, and concluded that "this low atavistic form"—the story—is also the "highest factor common" to novels and cannot be excised from those "complicated organisms" (153, 45, 48).

Practitioners and theorists of the new novel have nevertheless persisted in their search for ways to go beyond the stock of inherited fictional techniques in order to convey their own conceptions of the new realities produced by relativity in science and by totalitarianism and war, all of which overwhelmed the individual so dear to the traditional novel as well as to the writer, who began to find the new reality strange and unmanageable. Extending Flaubert's insights, Robbe-Grillet, in *For a New Novel,* attacked stories once more as "prefabricated schemas people are used to" and as reassuring representations of a familiar order (31). The story imposes "the image of a stable, coherent, continuous, unequivocal, entirely decipherable universe," all of which science and social change presumably belie (32). Such a fictional world is, to Robbe-Grillet, not natural but an invention of novelists. They ought therefore to use their freedom to invent not such a story of the world but new realities of their own with new forms. As he puts it, "literary revolutions have always been made in the name of realism," for old formulas do not suffice and "a return to the real" is necessary to cut through them (158). The novel does not "seek to inform"; rather, it is, as Flaubert, Wilde, and Joyce also said, pure invention, "invention of the world and of man, constant invention," and what it invents "*constitutes* reality" (161). Since the world is so complex, the novelist cannot know it all and must get away from the pose of omniscience. Instead, the new novelists seem to say, the novel must use an unrestricted imagination to deal with a more restricted domain or at least to present things to the reader from various and limited points of view stated frankly. Such positions have brought novelists in France since World War Two into close relation with philosophers, if not scientists.[7]

Though the new novelists have left much more to the reader to supply, the author has remained in view, as Forster suggested. It is he who decides what the reader has before him to work on. True, the new novelist does not intrude his generalizations or lead the reader openly to think about scenes, events, and characters in a certain way, but the author still influences the reader and cannot help but do so. Robbe-Grillet's *Jealousy*, for example, tries to be objective or neutral by placing the observer outside the novel looking in on it from various angles and by presenting only observable, measured facts. Yet precisely by this manner Robbe-Grillet gives the reader an impression of coldness and impending trouble, a sense that the entire scene is dominated by self-assured forces which have created a landscape in order to control it.

The modern artist prefers to give the audience clues rather than to persuade or inform openly. More than a century and a half ago, Sir Walter Scott saw the alternatives facing novelists and indicated the choice made by his predecessors and contemporaries. In an essay on Fielding in *The Lives of the Novelists* Scott pointed out that the novelist had to work "without the assistance of material objects" available either to the painter, who could "present a visible and tangible representation" of a scene, or to the dramatist, who could present living people on a stage speaking and looking in a certain way. The novelist had to achieve his effects by "the mere force of an excited imagination," and hence it was his purpose to supply the reader everything he could in order to help him see what the author saw. This need comprised the strength and the weakness of the novelist. Lacking material objects, he had the possibility of achieving an even greater effect by skillfully "awakening the imagination of a congenial reader" (49-50). At that time novelists chose to awaken the reader's imagination by supplying a great deal of description and direction; since then, many novelists have preferred to do so by presenting less and less and leaving more and more to the reader.

Arthur Koestler calls this process in art the "law of infolding." The artist "folds" the meaning within the work, making it more economical and subtle and thus requiring the audience to exercise considerable imagination in approaching it. Koestler considers this trend as part of a succession of styles, akin to the succession advanced by Thomas Peacock. Any style reaches a "saturation" point when writers and readers are no longer challenged: "Yesterday's daring metaphors are today's clichés." One response of writers is to reach for new and subtler modes of expression which enable the reader to be more creative in interpreting the work. This technique, Koestler adds, can lead to "deliberate obscurity," as in some examples of the "nouveau roman" (43-45). Jacques Barzun, in a similar spirit in *The Use and Abuse of Art,* finds a "remarkable parallel" in the growing difficulty of both science and art in the nineteenth century. Science went from "organized common sense" to being "mathematical, statistical, abstract, invisible," while movements in art, such as impressionism and symbolism, "denied the beholder simple representative effects" (101).

Convergence of the Novel and Social Science

Among the social sciences, history at least has, like the novel, recently given less emphasis to narrative. Critics have once more discovered a convergence between the novel and social science, now mainly sociology.[8] There is also recently the same humanistic opposition to the "sociological" novel as a diminution of art. Social science and novels have both resorted to the tape recorder, producing a certain similarity in what is offered the reader, as noted by Jonathan Raban and John Coleman. Oscar Lewis, an anthropologist, makes *La Vida,* his study of a family, sound like a novel in places, and Erving Goffman, a sociologist, uses incidents in novels to illustrate his ideas about interpersonal behavior. Two other authors, Dorothy Rabinowitz and Yedida Nielson, in writing about old age, have "pooled the resources of a shared vision and shared experience," producing a "documentary, which employs some of the techniques of fiction" or "an imaginative rendering of factual experience" (ix).

Some sociological studies have been regarded as similar to fiction even when the authors make no such claims. Elliot Liebow's *Tally's Corner* (1967), subtitled *A Study of Negro Streetcorner Men* and based on field work in Washington, D.C., in 1962-1963, is said by a sociologist in a foreword to it to be "as akin in preoccupation and point to Ralph Ellison's fictional classic, *Invisible Man,* as it is to William Foote Whyte's sociological classic, *Street Corner Society.*" Whyte himself, studying an Italian section of Boston in the late 1930s, did not use fictional techniques; his characters, conversations and monologues are not invented but taken from his field notes. At one point he perhaps senses that his study is comparable to fiction: "If this were a work of fiction, the story would now be finished," but he carries it on for another 200 pages (42). In the early 1930s W. L. Warner, an anthropologist, turned from studying Stone Age people in Australia to the community of Newburyport, Massachusetts, which he called Yankee City. To show "how it feels to live in the class system of Yankee City," he resorts to a chapter of avowedly imaginary portraits of individuals and families (127). The popular novelist John P. Marquand, known for his own portraits of social classes, had spent his boyhood in Newburyport and was unimpressed by Warner's social science survey. In *Point of No Return* (1949), Marquand tells of a young man growing up in "Clyde" at a time when the community is the object of study by an anthropologist, who calls it Yankee Persepolis. The novelist disparages social science technique, jargon, and generalizations, which cannot grasp the realities of individual and social life. Yet Marquand occasionally writes on social class and ethnic differences much as a social scientist might. Granville Hicks, literary critic, calls the novel superior to Warner's study in portraying classes: the novelist "beats" the social scientists "at their own game" (104).

Just as contemporary social treatises have turned to fictional techniques, so have novels sought to capitalize on public interest in social problems. Two anthologists of fiction, Penney and L. Rust Hills, calling their collection *How We Live: Contemporary Life in Contemporary Fiction,* believe that even though fiction is declining in popularity, it is not declining in the capacity to illuminate individual and social behavior. Concluding a section entitled "Alone," the editors report: "Each of the stories in this section dramatizes a different aspect of the modern condition of the non-hero: trapped in immobility; questing identity; longing for love and meaning; preoccupied with self and unable to accept responsibility for others; powerless to express his own uniqueness; alone in an absurd and meaningless world" (121-122). These broad themes are not peculiar to modern times but are perennial in the history of the novel. Nonfiction works on social problems sell much better than novels on the same or any other subjects. In a time of such serious problems — war, racial trouble, environmental issues, economic difficulty — people go to the genres that deal with them directly and point to solutions. Fiction does not perform this function today and did not, for example, in the early Victorian era, a time also beset by problems.[9]

Yet today, as before, the novel still seeks to attract the public interested in social evils and reform, as did Harriet Martineau a century and a half ago. Somerset Maugham, in his perhaps premature *The Summing Up* (1938 — he lived until 1965), observes in ch. 58 that in this century authors have written journalistic novels for an increasing audience wanting knowledge without working for it. But other writers have soon produced easily-understood books on social issues, killing what he calls the "propaganda novel." Novelists and critics have not allowed a decent burial for the novel's claim to the world of fact. Indeed, there seems to have been an increase in such novels in America since just before World War Two. They are the American counterpart to the French new novel, characteristically competing with journalism rather than science. The trend was first noted by its critics, then by its advocates. In 1934 Robert Penn Warren attacked T. S. Stribling's "critical realism" as artless propaganda based on a "pseudo-science, sociology" (463-464). In 1946 Jacques Barzun found that he disliked the works of "nonfiction novelists" who tried to copy reality too closely (129). He preferred novelists who used their imaginations and, as he later observed, returned to the "tale." In 1960 Geoffrey Wagner criticized some best-selling nonfiction novels not only as artless but also as less informative than journalism.

Meanwhile, the nonfiction novels kept on coming. Three of them are noteworthy. *The Ugly American* (1958), by William Lederer and Eugene Burdick, followed hard upon Graham Greene's *The Quiet American* (1955) and touched upon a similar theme more journalistically. The authors resorted to fiction to warn that the United States was losing the world-wide competition against communism because its representatives abroad did not understand or live close to the people they were sent to help. Lederer and Burdick added "A Factual Epilogue" differentiating fact and fiction in the book. A few years later Truman Capote's *In Cold Blood* (1965) appeared amid fanfare about the nonfiction novel. Once more the fictional use of fact, here a murder case, was hailed as an innovation. At the end of the book a note "About the Author" solemnly reported that Capote intended it to be "a contribution toward the establishment of a serious new literary form: the Nonfiction Novel." Critics joined the pontification. "The appearance of the 'nonfiction novel'," William Nance pronounced, "is a significant phenomenon on the American cultural scene" (238). Recently still another runaway best-selling story, only more nostalgic, has appeared in E. L. Doctorow's *Ragtime* (1975), which carries to its farthest point to date the novel mixing history and fiction. It combines several time-honored techniques of connecting imaginary characters and events to historical ones. Several of its themes closely resemble those of a superior novel published only three years earlier, Ishmael Reed's *Mumbo Jumbo,* which did not sell nearly so well. Journalistic chroniclers of culture have kept the public aware of these developments, reporting on "faction," or fiction based on fact, and "fictive nonfiction."[10]

One of the most apparently earnest, but also confusing and pretentious, of the efforts to combine journalism, history, and the novel is Norman Mailer's *The Armies of the Night.* He calls book one "History as a Novel: The Steps of the Pentagon," in which he presents a narrative with dialogue and characterization, referring to the author in the third person. At the end of the book he notes that it became a "history of himself over four days, and therefore was history in the costume of a novel." The next section will be a "concise Short History, a veritable précis of a collective novel," which "will seek as History, no, rather as some Novel of History, to elucidate the mysterious character of that quintessentially American event" (215-216). At the beginning of book two, called "The Novel as History: The Battle of the Pentagon," Mailer indicates that he is putting himself and the reader on a tower, enabling them to see further than the history permitted. The novel, "a telescope upon a tower," seems to correct false history and to provide meaning (219). It may be that Mailer is deliberately confusing, for halfway through book two he admits that he must abandon the pretense of writing a history and "will now unashamedly enter that world of strange lights and intuitive speculation which is the novel," because history reaches its limit and the "novel must replace history at precisely that point where experience is sufficiently emotional, spiritual, psychical, moral, existential, or supernatural" (255).

If Mailer is not merely setting out to confuse readers, he means that history tells merely what happened and can be told as a story. The novel, however, explains the meaning of the narrative. But Mailer confuses the categories and does not retain such a sharp division between the narrative and the explanation, which is perhaps his point. If so, it is an old one. Writing a social analysis of contemporary England, the enormously popular historical novelist Edward Bulwer-Lytton stated in 1833 that in this book he "wrote for the most part rather on causes, as in my fictions I have written rather on effects" (I, 8). He seems to have meant, like Mailer, that a history exposes conditions or facts, a novel explains them.

In these convergences, in various periods, the influences may go in either direction. Novelists and social thinkers find the germs of ideas in experience and all sorts of books, and some who resemble each other may both be responding to the same works of others. This seems to have been the case, for example, with Thorstein Veblen and Edith Wharton early in this century, especially in their treatment of the upper class — Veblen in *The Theory of the Leisure Class* (1899) and Wharton in *The House of Mirth* (1905), *The Custom of the Country* (1913), and *The Age of Innocence* (1920). Both considered this class from an anthropological viewpoint, stressing clan loyalty, ritual, matriarchy, unproductive roles, predation, power, money, and honor through sport and conflict. The main biographer of each, Joseph Dorfman and R. W. B. Lewis, does not mention the other, so there is perhaps no reason to believe that Veblen and Wharton exerted any mutual influence. As well-known contemporaries, they may have been only aware of each other's existence, yet almost certainly each was influenced by the same intellectual trends in evolutionary thought and anthropology.

Spheres of the Novel and Social Science

Plato observed a long time ago that "there is a long-standing quarrel between poetry and philosophy" (X. 606). It should be sobering to consider that this dispute, which is even now approached by the adversaries with eagerness and a sense of novelty, was already old stuff in ancient Greece. To say the least, there must be something fundamental in such a conflict; its continuation suggests that it meets a deep need among literary people, who appear to be the ones chiefly involved on both sides.

One example not too far back is the powerful attack by Thomas Love Peacock in 1820 upon Romantic poetry, in *The Four Ages of Poetry,* notwithstanding his friendship for and admiration of Shelley. Annoyed by the poetry of his own day, Peacock divided ancient and modern poetry into the ages of iron, gold, silver, and brass. At its origin, oral poetry mainly celebrated the chief warrior in an era when the sword was the nearest thing to law. Iron age poets were "the only historians and chroniclers of their time, and the sole depositories of all the knowledge of their age; and though this knowledge is rather a crude congeries of traditional phantasies than a collection of useful truths, yet, such as it is, they have it to themselves." In the golden age, "when something like a more extended system of civil polity is established," poetry is more artful but still "has no rivals in history, nor in philosophy, nor in science." Harking back to the themes of the previous age, it reaches perfection with Homer. As civilizaton and reason advance, however, "facts become more interesting than fiction," and thus the "maturity of poetry may be considered the infancy of history." The silver age repeats the most beautiful elements of experience, thereby becoming monotonous in its harmony. In this period of "civilized life," poetry is moving toward "extinction," for the "empire of thought is withdrawn from poetry, as the empire of facts had been before," leaving to silver-age poetry only a certain "polish and learning." Rejecting this excessive cultivation and seeking something new, the brass age "professes to return to nature and revive the age of gold"; this is the period of Roman decline. Peacock sees a repetition of these stages in the modern world, which in his lifetime, with the Romantic poets, is in another brass age. Poets now see nature "in a new light," cultivating such "phantasy only at the expense of the memory and the reason." They are "studiously ignorant of history, society, and human nature"; they retreat from the world to nature and end up not seeing or understanding either. "While the historian and the philosopher," Peacock concludes, "are advancing in, and accelerating, the progress of knowledge, the poet is wallowing in the rubbish of departed ignorance." Exaggerating to make his point, Peacock describes the poet as a "semi-barbarian in a civilized community" (3-16). His friend Shelley went to the "defense of poetry" but hardly against the particular indictment Peacock had made.

Peacock and Shelley were both literary men. The debate over science and literature reached another high point sixty years later in an exchange between a scientist, Thomas Huxley, and a poet, critic, and moralist, Matthew Arnold. In an essay collected in his *Essays in Criticism* in 1865, Arnold held that criticism of life was needed and that it required "a disinterested endeavor to learn and propagate the best that is known and thought in the world" (37). Huxley, in a lecture on "Science and Culture" in 1880, accused Arnold of believing that literature contained all that was needed. Huxley stressed the importance of science, advocating its introduction and enlargement throughout British education. He attacked the opponents of science education among the "practical men" who worshipped the "rule of thumb" and regarded science as "speculative rubbish," as well as among the humanists who defended the primacy of classical literature (137). Arnold, in *Discourses in America,* gave his reply. Not denying a place to science, Arnold nevertheless reaffirmed that literature should continue to predominate in the education of the general population, and he predicted that science would not replace it. Humane letters, he insisted, would always be needed to relate lives to beauty and even to show the place of modern science itself in the pursuit of right conduct.

Writing a half-century later, Max Eastman, a philosopher, radical journalist, poet, and critic, proclaimed that Arnold was wrong in both his sentiment and his prediction, for "scientific method" was already fast displacing humane letters "in the study of man himself" (10). To Eastman, this challenge of science explained the weakness of modern literary criticism, fiction, and poetry. As the natural sciences in the seventeenth century displaced poetry in knowledge of nature, so the psychological and social sciences, including Marxism, were in the twentieth century displacing literature in the knowledge of man.

As the 1960s approached, the old dispute broke out once more. C. P. Snow, trained in science and a writer of many novels, gave a lecture on "The Two Cultures and the Scientific Revolution" at Cambridge in 1959, in the same series in which Arnold had replied to Huxley in 1882. He deplored the lack of communication between scientists and "literary intellectuals." The latter regard the scientists as "brash and boastful," as well as "shallowly optimistic, unaware of man's condition," while the scientists "believe that the literary intellectuals are totally lacking in foresight, peculiarly unconcerned with their brother men, in a deep sense anti-intellectual." Snow found much of this mutual suspicion to be based on "misinterpretations which are dangerous," and he believed each group to be "impoverished" by its failure to see the value in the other's approach and achievements. He made a special plea' to the literary men to understand the role that the "scientific revolution" plays in reducing poverty and improving the condition of the world. Four years later Snow himself briefly reviewed the extraordinary controversy his lecture had touched off. He referred to a few articles by others and himself which had anticipated his lecture without arousing such a response. The response to his lecture was so great that Snow concluded that "a nerve had been touched almost simultaneously in different intellectual societies, in different parts of the world." He was right, for the nerve, though old and often touched, was still sensitive.

This dispute was only a prelude to the attack upon science in the 1960s. This attack raked over the old issues, but now the counterculture advocates ranged the traditional humanists with the scientists in a wholesale critique of reason and the intellectual establishment. Supported by college youth and members of the very intellectual community under attack, this movement found, perhaps coincidentally, a temporary ally in the scientific community. Thomas Kuhn, in *The Structure of Scientific Revolutions* (1962), supported new approaches that he described as a "historiographic revolution in the study of science, though one that is still in its early stages." Two important questions arose out of the difficulties encountered in the history of science. First, since it becomes increasingly difficult to say exactly who made certain discoveries in science and precisely when, some historians began to ask whether science really develops "by the accumulation of individual discoveries and inventions." Second, historians began to question the tendency of scientists to regard superseded beliefs about nature as "myths," for these "myths" were not so different from current science (2-3). "Observation and experience," Kuhn noted, "cannot alone determine" a scientific belief. "An apparently arbitrary element," he suggested, "compounded of personal and historical accident, is always a formative ingredient of the beliefs espoused by a given scientific community at a given time" (4). He also pointed to the importance of familiar "subjective and esthetic considerations" in the acceptance of new scientific theories or "paradigms," although he did not mean to "suggest that new paradigms triumph ultimately through some mystical esthetic" (156, 158). Yet he also asserted that "scientific training is not well designed to produce the man who will easily discover a fresh approach" (166).

Coming at a time when reason in both science and letters was under attack, these ideas were welcomed by many who challenged what they regarded as its restriction upon imagination and its support for the entire social setup. Kuhn's ideas were used in a wide variety of scholarship and even journalism to reduce the authority of science.[11] In a postscript of 1969, Kuhn noted the application of his ideas to many other fields, remarking that this was not surprising, for these ideas themselves had been "borrowed from other fields." What "puzzled" Kuhn, in this reaction of others, was that he had sought also to show that though "scientific development may resemble that in other fields more closely than has often been supposed, it is also strikingly different" (208-209). But the need supplied by some of Kuhn's ideas has precluded general understanding of all of them.

The persistence of the issues between science and literature should finally confirm that there are indeed two "cultures" and that their separate if related spheres should be recognized instead of trying to make them identical by fusing both or eliminating one. In one sense, the contest goes back to the seventeenth century "quarrel between the ancients and the moderns" in literature and thought, in which the moderns triumphed. It was a dispute between contemporaries, not between eras, and the advocates of modern freedom from the cult of the ancients won. One of their allies was the new physical science, and since then literature and science have seldom been on the same side. As so often happens, the toppling of one tyranny led to another, so that modernism became a cult fostering the notion that the new in art starts out with some kind of superiority over the old. This attitude disparages reason and thought no less than does the cult of antiquity. One must sympathize with scientists and artists, and with the general public, who in any generation want to express themselves in contemporary terms. But this impulse must not be allowed to denigrate earlier achievements and sources of understanding.

The world would seem to be doomed to struggles between extremes. The British scientist P. B. Medawar, for example, compares "poetism" to "scientism." The latter concept asserts that science can or will answer every question. Poetism, on the contrary, is "an aberration of imaginative literature" which assumes that all the answers are or will be produced by "imaginative insight and a mysteriously privileged sensibility" (23). Thus, many scholars and intellectuals find it impossible to hold two separate ideas on one theme at the same time. Certainly life of all kinds presents enough variety and complexity to warrant maintaining several ideas together. Medawar may be right when he argues that even though science and literature have "very important things to say" in many domains, they compete rather than cooperate. Probably, though, it is the theorists and critics who are competing, while most scientists and novelists are simply going about their separate tasks, each ignoring the other to the dismay of the articulate few who want to see them either joined or humbled.

The novel illuminates human behavior and social institutions without suppressing the imagination. Science, and especially social science, no matter what its contribution, has not yet eliminated a place for the novel, if only the theorists of literature and science will allow the novelists to occupy it confidently. There may be little that is new in this achievement of novels, speaking on a highly abstract level. From that height, there is unfortunately little that is new in social science either. Many modern novels suffer from the desire to be like science or to compete with it, instead of seeking, as Arnold suggested, to comprehend it, that is, both to understand and to include it, both as a human and social activity of the sort novels often deal with, and as a kind of knowledge that novelists, like the rest of humanity, must incorporate into their own view of things. Surely the novel is broad enough to make this effort. The point is not for the novel to imitate what it was in the nineteenth century or to try to be like the science of the twentieth. Rather, one would like to see it deal with the moral issues of today as successfully as so many earlier novelists did in their time, or indeed as such novelists as Forster, Silone, Cary, Wright, and Ellison have done in this century.

The need, as usual, is to achieve balance in an approach to life and in the attempts of science and literature to understand it. The science and literature of earlier times must be appreciated without stifling their growth in modern times. The separate spheres of science and literature must also be appreciated without trying to impose a spurious unity or to stir up a contest.

Bibliography

Notes

Index

Bibliography

This list includes only books and articles referred to in the text and footnotes. Where later editions are used, the year of first publication is given in parentheses following the title.

Aarsleff, Hans. "The State of Nature and the Nature of Man in Locke." *John Locke: Problems and Perspectives,* ed. John W. Yolton. Cambridge, Cambridge University Press, 1969.

Abercrombie, Lascelles. *Progress in Literature.* Cambridge, Cambridge University Press, 1929.

Achebe, Chinua. *No Longer at Ease.* London, Heinemann, 1960.

Adburgham, Alison. *Women in Print: Writing Women and Women's Magazines from the Restoration to the Accession of Victoria.* London, Allen and Unwin, 1972.

Albee, Edward. "The Death of Bessie Smith" (1959). *Three Plays.* New York, Coward-McCann, 1960.

Albertson, Chris. *Bessie.* New York, Stein and Day, 1972.

Alden, Raymond Macdonald. "The Doctrine of Verisimilitude in French and English Criticism of the Seventeenth Century." *Stanford University Publications. University Series,* no. 7, 1911, pp. 38-48.

Allott, Miriam, ed. *Novelists on the Novel.* London, Routledge and Kegan Paul, 1959.

Allsop, Kenneth. "Ignazio Silone." *Encounter,* March 1962, pp. 49-51.

Alter, Robert. *Fielding and the Nature of the Novel.* Cambridge, Harvard University Press, 1968.

————. *Partial Magic: The Novel as a Self-Conscious Genre.* Berkeley, Los Angeles, and London, University of California Press, 1975.

Anon. "The Plagiarisms of S. T. Coleridge." *Blackwood's Magazine* 47 (1840): 287-299.

Aristotle. "On the Art of Poetry." *Classical Literary Criticism,* tran. T. S. Dorsch. Harmondsworth, Eng., Penguin Books, 1965

Arnold, Matthew. *Discourses in America* (1885). New York, Macmillan, 1924.

————. *Essays in Criticism.* First Series (1865). New York, Macmillan, 1916.

Austen, Jane. *Emma* (1816). London, Oxford University Press, 1971.

————. *Fragment of a Novel* (also known as *Sanditon*). Oxford, Oxford University Press, 1925.

————. *Northanger Abbey* (1818). London, Oxford University Press, 1971.

————. *Pride and Prejudice* (1813). New York, Modern Library, 1950.

————. *Sense and Sensibility* (1811). New York, Modern Library, 1950.

Aydelotte, William O. "The England of Marx and Mill as Reflected in Fiction." *The Journal of Economic History,* Supplement 8 (1948), pp. 42-58.

Babbitt, Irving. *Masters of Modern French Criticism.* Boston, Houghton Mifflin, 1912.

Bacon, Francis. *The Advancement of Learning* (1605), ed. James Spedding et al. *The Works of Francis Bacon,* vol. 4. London, Longmans et al., 1860.

Ballantyne, Robert M. *The Coral Island* (1858). London, Everyman's Library, various editions.

Balzac, Honoré de. *Domestic Peace and Other Stories,* tran. M. A. Crawford. Harmondsworth, Eng., Penguin Books, 1958.

————. *Oeuvres Complètes de Honoré de Balzac. La Comédie Humaine,* ed. Marcel Bouteron and Henri Longnon. Vol. 1. *La Comédie Humaine,* 1912. Vol. 25. *Le Curé de Village* (1839), 1922. Vol. 29. *Les Employés* (1836), 1914. Vol 23. *Les Paysans* (1855), 1923. Paris, Conard, 1912-.

Barber, Bernard. *Social Stratification.* New York, Harcourt, Brace, 1957.

Barbey d'Aurevilly, J. A., ed. *H. de Balzac: Pensées et Maximes Recueillies et Classés* (1854). Paris, Alphonse Lemerre, 1909.

Barker, Ernest, ed. *Social Contract: Essays by Locke, Hume, and Rousseau.* Oxford, Oxford University Press, 1948.

Barzun, Jacques. "The Novel Turns Tale." *Mosaic* 4.3 (1971): 33-40.

―――. "Our Non-Fiction Novelists." *The Atlantic Monthly,* July 1946, pp. 129-132.

―――. *The Use and Abuse of Art.* Princeton, Princeton University Press, 1974.

Basch, Françoise. *Relative Creatures: Victorian Women in Society and the Novel,* tran. Anthony Rudolf. New York, Schocken, 1974.

Bate, Walter Jackson. *Coleridge.* New York, Macmillan, 1968.

Beach, Joseph Warren. *The Twentieth Century Novel* (1932). New York, Appleton-Century-Crofts, 1960.

Behn, Aphra. *Oroonoko: Or, The Royal Slave* (1688). *The Plays, Histories, and Novels of the Ingenious Mrs. Aphra Behn,* vol. 5. London, Pearson, 1871.

Bein, Alex. *Theodore Herzl: A Biography* (1941), tran. Maurice Samuel. New ed. London, East and West Library, 1957.

Bell, Thomas. *The Second Prince.* New York, Putnam, 1935.

Bellow, Saul. "Skepticism and the Depth of Life." *The Arts and Public Life,* ed. James E. Miller, Jr., and Paul D. Herring. Chicago, University of Chicago Press, 1968.

Berelson, Bernard, and Gary A. Steiner. *Human Behavior: An Inventory of Scientific Findings.* New York, Harcourt, Brace and World, 1964.

Berger, Morroe. *Equality By Statute: Legal Controls over Group Discrimination* (1952). Rev. ed. New York, Doubleday, 1967.

―――. "Thorstein Veblen's Literary Style." *Cairo Studies in English,* ed. Magdi Wahba, 1961-1962, pp. 17-35.

Bergonzi, Bernard. *The Situation of the Novel.* London, Macmillan, 1970.

Betsky, Seymour. "Society in Thackeray and Trollope." *From Dickens to Hardy,* ed. Boris Ford. Pelican Guide to English Literature, vol. 6. Baltimore, Penguin Books, 1964.

Birdwhistell, Ray L. *Kinesics and Context.* Philadelphia, University of Pennsylvania Press, 1970.

Blake, Fay M. *The Strike in the American Novel.* Metuchen, N. J., Scarecrow Press, 1972.

Blanchard, Frederic T. *Fielding the Novelist: A Study in Historical Criticism.* New Haven, Yale University Press, 1926.

Blodgett, Harriet. "Necessary Presence: The Rhetoric of the Narrator in *Vanity Fair.*" *Nineteenth-Century Fiction* 22 (1967): 211-223.

Blotner, Joseph. *The Modern American Political Novel, 1900-1960.* Austin, University of Texas Press, 1966.

Boas, George. "Il Faut Être de Son Temps." *The Journal of Aesthetics and Art Criticism* 1 (1941): 52-65.

Boorstin, Daniel J. *The Americans: The National Experience.* New York, Random House, 1965.

Booth, Wayne C. *The Rhetoric of Fiction.* Chicago, University of Chicago Press, 1961.

Bradbury, Malcolm. *The Social Context of Modern English Literature.* New York, Schocken, 1971.

Braudy, Leo. *Narrative Form in History and Fiction: Hume, Fielding and Gibbon.* Princeton, Princeton University Press, 1970.

Broch, Hermann. *The Sleepwalkers: A Trilogy,* tran. Willa and Edwin Muir. Boston, Little, Brown, 1932.

Broom, Leonard, and Philip Selznick. *Sociology: A Text with Adapted Readings.* 2nd ed. Evanston, Ill., Row, Peterson, 1958.

Bryant, Jerry H. *The Open Decision: The Contemporary American Novel and Its Intellectual Background.* New York, Free Press, 1970.

Bryson, Gladys. *Man and Society: The Scottish Inquiry of the Eighteenth Century.* Princeton, Princeton University Press, 1945.

Bullough, Edward. "Psychical Distance as a Factor in Art and as an Esthetic Principle" (1913). *A Modern Book of Esthetics* (1935), ed. Melvin Rader. 3rd ed. New York, Holt, Rinehart, and Winston, 1960.

Bulwer-Lytton, Edward. *England and the English.* New York, Harper, 1833.

Burke, Kenneth. *Counter-Statement.* New York, Harcourt, Brace, 1931.

Burton, Richard F. "Terminal Essay." *The Book of the Thousand Nights and a Night,* vol. 10. Privately Printed, The Burton Club, 1886.

Butterfield, Herbert. *The Historical Novel.* Cambridge, Cambridge University Press, 1924.

Campbell, Norman. *What Is Science?* London, Methuen, 1921.

Capote, Truman. *In Cold Blood.* New York, Random House, 1965.

Carroll, Kieran Joseph. *Some Aspects of the Thought of Augustin Thierry.* Washington, D.C., Catholic University of America Press, 1951.

Carter, A. E. *The Idea of Decadence in French Literature, 1830-1900.* Toronto, University of Toronto Press, 1958.

Cary, Joyce. *Mister Johnson* (1939). London, Joseph, 1952.

Cassinelli, C. W. "The Law of Oligarchy." *American Political Science Review* 47 (1953): 773-784.

Cazamian, Louis, *Le Roman Social en Angleterre (1830-1850)* (1934). New York, Russell and Russell, 1967.

Cervantes Saavedra, Miguel de. *Don Quijote de la Mancha* (1605, 1615), ed. Rodolfo Schevill and Adolfo Bonilla. Madrid, Gráficas Reunidas, 1928-1935.

Chapman, Raymond. *The Victorian Debate: English Literature and Society, 1832-1901.* London, Weidenfeld and Nicolson, 1968.

Chappelow, Allan. *Shaw—"The Chucker-Out."* London, Allen and Unwin, 1969.

Chassang, Alexis. *Histoire du Roman et de Ses Rapports avec l'Histoire dans l'Antiquité Grecque et Latine.* 2nd ed. Paris, Didier, 1862.

Chaudhuri, Nirad C. *The Continent of Circe.* New York, Oxford University Press, 1966.

Chilton, John. *Who's Who of Jazz.* London, Bloomsbury Book Shop, 1970.

Clor, Harry M. *Obscenity and Public Morality: Censorship in a Liberal Society.* Chicago, University of Chicago Press, 1969.

Clouard, Henri, ed. *Balzac, Pages Sociales et Politiques.* Paris, Nouvelle Librairie Nationale, 1910.

Clough, Shepard B. *The Rise and Fall of Civilization: An Enquiry into the Relationship Between Economic Development and Civilization.* New York, McGraw-Hill, 1951.

Cobban, Alfred. *Aspects of the French Revolution.* New York, Braziller, 1968.

————. *The Social Interpretation of the French Revolution.* Cambridge, Cambridge University Press, 1965.

Cockshut, A. O. J. *Anthony Trollope: A Critical Study.* London, Collins, 1955.

Cohen, Morris R. *American Thought.* Glencoe, Ill., Free Press, 1954.

————. *The Meaning of Human History.* La Salle, Ill., Open Court Press, 1947.

————. *A Preface to Logic.* New York, Holt, 1944.

Colby, Robert A. *Fiction with a Purpose.* Bloomington, Indiana University Press, 1967.

Colby, Vineta. *Yesterday's Woman: Domestic Realism in the English Novel.* Princeton, Princeton University Press, 1974.

Coleman, John. Review of *Exodus* by Leon Uris. *The Spectator,* July 10, 1959, p. 44.

Coleridge, Samuel Taylor. *Biographia Literaria* (1817), ed. J. Shawcross. Oxford, Oxford University Press, 1907.

————. *Complete Works of Samuel Taylor Coleridge*, ed. W. G. T. Shedd. New York, Shedd, Harper, 1853.

Condorcet, Marquis de. *Oeuvres de Condorcet*, vol. 6. *Esquisse d'un Tableau Historique des Progrès de l'Esprit Humain* (1795), ed. Arthur C. O'Connor and François Arago. Paris, Didot, 1847-1849.

Cook, Richard I. *Bernard Mandeville*. Boston, Twayne, 1974.

Coser, Lewis A., ed. *Sociology Through Literature*. Englewood Cliffs, N.J., Prentice-Hall, 1963.

Craig, David. "Towards Laws of Literary Development." *Mosaic* 5.2 (1971-1972): 11-30.

Crews, Frederick C. *The Sins of the Fathers: Hawthorne's Psychological Themes*. New York, Oxford University Press, 1966.

Cross, Wilbur L. *The History of Henry Fielding*. New Haven, Yale University Press, 1918.

Cruickshank, John, ed. *The Novelist as Philosopher: Studies in French Fiction, 1935-1960*. London, Oxford University Press, 1962.

Dabaghian, Jane, ed. *Mirror of Man: Readings in Sociology and Literature* (1970). 2nd ed. Boston, Little, Brown, 1975.

Daiches, David. "Society and the Artist." *New York Times Book Review,* Nov. 28, 1965.

Davis, David Brion. *Homicide in American Fiction, 1798-1860*. Ithaca, Cornell University Press, 1957.

————. "Violence in American Literature." *The Annals* 364 (1966): 28-36.

De Beer, Gavin. "Other Men's Shoulders." *Annals of Science* 20 (1964): 303-322.

Deegan, Dorothy Yost. *The Stereotype of the Single Woman in American Novels*. New York, King's Crown Press, 1951.

Defoe, Daniel. *Moll Flanders* (1722). *Defoe's Writings*. Published for Shakespeare Head Press: Oxford, Blackwell, 1927.

————. *Robinson Crusoe* (1719). *Defoe's Writings*. Published for Shakespeare Head Press: Oxford, Blackwell, 1927.

————. *A Treatise Concerning the Use and Abuse of the Marriage Bed* (1727). London, Clements, 1841.

De Voto, Bernard. *The Literary Fallacy*. Boston, Little, Brown, 1944.

Dewey, John. *Art as Experience*. New York, Minton, Balch, 1934.

Dickens, Charles. *A Cyclopedia of the Best Thoughts of Charles Dickens,* comp. F. G. de Fontaine. London, Hale, 1873.

————. *Hard Times* (1854). London, Chapman and Hall, 1911.

————. *The Life and Adventures of Nicholas Nickleby* (1839). London and New York, Everyman's Library, 1909.

Diderot, Denis. *Jacques the Fatalist and His Master* (1796), tran. J. Robert Loy. New York, New York University Press, 1959.

Dietrickson, Jan W. *The Image of Money in the American Novel of the Gilded Age.* New York, Humanities Press, 1969.

Dilworth, E. N. "Fielding and Coleridge: 'Poetic Faith.' " *Notes and Queries* n.s.5 (1958): 35-37.

Disraeli, Benjamin (Earl of Beaconsfield). *Sybil, or The Two Nations.* London, Colburn, 1845.

————. *Tancred, or The New Crusade* (1847). London, Longmans, Green, 1907.

Dobrée, Bonamy. *English Literature in the Early Eighteenth Century, 1700-1740.* Oxford, Oxford University Press, 1959.

Doctorow, E. L. *Ragtime.* New York, Randon House, 1975.

Dollard, John. *Caste and Class in a Southern Town* (1937). 2nd ed. New York, Harper, 1949.

Dorfman, Joseph. *Thorstein Veblen and His America.* New York, Viking, 1934.

Dos Passos, John. *U.S.A.* (1930, 1932, 1936). New York, Modern Library, 1939.

Dostoyevsky, Fyodor. *The Brothers Karamazov* (1880), tran. Constance Garnett. New York, Modern Library, 1937.

Durrell, Lawrence. *Mountolive.* New York, Dutton, 1959.

Earnest, Ernest. *The American Eve in Fact and Fiction, 1775-1914.* Urbana, University of Illinois Press, 1974.

Eastman, Max. *The Literary Mind.* New York, Scribner, 1931.

Eaves, T. C. Duncan, and Ben D. Kimpel. *Samuel Richardson: A Biography.* Oxford, Oxford University Press, 1971.

Egbert, Donald Drew. *Social Radicalism and the Arts: Western Europe.* New York, Knopf, 1970.

Eliot, George. *Adam Bede* (1859). London, Everyman's Library, 1960.

————. *Daniel Deronda* (1876). Boston, Estes, 1885.

————. *Essays of George Eliot,* ed. Thomas Pinney. New York, Columbia University Press, 1963.

————. *Felix Holt, The Radical* (1866). *The Works of George Eliot,* vols. 15-16. Boston, Small and Maynard, n.d. (c. 1908-1910).

————. *The George Eliot Letters,* ed. Gordon S. Haight. New Haven, Yale University Press, 1954-1955.

————. *Impressions of Theophrastus Such* (1879). *The Writings of George Eliot,* vol. 4. Boston, Little, Brown, 1900.

————. *Middlemarch* (1872). Boston, Estes, 1885.

————. *The Mill on the Floss* (1860). London, Longmans, 1960.

————. *Scenes of Clerical Life* (1858). Boston, Small, Maynard, 1908.

————. *Wise, Witty, and Tender Sayings in Prose and Verse Selected from the Works of George Eliot,* ed. Alexander Main. London, Blackwood, 1872.

————. *Wit and Wisdom of George Eliot.* Boston, Roberts Brothers, 1876, 1881.

Eliot, T. S. "The Function of Criticism." *English Critical Essays: Twentieth Century,* ed. Derek Hudson. London, Oxford University Press, 1958.

Ellison, Ralph. *Invisible Man.* New York, Random House, 1952.

Ellmann, Richard. *James Joyce* (1959). New York, Oxford University Press, 1965.

————, and Charles Feidelson, Jr., eds. *The Modern Tradition.* New York, Oxford University Press, 1965.

Ephron, Nora. "Yossarian Is Alive and Well in the Mexican Desert." *New York Times Magazine,* Mar. 16, 1969.

Epstein, E. L. "Notes on *Lord of the Flies*," in William Golding, *Lord of the Flies,* New York, Putnam, 1959.

Erikson, Erik H. *Identity: Youth and Crisis.* New York, Norton, 1968.

Felix, David. *Protest: Sacco-Vanzetti and the Intellectuals.* Bloomington, Indiana University Press, 1965.

Feuer, Lewis S. *Einstein and the Generations of Science.* New York, Basic Books, 1974.

Fielding, Henry. *The Complete Works of Henry Fielding,* ed. William Ernest Henley. Vols. 6-7. *Amelia* (1751) Vol. 13. *An Inquiry into the Causes of the late Increase of Robbers, Etc.* (1751) Vol. 14. "An Essay on the Knowledge of the Characters of Men" (1743), *Miscellaneous Writings* Vol. 2. *The History of the Life of the late Mr. Jonathan Wild* (1743) Vols. 3-5. *The History of Tom Jones* (1749). London, Heinemann, 1903.

————. *Joseph Andrews* (1742), ed. Martin C. Battestin. Middletown, Wesleyan University Press, 1967.

Fitzgerald, F. Scott. *The Crack-Up.* New York, New Directions, 1945.

————. *Tender is the Night.* New York, Scribner, 1934.

Flaubert, Gustave. *Correspondance,* vols. 2, 4-5. *Oeuvres Complètes de Gustave Flaubert.* Paris, Conard, 1926, 1927, 1929.

————. Preface to "Dernières Chansons." *Oeuvres de Louis Bouilhet.* Paris, Lemerre, 1881.

Fogel, Robert William, and Stanley L. Engerman. *Time on the Cross.* Boston, Little, Brown, 1974.

Ford, George H. *Dickens and His Readers.* Princeton, Princeton University Press, 1955.

Forster, E. M. *Aspects of the Novel* (1927). New York, Harcourt, Brace, 1947.

_____. *Howards End.* New York and London, Putnam, 1910.

_____. *A Room with a View* (1908). Norfolk, Conn., New Directions, 1943.

Forsyth, William. *The Novels and Novelists of the Eighteenth Century, in Illustration of the Manners and Morals of the Age.* New York, Appleton, 1871.

Franklin, Benjamin. *Autobiography* (1791). New Haven, Yale University Press, 1964.

Fredman, Alice Green. *Diderot and Sterne.* New York, Columbia University Press, 1955.

Friedman, Norman. "Point of View in Fiction: The Development of a Critical Concept." *Publications of the Modern Language Association* 70 (1955): 1160-1184.

Fruman, Norman. *Coleridge, the Damaged Archangel.* New York, Braziller, 1971.

Gaines, Francis Pendleton. *The Southern Plantation: A Study in the Development and the Accuracy of a Tradition.* New York, Columbia University Press, 1925.

Galbraith, John Kenneth. *The Affluent Society.* Boston, Houghton Mifflin, 1958.

Gallie, W. B. *Philosophy and the Historical Understanding.* New York, Schocken, 1964.

Galsworthy, John. *The Island Pharisees.* New York, Putnam, 1904.

Gerschenkron, Alexander. *Economic Backwardness in Historical Perspective.* Cambridge, Harvard University Press, 1966.

Gissing, George. *The House of Cobwebs and Other Stories.* London, Constable, 1906.

_____. *The Private Papers of Henry Ryecroft* (1903). New York, Modern Library, n.d.

Glasgow, Ellen. *A Certain Measure.* New York, Harcourt, Brace, 1943.

_____. *The Sheltered Life.* New York, Doubleday, 1932.

Goethe, Johann Wolfgang von. *Words of Goethe: Being the Conversations of Johann Wolfgang von Goethe Recorded by His Friend Johann Peter Eckermann* (1836, 1842). New York, Classic, 1933.

Goffman, Erving. *Behavior in Public Places.* New York, Free Press, 1963.

_____. *Relations in Public.* New York, Basic Books, 1971.

Golding, William. *Lord of the Flies.* New York, Coward-McCann, 1955.

Goldknopf, David. *The Life of the Novel.* Chicago, University of Chicago Press, 1972.

Gough, J. W. *The Social Contract: A Critical Study of Its Development* (1936). 2nd ed. Oxford, Oxford University Press, 1957.

Gove, Philip Babcock. *The Imaginary Voyage in Prose Fiction.* New York, Columbia University Press, 1941.

Grabo, Carl H. *The Technique of the Novel.* New York, Scribner, 1928.

Green, T. H. "The Value and Influence of Works of Fiction" (1862). *Works of Thomas Hill Green,* ed. R. L. Nettleship, vol. 3. 3rd ed. London, Longmans, Green, 1891.

Greene, Graham. *The Quiet American.* London, Heinemann, 1955.

Guerard, Albert J. "Hardy and the Modern Reader: A Revaluation" (1949). In Thomas Hardy, *Tess of the d'Urbervilles.* New York, Norton Critical Editions, 1965.

Guyau, Marie-Jean. *L'Art au Point de Vue Sociologique* (1889). 4th ed. Paris, Alcan, 1897.

Haight, Gordon S. *George Eliot: A Biography.* New York, Oxford University Press, 1968.

————, ed. *The George Eliot Letters.* New Haven, Yale University Press, 1954-1955.

Hardy, Thomas. *Far from the Madding Crowd* (1874). New York, Harper, 1905.

————. *Jude the Obscure* (1895). London, Macmillan, 1920.

————. *The Life of Thomas Hardy, 1840-1928,* comp. Florence Emily Hardy. London, Macmillan, 1962.

————. *The Mayor of Casterbridge* (1886). Harper, New York, 1922.

————. *The Return of the Native* (1878). New York, Harper, 1895.

————. *The Selected Writings of Thomas Hardy,* ed. Irving Howe. New York, Fawcett, 1966.

————. *Tess of the d'Urbervilles* (1891). New York, Harper, 1892.

————. *The Woodlanders* (1887). Harper, New York, 1896.

Harris, Neil. *The Artist in American Society: The Formative Years, 1790-1860.* New York, Braziller, 1966.

Hatfield, Glenn W. *Henry Fielding and the Language of Irony.* Chicago, University of Chicago Press, 1968.

Hawthorne, Nathaniel. *The Blithedale Romance* (1852). Columbus, Ohio State University Press, 1964.

————. *The House of the Seven Gables* (1851). Columbus, Ohio State University Press, 1965.

Haywood, Eliza. *The Tea-Table*. London, Roberts, 1725.

Hazelrigg, Lawrence E., ed. *Prison Within Society: A Reader in Penology*. New York, Doubleday, 1968.

Hegel, G. W. F. *On Art, Religion, Philosophy* (1820), ed. J. Glenn Gray, tran. Bernard Bosanquet. New York, Harper Torchbooks, 1970.

Henkin, Leo J. *Darwinism in the English Novel, 1860-1910*. New York, Corporate Press, 1940.

Herzl, Theodore. *The Diaries of Theodore Herzl*, ed. and tran. Marvin Lowenthal. New York, Dial, 1956.

Hicks, Granville. "Marquand of Newburyport." *Harper's Magazine*, April 1950, pp. 101-108.

Highet, Gilbert. *A Clerk of Oxenford: Essays on Literature and Life*. New York, Oxford University Press, 1954.

Hill, Christopher. *Puritanism and Revolution*. London, Secker and Warburg, 1958.

Hills, Penney Chapin, and L. Rust Hills, eds. *How We Live: Contemporary Life in Contemporary Fiction*. New York, Macmillan, 1968.

Himes, Chester B. *If He Hollers Let Him Go*. New York, Doubleday, Doran, 1945.

Hobbes, Thomas. *Leviathan* (1651). Oxford, Oxford University Press, 1909.

Hoggart, Richard. *Speaking to Each Other*. New York, Oxford University Press, 1970.

Horace. "On the Art of Poetry." *Classical Literary Criticism*, tran. T. S. Dorsch. Harmondsworth, Eng., Penguin Books, 1965.

Hornbeak, Katherine. "Richardson's Familiar Letters and the Domestic Conduct Books." *Smith College Studies in Modern Languages* 19 (1938): 1-29.

Horne, C. J. "Literature and Science." *From Dryden to Johnson,* ed. Boris Ford. Pelican Guide to English Literature, vol. 4. Baltimore, Penguin Books, 1957.

Horner, Joyce M. *The English Women Novelists and Their Connection with the Feminist Movement (1688-1797)*. Smith College Studies in Modern Languages, vol. 11. Northampton, 1929-1930.

Hospers, John. "Implied Truths in Literature." *Philosophy Looks at the Arts,* ed. Joseph Margolis. New York, Scribner, 1962.

————. *Meaning and Truth in the Arts*. Chapel Hill, University of North Carolina Press, 1946.

Howe, Irving. *Politics and the Novel*. New York, Horizon Press, 1957.

Howells, William Dean. *Literature and Life*. New York, Harper, 1902.

Hubbell, Jay B. *Southern Life in Fiction.* Athens, University of Georgia Press, 1960.

Hunter, Paul. *The Reluctant Pilgrim.* Baltimore, The Johns Hopkins Press, 1966.

Huxley, Aldous. *Brave New World.* New York, Doubleday, 1932.

———. *Brave New World Revisited.* New York, Harper, 1958.

Huxley, Thomas H. *Science and Education: Essays* (1893). New York, Appleton, 1910.

Ibn Tufayl, Abu Bakr Muhammad. *The History of Hayy Ibn Yaqzan,* tran. Simon Ackley, rev. A. S. Fulton. London, Chapman and Hall, 1929. Also tran. Lenn Evan Goodman. New York, Twayne, 1972.

Iknayan, Marguerite. *The Idea of the Novel in France: The Critical Reaction, 1815-1848.* Geneva, Droz, 1961.

Jamalzadeh, Muhammad Ali. Preface to *Yiki Bud, Yiki Nabud* (Once upon a Time), tran. Haideh Daraghi. *The Literary Review* 18 (1974): 18-37.

James, Henry. *The Art of the Novel: Critical Prefaces,* intro. R. P. Blackmur. New York, Scribner, 1947.

———. *The Future of the Novel,* ed. Leon Edel. New York, Vintage, 1956.

———. "The Real Thing" (1893). *Stories of Artists and Writers.* New York, New Directions, 1944.

Jeffares, A. Norman. *Language, Literature and Science.* Cambridge, Eng., Leeds University Press, 1959.

Johnson, Edgar. "Scott and the Corners of Time." *Scott Bicentenary Essays,* ed. Alan Bell. Edinburgh and London, Scottish Academic Press, 1973.

Johnson, Samuel. *The Rambler,* no. 4, Mar. 31, 1750. *Novel and Romance, 1700-1800: A Documentary Record,* ed. Ioan Williams. New York, Barnes and Noble, 1970.

Jones, Ernest. *The Life and Work of Sigmund Freud.* New York, Basic Books, 1953-1957.

Jones, William Powell. *The Rhetoric of Science.* Berkeley and Los Angeles, University of California Press, 1966.

Joughin, G. Louis, and Edmund M. Morgan. *The Legacy of Sacco and Vanzetti.* New York, Harcourt, Brace, 1948.

Joyce, James. *A Portrait of the Artist as a Young Man* (1916). New York, Viking, 1964.

Kafka, Franz. *The Trial* (1925), tran. Willa and Edwin Muir. New York, Knopf, 1937.

Kakonis, Thomas E., and Barbara G. T. Desmarais, eds. *The Literary Artist as Social Critic.* Beverly Hills, Glencoe Press, 1969.

Kanin, Garson. *Remembering Mr. Maugham.* New York, Atheneum, 1966.

Kanter, Rosabeth Moss. *Commitment and Community.* Cambridge, Harvard University Press, 1972.

Karl, Frederick R. *The Adversary Culture: The English Novel in the Eighteenth Century.* New York, Farrar, Straus and Giroux, 1974.

Katz, Elihu, and Paul F. Lazarsfeld. *Personal Influence.* Glencoe, Ill., Free Press, 1955.

Kaul, A. N. *The American Vision: Actual and Ideal Society in Nineteenth-Century Fiction.* New Haven, Yale University Press, 1963.

Kellett, E. E. "The Press." *Early Victorian England, 1830-1865,* ed. G. M. Young, vol. 2. London, Oxford University Press, 1934.

Kerr, Walter. " 'Inquest': Kerr Votes Against It." *The New York Times,* May 3, 1970, sec. 2, p. 3.

Kipling, Rudyard. *Kim* (1901). New York, Doubleday, Page, 1920.

Kirby, Michael, ed. *Happenings: An Illustrated Anthology.* New York, Dutton, 1966.

Klapper, Joseph T. "Communication, Mass: Effects." *International Encyclopedia of the Social Sciences,* vol. 3. New York, Macmillan and Free Press, 1968.

————. *The Effects of Mass Communication.* Glencoe, Ill., Free Press, 1960.

Koestler, Arthur. "Literature and the Law of Diminishing Returns." *Encounter,* May 1970, pp. 39-45.

Krook, Dorothea. *The Ordeal of Consciousness in Henry James.* Cambridge, Cambridge University Press, 1962.

Kuhn, Thomas S. *The Structure of Scientific Revolutions* (1962). 2nd ed. Chicago, University of Chicago Press, 1970.

Ladd, Everett Carll, Jr., and Seymour Martin Lipset. *The Divided Academy: Professors and Politics.* New York, McGraw-Hill, 1975.

Lawrence, D. H. *Sons and Lovers* (1913). New York, Modern Library, n.d.

Lazarsfeld, Paul F., and Robert K. Merton. "Mass Communication, Popular Taste and Organized Social Action." *The Communication of Ideas,* ed. Lyman Bryson. New York, Harper, 1948.

Leavis, F. R., and Q. D. Leavis. *Lectures in America.* London, Chatto and Windus, 1969.

Lederer, William J., and Eugene Burdick. *The Ugly American.* New

York, Norton, 1958.

Legman, Gershon. *Love and Death: A Study in Censorship*. New York, Breaking Point, 1949.

Leith, James A. *The Idea of Art as Propaganda in France, 1750-1799*. Toronto, University of Toronto Press, 1965.

Leonard, Irving A. *Books of the Brave*. Cambridge, Harvard University Press, 1949.

Lesser, Simon. *Fiction and the Unconscious*. Boston, Beacon Press, 1957.

Lewis, Oscar. *La Vida: A Puerto Rican Family in the Culture of Poverty*. New York, Random House, 1966.

Lewis, R. W. B. *Edith Wharton: A Biography*. New York, Harper and Row, 1975.

Lewis, Sinclair. *Babbitt*. New York, Harcourt, Brace, 1922.

––––––. *Elmer Gantry* (1927). New York, Harcourt, Brace, 1928.

Liebow, Elliot. *Tally's Corner: A Study of Negro Streetcorner Men*. Boston, Little, Brown, 1967.

Lifschitz, Michail, ed. *Karl Marx-Friedrich Engels uber Kunst und Literatur*. Berlin, Henschelverlag, 1953.

Lippmann, Walter. *Public Opinion*. New York, Harcourt, Brace, 1922.

Locke, John. *Essay Concerning Human Understanding* (1690), ed. John W. Yolton. London, Everyman's Library, 1964.

––––––. *Of Civil Government (Two Treatises of Government)* (1690). London, Everyman's Library, 1924.

Lowell, James Russell. "Disraeli as a Novelist" (1847). *The Round Table*. Boston, Gorham Press, 1913.

Lubbock, Percy. *The Craft of Fiction*. London, Cape, 1921.

Lukacs, Georg. *Studies in European Realism*. New York, Grosset and Dunlap, 1964.

Lukacs, John. *History and Consciousness*. New York, Harper and Row, 1968.

Lundberg, George A. *Can Science Save Us?* (1947). 2nd ed. New York, Longmans, Green, 1961.

Lynn, Kenneth, "Violence in American Literature and Folklore." *Violence in America: Historical and Comparative Perspectives. A Report Submitted to the National Commission on the Causes and Prevention of Violence*, ed. Hugh Davis Graham and Ted Robert Gurr. New York, Bantam Books, 1969.

Macdonald, Margaret. "The Language of Fiction." *Belief and Will*, Aristotelian Society, London, supp. 28 (1954): 165-184.

Mach, Ernst. *Popular Scientific Lectures* (1894), trans. Thomas J. McCormack. Chicago, Open Court, 1898.

MacIver, R. M. *Social Causation*. Boston, Ginn, 1942.

MacLean, Kenneth. "Imagination and Sympathy: Sterne and Adam Smith." *Journal of the History of Ideas* 10 (1949): 399-410.

_____. *John Locke and English Literature of the Eighteenth Century*. New Haven, Yale University Press, 1936.

Mailer, Norman. *The Armies of the Night: History as a Novel. The Novel as History*. New York, New American Library, 1968.

Malamud, Bernard. *The Fixer*. New York, Farrar, Straus and Giroux, 1966.

Mandelbaum, Maurice. "A Note on History as Narrative." *History and Theory* 6 (1967): 413-419.

Mandeville, Bernard. *An Enquiry into the Causes of the Frequent Executions at Tyburn* (1725), intro. Malvin R. Zirker, Jr. Augustan Reprint Society, no. 105. Los Angeles, 1964.

_____. *The Fable of the Bees* (1714), ed. F. B. Kaye. Oxford, Oxford University Press, 1924.

_____. *The Virgin Unmask'd: or, Female Dialogues Betwixt an Elderly Maiden Lady, and Her Niece*. London, Morphew and Woodward, 1709.

Mann, Thomas. *Buddenbrooks* (1901), tran. H. T. Lowe-Porter. New York, Knopf, 1964.

_____. *Doctor Faustus* (1947), tran. H. T. Lowe-Porter. New York, Knopf, 1948.

_____. *The Magic Mountain* (1924), tran. H. T. Lowe-Porter. New York, Knopf, 1927.

_____. *The Story of a Novel: The Genesis of Doctor Faustus* (1949), tran. R. and C. Winston. New York, Knopf, 1961.

Mannoni, O. *Prospero and Caliban: The Psychology of Colonization* (1950), tran. Pamela Powesland. New York, Praeger, 1964.

Marcus, Steven. *The Other Victorians*. New York, Basic Books, 1966.

Margolis, Joseph. *The Languages of Art and Art Criticism*. Detroit, Wayne State University Press, 1965.

Marquand, John P. *Point of No Return*. Boston, Little, Brown, 1949.

Martineau, Harriet. "Achievements of the Genius of Scott" (1832). *Miscellanies*. Boston, Hilliard, Gray, 1836.

_____. *Harriet Martineau's Autobiography*, ed. Maria Weston. Boston, Osgood, 1877.

_____. *Illustrations of Political Economy*. London, Charles Fox, 1834.

_____. *Poor Laws and Paupers Illustrated*. London, Charles Fox, 1833-1834.

_____. *The Positive Philosophy of Auguste Comte: Freely Translated and Condensed by Harriet Martineau.* New York, Appleton, 1854.

Masterman, C. F. G. *The Condition of England.* London, Methuen, 1909.

Maugham, W. Somerset. *Cakes and Ale.* New York, Doubleday, Doran, 1930.

———. *The Summing Up.* New York, Doubleday, 1938.

Maurois, André. *Prometheus: The Life of Balzac,* tran. Norman Denny. New York, Harper and Row, 1966.

Mayfield, Julian. *The Grand Parade.* New York, Vanguard, 1961.

Mayo, Robert D. *The English Novel in the Magazines, 1740-1815.* Evanston, Ill., and London, Northwestern University Press, 1962.

Mebane, Mary E. "Daddy Wasn't a Numbers Runner." *The New York Times,* Feb. 18, 1971, p. 35.

Medawar, P. B. "Science and Literature." *Encounter,* January 1969, pp. 15-23.

Melville, Herman. *Moby Dick* (1851). New York, Oxford University Press, 1947.

Merton, Robert K. *Social Theory and Social Structure.* New York, Free Press, 1968.

———. "The Unanticipated Consequences of Purposive Social Action." *American Sociological Review* 1 (1936): 894-904.

Michels, Robert. *Political Parties* (1911), tran. Eden and Cedar Paul. Glencoe, Ill., Free Press, 1949.

Mills, C. Wright. *The Sociological Imagination.* New York, Oxford University Press, 1959.

———. *White Collar: The American Middle Classes.* New York, Oxford University Press, 1951.

Milstead, John W., et al., eds. *Sociology Through Science Fiction.* New York, St. Martin's, 1974.

Miner, Ward L. *The World of William Faulkner* (1952). New York, Cooper Square, 1963.

Mittelholzer, Edgar. *Sylvia* (1953). London, New English Library, 1963.

Monro, Hector. *The Ambivalence of Bernard Mandeville.* London, Oxford University Press, 1975.

Montaigne, Michel de. *The Complete Works of Montaigne,* ed. and tran. Donald M. Frame. Stanford, Stanford University Press, 1957.

Moore, John Robert. "The Tempest and Robinson Crusoe." *Review of English Studies* 21 (1945): 52-56.

Moore, L. Hugh. *Robert Penn Warren and History.* The Hague and Paris, Mouton, 1970.

Moravia, Alberto. *The Lie* (1965), tran. Angus Davidson. New York, Farrar, Straus and Giroux, 1966.

Moreno, J. L., et al., eds. *The Sociometry Reader.* Glencoe, Ill., Free Press, 1960.

Morgan, Charlotte E. *The Rise of the Novel of Manners.* New York, Columbia University Press, 1911.

Morris, Wright. "How Things Are." *The Arts and the Public,* ed. James E. Miller, Jr., and Paul D. Herring. Chicago, University of Chicago Press, 1967.

Munroe, David. "Sir Walter Scott and the Development of Historical Writing." *Queen's Quarterly* 45 (1938): 216-227.

Mylne, Vivienne. *The Eighteenth-Century French Novel.* New York, Barnes and Noble, 1965.

Nagel, Ernest. *The Structure of Science.* New York, Harcourt, Brace, 1961.

Nance, William L. *The Worlds of Truman Capote.* New York, Stein and Day, 1970.

Neal, John. *Randolph.* Baltimore, "Published for Whom It May Concern," 1823.

Neill, Robert. "The Historical Novelist." *The Writer in the Market Place,* ed. Raymond Astbury. London, Bingley, 1969.

Nelson, William. *William Golding's Lord of the Flies: A Source Book.* New York, Odyssey Press, 1963.

Nisbet, Robert A. *Tradition and Revolt.* New York, Random House, 1968.

Norris, Frank. *The Responsibilities of the Novelist.* New York, Doubleday, Doran, 1928.

Novak, Maximillian E. *Defoe and the Nature of Man.* Oxford, Oxford University Press, 1963.

————. *Economics and the Fiction of Daniel Defoe.* Berkeley and Los Angeles, University of California Press, 1962.

Orwell, George. *Nineteen Eighty-Four.* New York, Harcourt, Brace, 1949.

Oswalt, Wendell H. *Other Peoples, Other Customs: World Ethnography and Its History.* New York, Holt, Rinehart and Winston, 1972.

Pagès, Alphonse, ed. *Balzac Moraliste.* Paris, Levy, 1866.

Parker, De Witt H. *The Analysis of Art.* New Haven, Yale University Press, 1926.

Parkinson, C. Northcote. *Parkinson's Law or the Pursuit of Progress.* London, Murray, 1958.

Patterson, Charles I. "Coleridge's Conception of Dramatic Illusion in the Novel." *ELH* 18 (1951): 123-137.

Peacock, Thomas Love. *Peacock's Four Ages of Poetry, Shelley's Defense of Poetry, Browning's Essay on Shelley*, ed. H. F. B. Brett-Smith. Oxford, Blackwell, 1937.

Peckham, Morse. *Man's Rage for Chaos*. Philadelphia, Chilton Books, 1965.

Pelles, Geraldine. *Art, Artists and Society*. Englewood Cliffs, N.J., Prentice-Hall, 1963.

Peterson, Theodore. *Magazines in the Twentieth Century*. Urbana, University of Illinois Press, 1964.

Peytel, Adrien. *Balzac Juriste Romantique*. Paris, Ponsot, 1950.

Pinion, F. B. *A Hardy Companion: A Guide to the Works of Thomas Hardy and Their Background*. London, Macmillan, 1968.

Plath, Sylvia. *The Bell Jar*. New York, Harper and Row, 1971.

Plato. *The Republic,* tran. F. M. Cornford (1941). New York, Oxford University Press, 1945.

Pope, Alexander. *Literary Criticism of Alexander Pope,* ed. Bertrand A. Goldgar. Lincoln, University of Nebraska Press, 1965.

Powell, Chilton Latham. *English Domestic Relations, 1487-1653*. New York, Columbia University Press, 1917.

Proust, Marcel. *The Guermantes Way* (1920-1921), tran. C. K. Scott Moncrieff. New York, Modern Library, 1933.

———. *The Past Recaptured* (1928), tran. Frederick A. Blossom. New York, Boni, 1932.

Raban, Jonathan. *The Techniques of Modern Fiction* (1968). Notre Dame, University of Notre Dame Press, 1969.

Rabinowitz, Dorothy, and Yedida Nielsen. *Home: A Story of Old Age*. New York, Macmillan, 1971.

Raper, J. R. *Without Shelter: The Early Career of Ellen Glasgow*. Baton Rouge, Louisiana State University Press, 1971.

Read, Herbert. *The Grass Roots of Art*. New York, Wittenborn, 1947.

Reed, Ishmael. *Mumbo-Jumbo*. New York, Doubleday, 1972.

Richardson, Samuel. "Advice to Unmarried Ladies." *The Rambler,* no. 97, Feb. 19, 1751. London, 1800.

———. *Clarissa* (1747-1748). London, Everyman's Library. 1967.

———. *Familiar Letters on Important Occasions* (1741), ed. Brian W. Downs. London, Routledge, 1928.

Rickel, Harry, ed. *The Wisdom of Balzac*. New York, Putnam, 1923.

Riedel, Frederick Carl. *Crime and Punishment in the Old French Romances*. New York, Columbia University Press, 1938.

Robbe-Grillet, Alain. *For a New Novel,* tran. Richard Howard. New York, Grove Press, 1965.

———. *Two Novels by Robbe-Grillet: Jealousy* (1957), trans. Richard Howard. New York, Grove Press, 1965.

Robbins, Frank E. "Chronology and History in Trollope's Barset and Parliamentary Novels." *Nineteenth-Century Fiction* 5 (1951): 303-316.

Roberts, Warren. *Morality and Social Class in Eighteenth-Century French Literature and Painting.* Toronto, University of Toronto Press, 1974.

Roby, Kinley E. "Irony and the Narrative Voice in *Howards End."* The *Journal of Narrative Technique* 2 (1972): 116-123.

Rockwell, Joan. *Fact in Fiction: The Use of Literature in the Systematic Study of Society.* London, Routledge and Kegan Paul, 1974.

Rogers, Pat. *Grub Street: Studies in a Subculture.* London, Methuen, 1972.

Rosenbaum, S. P., ed. *English Literature and British Philosophy.* Chicago, University of Chicago Press, 1971.

Ross, Stephen D. *Literature and Philosophy.* New York, Appleton-Century-Crofts, 1969.

Roszak, Theodore. *The Making of a Counter Culture.* New York, Doubleday, 1969.

Rubin, Louis D., Jr. *The Teller in the Tale.* Seattle, University of Washington Press, 1967.

Russell, Francis. *Tragedy in Dedham: The Story of the Sacco-Vanzetti Case* (1962). New York, McGraw-Hill, 1971.

Rustow, Dankwart A., ed. *Philosophers and Kings: Studies in Leadership.* New York, Braziller, 1970.

Sacks, Sheldon. *Fiction and the Shape of Belief.* Berkeley and Los Angeles, University of California Press, 1964.

Sale, William Merritt, Jr. *Samuel Richardson: A Bibliographical Record of His Literary Career with Historical Notes.* New Haven, Yale University Press, 1936.

Samuel, Maurice. *Blood Accusation: The Strange History of the Beiliss Case.* New York, Knopf, 1966.

Sarraute, Nathalie. *The Age of Suspicion: Essays on the Novel* (1956), tran. Maria Jolas. New York, Braziller, 1963.

———. *Tropisms,* tran. Maria Jolas. New York, Braziller, 1963.

Sartre, Jean-Paul. *What Is Literature?* tran. Bernard Frechtman. New York, Philosophical Library, 1949.

Schapiro, Meyer. "Style" (1953). *Aesthetics Today,* ed. Morris Philipson. New York, World, 1961.

Scheflen, Albert E., and Alice. *Body Language and the Social Order.* Englewood Cliffs, N.J., Prentice-Hall, 1972.

Schneider, Daniel J. "Techniques of Cognition in Modern Fiction." *The Journal of Aesthetics and Art Criticism* 26 (1968): 317-328.

Schneider, Louis, ed. *The Scottish Moralists on Human Nature.* Chicago, University of Chicago Press, 1967.

Schur, Edwin M. *Labeling Deviant Behavior.* New York, Harper and Row, 1971.

Scott, Sir Walter. "Essay on Romance" (1824). *Miscellaneous Prose Works,* vol. 6. Edinburgh, Cadell, 1827.

————. *The Lives of the Novelists* (1821). London, Everyman's Library, various dates.

————. Review of *Emma* by Jane Austen (1815). *Novelists on the Novel,* ed. Miriam Allott. London, Routledge and Kegan Paul, 1959.

Scriven, Michael. "The Language of Fiction." *Belief and Will,* Aristotelian Society, London, supp. 28 (1954): 185-196.

Scudder, Vida. *Social Ideals in English Letters* (1898). New York, Johnson Reprint, 1969.

Sedlmayr, Hans. *Art in Crisis: The Lost Center* (1953), tran. Brian Battershaw. Chicago, Regnery, 1958.

Sherrington, R. J. *Three Novels by Flaubert: A Study of Techniques.* Oxford, Oxford University Press, 1970.

Sherwood, Irma Z. "The Novelists as Commentators." *The Age of Johnson: Essays Presented to Chauncey Brewster Tinker.* New Haven, Yale University Press, 1949.

Showalter, English, Jr. *The Evolution of the French Novel, 1641-1782.* Princeton, Princeton University Press, 1972.

Sills, Xole G. "Social Science Fiction." *International Encyclopedia of the Social Sciences,* vol. 14. New York, Macmillan and Free Press, 1968.

Silone, Ignazio. *Bread and Wine,* tran. Gwenda David and Erich Mosbacher. New York, Harper, 1937.

————. *Bread and Wine: A New Version . . .* (1955), tran. Harvey Fergusson II. New York, Atheneum, 1962.

————. *Emergency Exit,* trans. Harvey Fergusson II. New York, Harper and Row, 1968.

————. *Fontamara* (1930), tran. Michael Wharf. New York, Random House, 1934.

————. "Of Heretics and Intellectuals: An Interview." *Encounter,* July 1970, pp. 59-61.

————. *The Story of a Humble Christian* (1968), tran. William Weaver. New York, Harper and Row, 1970.

Simmons, James C. *The Novelist as Historian: Essays on the Victorian Historical Novel.* The Hague and Paris, Mouton, 1973.

Sinclair, Upton. *Money Writes!* New York, Boni, 1927.

Smith, LeRoy W. "Fielding and Mandeville: The War Against 'Virtue.' " *Criticism* 3 (1961): 7-15.

Smith, Raymond T. *British Guiana.* London, Oxford University Press, 1962.

Smith, Sheila M. "Willenhall and Wodgate: Disraeli's Use of Blue Book Evidence." *The Review of English Studies* n.s.13 (1962): 368-384.

Snow, C. P. *The Two Cultures: And a Second Look.* Cambridge, Cambridge University Press, 1964.

Snowden, Frank. *Blacks in Antiquity: Ethiopians in the Greco-Roman Experience.* Cambridge, Harvard University Press, 1970.

Solzhenitsyn, Aleksandr I. *The First Circle,* tran. Thomas P. Whitney. New York, Harper and Row, 1968.

Somekh, Sasson. *The Changing Rhythm: A Study of Najib Mahfuz's Novels.* Leiden, Brill, 1973.

Sontag, Susan. *Against Interpretation.* New York, Farrar, Straus and Giroux, 1966.

Sorokin, Pitirim A. *The Crisis of Our Age.* New York, Dutton, 1941.

_____. *Social and Cultural Dynamics.* New York, American Book Company, 1937-1941. Also rev. and abr. in one vol. by the author. Boston, Porter Sargent, 1957.

Spark, Muriel. *The Comforters.* Philadelphia and New York, Lippincott, 1957.

_____. *Robinson.* Philadelphia and New York, Lippincott, 1958.

Sparshott, F. E. "Truth in Fiction." *The Journal of Aesthetics and Art Criticism* 26 (1967): 3-7.

Speare, Morris Edmund. *The Political Novel: Its Development in England and America.* New York, Oxford University Press, 1924.

Spearman, Diana. *The Novel and Society.* New York, Barnes and Noble, 1966.

Staël, Madame de. *De l'Allemagne* (1813). Paris, Hachette, 1958-1960.

_____. *Dix Années d'Exil* (1818). Paris, Guillequin, n.d.

_____. *Madame de Staël on Politics, Literature and National Character,* ed. and tran. Morroe Berger. New York, Doubleday, 1964.

Stang, Richard. *The Theory of the Novel in England, 1850-1870.* London, Routledge and Kegan Paul, 1959.

Starr, G. A. *Defoe and Spiritual Autobiography.* Princeton, Princeton University Press, 1965.

Steinbeck, John. *The Grapes of Wrath.* New York, Viking, 1939.

Steinmann, Martin, Jr. "The Old Novel and the New." *From Jane Austen to Joseph Conrad*, ed. Robert C. Rathburn and Martin Steinmann, Jr. Minneapolis, University of Minnesota Press, 1958.

Stephen, Fitzjames. "The Relation of Literature to Life." *Cambridge Essays*. London, Parker, 1855.

Stephen, Leslie. *English Literature and Society in the Eighteenth Century.* New York, Putnam, and London, Duckworth, 1904.

_____. *Essays on Freethinking and Plainspeaking.* London, Smith, 1907.

_____. *History of English Thought in the Eighteenth Century* (1876). 3rd ed. New York, Putnam, 1902.

_____. "Nathaniel Hawthorne" (1872). *Hours in a Library.* New ed., vol. 1. London, Smith, 1907.

Stern, Laurent. "Fictional Characters, Places, and Events." *Philosophy and Phenomenological Research* 26 (1965): 202-215.

Sterne, Laurence. *The Life and Opinions of Tristram Shandy, Gentleman* (1760-1767). New York, Odyssey, 1940.

Stevenson, Lionel. "Darwin and the Novel." *Nineteenth-Century Fiction* 15 (1960): 29-38.

Stewart, Philip. *Imitation and Illusion in the French Memoir-Novel, 1700-1750.* New Haven, Yale University Press, 1969.

Stoll, Elmer Edgar. *From Shakespeare to Joyce.* New York, Doubleday, 1944.

_____. *Shakespeare Studies, Historical and Comparative in Method.* New York, Macmillan, 1927.

Stribling, T. S. *Birthright.* New York, Century, 1922.

_____. *Fombombo.* New York, Century, 1923.

_____. *The Forge.* New York, Doubleday, Doran, 1931.

_____. *Unfinished Cathedral.* New York, The Literary Guild, 1934.

Sturrock, John. *The French New Novel.* London, Oxford University Press, 1969.

Swann, George Rogers. *Philosophical Parallelisms in Six English Novelists.* Philadelphia, University of Pennsylvania Press, 1929.

Taylor, John Tinnon. *Early Opposition to the English Novel: The Popular Reaction from 1760 to 1830.* New York, King's Crown Press, 1943.

Thackeray, William. *The Newcomes* (1854-1855). London, Everyman's Library, various dates.

_____. *Vanity Fair* (1848). London, Methuen, 1963.

Theroux, Paul. *Jungle Lovers.* Boston, Houghton, Mifflin, 1971.

Tillett, Nettie S. "Is Coleridge Indebted to Fielding?" *Studies in Philology* 43 (1946): 675-681.

Tillotson, Kathleen. *Novels of the Eighteen-Forties.* Oxford, Oxford University Press, 1954.

Tocqueville, Alexis de. *Democracy in America* (1835), tran. Henry Reeve. New York, Appleton, 1899.

Tournier, Michel. *Friday* (1967), tran. Norman Denny. New York, Doubleday, 1969.

Trevelyan, G. M. *An Autobiography and Other Essays.* London, Longmans, Green, 1949.

Trilling, Lionel. *Beyond Culture.* New York, Viking, 1965.

Trollope, Anthony. *An Autobiography* (1883). Berkeley and Los Angeles, University of California Press, 1947.

————. *Barchester Towers* (1857). Oxford, Oxford University Press, 1953.

————. *Doctor Thorne.* New York, Harper, 1858.

————. *The Warden* (1855). Oxford, Oxford University Press, 1952.

————. *The Way We Live Now* (1875). New York, Knopf, 1950.

Turgenev, Ivan. *Fathers and Sons* (1867), tran. C. J. Hogarth. London, Everyman's Library, 1921.

Twain, Mark. *Huckleberry Finn* (1884). New York, Harper, 1899.

Tye, J. R. "George Eliot's Unascribed Mottoes." *Nineteenth-Century Fiction* 22 (1967): 235-249.

United States Commission on Obscenity and Pornography. *Report,* Sept. 30, 1970. New York, Bantam Books, 1970.

United States National Commission on the Causes and Prevention of Violence. *To Establish Justice, To Insure Domestic Tranquillity: Final Report.* Washington, D.C., Government Printing Office, 1969.

United States Surgeon General's Scientific Advisory Committee on Television and Social Behavior. *Television and Growing Up.* Washington, D.C., Government Printing Office, 1972.

Valentine, Charles A. *Culture and Poverty.* Chicago, University of Chicago Press, 1968.

Van Ghent, Dorothy. *The English Novel: Form and Function.* New York, Rinehart, 1953.

Veblen, Thorstein. *Absentee Ownership and Business Enterprise.* New York, Viking, 1923.

————. *The Theory of the Leisure Class* (1899). New York, Huebsch, 1924.

Vichert, Gordon S. "Bernard Mandeville's *The Virgin Unmask'd.*" *Man-*

deville Studies. New Explorations in the Art and Thought of Dr. Bernard Mandeville (1670-1733), ed. Irwin Primer. The Hague, Martinus Nijhoff, 1975.

Vincent, Howard P. *The Trying-Out of Moby Dick*. Boston, Houghton Mifflin, 1949.

Wagner, Geoffrey. "Sociology and Fiction." *Twentieth Century* 167 (1960): 108-114.

Walsh, Dorothy. *Literature and Knowledge*. Middletown, Wesleyan University Press, 1969.

Waples, Douglas, et al. *What Reading Does to People*. Chicago, University of Chicago Press, 1940.

Warner, Charles Dudley. *The Relation of Literature to Life*. New York, Harper, 1897.

Warner, W. L., and Paul S. Lunt. *The Social Life of a Modern Community*. New Haven, Yale University Press, 1941.

Warren, Robert Penn. "A Note to *All the King's Men*." *Sewanee Review* 61 (1953): 476-480.

———. "T. S. Stribling: A Paragraph in the History of Critical Realism." *The American Review* 2 (1934): 463-486.

Watkins, Floyd C. *The Death of Art: Black and White in the Recent Southern Novel*. Athens, University of Georgia Press, 1970.

Watt, Ian. *The Rise of the Novel: Studies in Defoe, Richardson and Fielding*. London, Chatto and Windus, 1957.

Waugh, Evelyn. *Black Mischief*. New York, Farrar and Rinehart, 1932.

Webb, R. K. *The British Working Class Reader, 1790-1848*. London, Allen and Unwin, 1955.

———. *Harriet Martineau: A Radical Victorian*. London, Heinemann, 1960.

Weber, Max. *The Protestant Ethic and the Spirit of Capitalism*, tran. Talcott Parsons. New York, Scribner, 1958.

Weiss, Walter. "Effects of the Mass Media of Communication." *The Handbook of Social Psychology*, ed. Gardner Lindzey and Elliot Aronson, vol. 5. 2nd ed. Reading, Mass., Addison-Wesley, 1969.

Weitz, Morris. *Philosophy in Literature*. Detroit, Wayne State University Press, 1963.

Wellek, René, and Austin Warren. *Theory of Literature*. New York, Harcourt, Brace, 1949.

Wells, H. G. *Henry James and H. G. Wells*, ed. Leon Edel and Gordon N. Ray. Urbana, University of Illinois Press, 1958.

———. *Tono-Bungay*. New York, Grosset and Dunlap, 1908.

Werlin, Herbert H. "The Consequences of Corruption: The Ghanaian Experience." *Political Science Quarterly* 88 (1973): 71-85.

Wharton, Edith. *The Age of Innocence*. New York, Appleton, 1920.

————. *A Backward Glance*. New York, Scribner, 1934.

————. *The Custom of the Country*. New York, Scribner, 1913.

————. *The Descent of Man and Other Stories*. New York, Scribner, 1904.

————. *The House of Mirth*. New York, Scribner, 1905.

————. *The Reef* (1912). New York, Scribner, 1965.

Whistler, James A. McNeil. *"Ten O'Clock": A Lecture by James A. McNeil Whistler* (1885). Portland, Me., Mosher, 1925.

Whorf, Benjamin. "The Relation of Habitual Thought and Behavior to Language" (1941). *Language, Thought, and Reality*. Cambridge, Massachusetts Institute of Technology Press, 1956.

Whyte, William Foote. *Street Corner Society: The Social Structure of an Italian Slum*. Chicago, University of Chicago Press, 1943.

Wilde, Oscar. *The Artist as Critic: Critical Writings of Oscar Wilde*, ed. Richard Ellmann. New York, Random House, 1968.

Williams, Ioan, ed. *Novel and Romance, 1700-1800: A Documentary Record*. New York, Barnes and Noble, 1970.

Williams, John A. *The Man Who Cried I Am*. Boston, Little, Brown, 1967.

Woolf, Virginia. *The Letters of Virginia Woolf*, vol. 1. *1888-1912*, ed. Nigel Nicolson and Joanne Trautmann. New York and London, Harcourt Brace Jovanovich, 1975.

————. *A Room of One's Own*. New York, Harcourt Brace, 1929.

————. *The Voyage Out*. London, Duckworth, 1927.

Wright, Richard. *Lawd Today*. New York, Walker, 1963.

Wyss, Johann Rudolf. *The Swiss Family Robinson* (1813), various translations and editions.

Young, G. M. *Last Essays*. London, Hart-Davis, 1950.

Zola, Emile. *Le Roman Experimental* (1880). *Les Oeuvres Complètes*, vol. 46. Paris, Bernouard, 1928.

Notes

1. Approaches to Social Life

1. Engels in Lifschitz, p. 122.
2. Wells, *Henry James and H. G. Wells*, pp. 155-156, 223; Woolf, *Letters*, p. 356; Zola, p. 46.
3. Trollope, *Autobiography*, pp. 106-107; Robbe-Grillet, *For a New Novel*, pp. 29, 33; Balzac, *Les Paysans*, pt. 1, ch. 9.
4. Flaubert, *Bouilhet*, p. 280; Babbitt, pp. 338-339.
5. Flaubert, *Correspondence*, V, 160; T. S. Eliot, pp. 45-46.
6. Schapiro, pp. 112-113; Bradbury, p. xviii.

2. Common Origins in the Eighteenth Century

1. On the Scottish philosophers and their elaboration of certain themes, see Bryson, pp. 83, 105-106, 142-143, 242-243, and excerpts from their works in L. Schneider.
2. Stephen's account of this "revolution in thought" presaged Kuhn's recent one.
3. See e.g. MacLean, *Locke*.
4. On Diderot in relation to Sterne, see Fredman, pp. 16-18, 34, 88-91, 130. On Sterne and Adam Smith, see MacLean, "Imagination and Sympathy," p. 410. On Fielding and Hume, see Braudy, p. 5.

5. Mandeville, *Fable,* I, 230, 349; Fielding, *Miscellaneous Writings,* pp. 281-305. For a comparison of Mandeville and Fielding, see L. Smith.

6. Intro. to Mandeville, *Tyburn,* Zirker, p. iii.

7. Jeffares, pp. 8-9, 12-18, examines the effort in the seventeenth century to substitute a new simplified language to express scientific ideas, and the acceptance of such a "plain style" in the eighteenth century.

8. Mandeville's essay, "An Inquiry into the Origin of Moral Virtue," was incorporated into *Fable,* I, 39-57. See Kaye's Introduction, p. xxxiii. For the gist of Mandeville's explanation, see I, 41-46.

9. Mandeville used fictional methods in works other than *The Fable of the Bees,* most notably in the long dialogue *The Virgin Unmask'd* (1709), in which two stories are related. Vichert argues (p. 10) that Mandeville's creation of several "highly individualistic women" in these tales "anticipates the techniques of novelists to come." See also Cook, p. 51; Monro, pp. 38-39.

10. On natural law, state of nature, and social contract, see Barker, Intro., Gough, pp. 105, 113-114, 119-120, 182, 189, 244, 154.

11. Locke, *Two Treatises* (1690), bk. 2, ch. 8. See also Aarsleff, pp. 103-104.

12. On fictional travel literature, see Gove. On new societies in the Americas, Africa, and the Pacific, see Oswalt, ch. 1; Dobrée, pp. 368-377, 607-608. For a comparison of fiction and treatises, see Novak, *Defoe and the Nature of Man,* p. 66.

13. Hunter, ch. 5 and pp. 74-75, 93-94, 103, 113-116; Franklin, p. 72. See also Starr, pp. vii-viii and ch. 3.

14. On conduct books, see Powell, pp. 101-102, 139-140; Morgan, pp. 89-91, 136-137.

15. On Richardson's *Familiar Letters* in relation to conduct books, see Hornbeak.

16. Wharton, *A Backward Glance,* pp. 65-66. On Egypt, see Somekh, pp. 8, 11-12, 23-24.

17. On the banality of the novel's themes, see Scott's review of *Emma,* pp. 64-65.

18. Advertisement in Bulwer-Lytton, end of vol. 1; Trollope, *Autobiography,* p. 124.

19. G. Eliot, *Essays,* pp. 300-324; *Madame de Staël on Politics,* pp. 233-234.

20. Mayo, pp. 28, 32. On periodicals for and by women, see also Adburghum.

21. *Madame de Staël on Politics,* pp. 259-260, 264. For her comments on women in relation to the novel and other forms of literature, see pp. 157, 164, 205-207.

22. See e.g., Cockshut, p. 213; Betsky, pp. 166-167.

23. Hamilton, quoted in V. Colby, pp. 34-35; *Madame de Staël on Politics,* pp. 205-206.

24. See Hill, p. 382; Hunter, *passim;* Starr, *passim;* Watt, pp. 13-31.

25. *Madame de Staël on Politics,* p. 259; Scott, review of *Emma,* p. 65. See also Allott, pp. 59-82; I. Williams.

26. *Madame de Staël on Politics,* pp. 315-316, 127-129, 207-208.

27. For a critique of Spearman, see Rockwell, pp. 98-99; Craig, pp. 24-28.

28. Cobban, *Social Interpretation,* ch. 2, 4, and *Aspects,* ch. 15; Mayo, pp. 13-14; Karl, p. 5; Roberts, pp. xvi, 86-87, 102, 146-149. On the confusion over the term "bourgeois," see Barzun, *Use and Abuse,* pp. 58-66.

3. Human Association and Culture in the Novel

1. The similarity in plot between *Robinson Crusoe* and *The Tempest* was pointed out by John Robert Moore in 1945, but the more important similarity, in the theme of the superiority of the European Prospero over the "native" Caliban, was not discussed until 1950 by Mannoni.

2. Quoted in Epstein, p. 250.

3. On corruption, a theme in both novels, see Werlin, whose analysis of Ghana also applies to Nigeria as portrayed in these two novels.

4. Warren, "T. S. Stribling," pp. 472, 476, 477. See also Watkins, pp. 2-3.

4. Political Power and Social Class in the Novel

1. There are various approaches to the political novel. Irving Howe, ch. 1, sees it mainly as involving "political ideas" or ideologies and the "political milieu" or the actions that follow from ideologies. Joseph Blotner limits political novels about America to the "overt, institutionalized politics of the officeholder, the candidate, the party official, or the individual who performs political acts as they are conventionally understood" (8). For an earlier treatment of political novels, see Speare.

2. Silone, *Emergency Exit,* p. 164.

3. Silone, *Emergency Exit,* p. 155.
4. Silone, *Emergency Exit,* p. 207.
5. Silone, "Of Heretics and Intellectuals," pp. 60-61.
6. Silone, "Of Heretics and Intellectuals," p. 61.
7. Allsop, p. 49.
8. Silone, *Emergency Exit,* p. 207.
9. On the culture of poverty, see Oscar Lewis, pp. xlii-lii; Valentine, pp. 141-171.
10. On the narrator in *Howards End,* see Roby.

5. The Novel as a Vehicle for Social Commentary

1. Alter, *Fielding,* p. 34.
2. Alter has written perceptively in *Partial Magic,* esp. chs. 4 and 5, on the "novel as a self-conscious genre." His study was published too recently to enable me to profit from it here.
3. Sarraute, *The Age of Suspicion,* pp. 70-71.
4. Plath, ch. 12. Plath does the same thing in ch. 13.
5. On Sterne's digressions, see vol. 1, ch. 22; Fielding's similar point is in *Tom Jones,* bk. 5, ch. 1. Sterne invites the reader to supply his own description, vol. 6, ch. 38; Fielding does so in *Joseph Andrews,* bk. 3, ch. 4.
6. On the case for intrusions, see e.g. Booth, Friedman, Blodgett, and Chapman.
7. See, e.g. Rubin, pp. 9-14; Sacks, pp. 231-233, 249-251.
8. Glasgow, *A Certain Measure,* p. 204; Hardy, "The Profitable Reading of Fiction" (1888), *Selected Writings,* p. 149.
9. James, "Anthony Trollope" (1883) and "The Art of Fiction" (1884), in *The Future of the Novel,* pp. 248, 6.
10. Stewart, pp. 15, 18-19; Dietrickson, p. 64. See also Nassau Senior's similar point cited in Stang, p. 107.

6. Sociopsychological Insights in the Novel

1. Similar ideas were expressed almost two centuries earlier by Mandeville, *Fable,* I, 127-130, 170.
2. This skeptical attitude about the Greeks' racial tolerance has been shown to be overly harsh, since the Greeks did know Ethiopians well and were indeed not so prejudiced as has been assumed. See Snowden, pp. 183, 216-218.
3. See also Cassinelli, p. 778.
4. Hazelrigg, chs. 4-5.

5. For a social science treatment of law as a means of social control and in relation to equality, see Berger, ch. 5. For a survey of law as treated by Balzac, see Peytel.

6. Hardy, *Selected Writings*, pp. 330-331.

7. Before Wells' *Tono-Bungay*, such ideas appeared in Veblen's *The Theory of the Leisure Class*, ch. 4, in 1899. In recent times, similar notions have appeared. On hotels, see Boorstin, pp. 134-147. On affluence and its concomitants, see Galbraith, pp. 90-94, 289-291. On the mass media as guides to consuming, see Lazarsfeld and Merton, pp. 101-102; Peterson, pp. 4, 11-12, 14, 42-43; Waples, p. 13; Katz and Lazarsfeld, *passim;* Mills, *White Collar*, pp. 253-258.

8. Thackeray puts the same idea into dialogue in *The Newcomes*, I, ch. 32.

9. Madame de Staël, *Dix Années d'Exil*, p. 53, quoted in *Madame de Staël on Politics*, p. 15. These two writers, Austen and de Staël, of very different temperaments and careers, were born four months apart in 1775-1776 and died four days apart in July 1817. These two books were both published posthumously, Austen's in 1818, de Staël's in 1821.

10. G. Eliot, "Moral Swindlers," *Impressions of Theophrastus Such*, p. 133.

11. See Madame de Staël's comment in an essay of 1799 that "reason is not a shade of meaning between extremes, but the primary color given off by the purest rays of the sun." *Madame de Staël on Politics*, p. 136.

12. Weber, pp. 170-171; R. H. Tawney, foreword to Weber, p. 2.

13. On kinesics, see Birdwhistell, p. xi; Scheflen, pp. 27, 131-132. On sociometry, see Moreno, pp. vii, 707, 750. On ethnomethodology, see Schur, pp. 122-123.

14. Merton 1968, pp. 475, 477.

15. On compilations from Balzac, see Barbey d'Aurevilly, Pagès, Clouard, and Rickel. For Dickens, see his *Cyclopedia*. For Richardson, see Sale, pp. 95-97; Eaves and Kimpel, pp. 313, 420-422. For Eliot, see Bibliography under Eliot; Haight, ed., *The George Eliot Letters*, V, 459; Haight, *George Eliot*, p. 440; Tye, p. 248.

7. Fiction and History

1. Chassang, pp. 6-12.

2. See Ford, ch. 7.

3. See Vincent, pp. 126-42; Ellmann, pp. 238-239, 385-386; Mann, *Doctor Faustus*, ch. 7, 8, 22, Author's Note; Mann, *The Story of a Novel*.

4. For an author's account of the role of imagination in writing a

historical novel, see e.g. Neill, pp. 68-69.

5. On Disraeli's *Sybil,* see S. M. Smith; Cazamian, pp. 9, 12, 252; Aydelotte, p. 43.

6. On *Illustrations,* see Martineau, *Autobiography,* I, 122-148; Webb, *Harriet Martineau,* pp. 99-125. On *Poor Laws,* see Martineau, *Autobiography,* I, 165-170; Webb, *Harriet Martineau,* pp. 125-129; Webb, *British Working Class Reader,* pp. 124-126. On her fiction as a whole, see V. Colby, ch. 5.

7. On Scott, see Martineau, "Achievements of the Genius of Scott." On Comte, see Martineau, preface to her translation, p. ix; Martineau, *Autobiography,* II, 58, 66-67, 70-76.

8. Eliot, *Essays,* p. 447. For a similar, more recent statement, see Butterfield, pp. 18, 51-52, 73-75.

9. For Scott's influence, see Carroll, pp. 5-7, 95; Young, pp. 17-40; Trevelyan, pp. 200-205; Munroe; Edgar Johnson, pp. 35-36; Simmons. For the differences between history and fiction, see Mandelbaum.

10. Warren, "A Note," pp. 478-480. For Warren's use of history in fiction, see also L. Moore.

11. *Mme. de Staël on Politics,* pp. 260-261; Hardy, *Selected Writings,* p. 144. For the relation between the novel and history, see also J. Lukacs, pp. 115-124.

12. Ellman and Feidelson, p. 310; Hardy, *Selected Writings,* p. 145; Glasgow, *A Certain Measure,* pp. 211-213, 63.

13. Locke, *Essay,* II, 262-263.

14. Montaigne, p. 75; Pope, p. 109 (preface to his translation of the *Iliad*); Reeve, excerpts in Allott, pp. 45, 47 (prefaces to *The Old English Baron,* 1778, and *The Progress of Romance,* 1785); Scott, "Essay on Romance" (1824), p. 156; Trollope, *Autobiography,* p. 107; Balzac, *Les Paysans,* bk. 1, ch. 6; Hardy, *The Life,* p. 150; Gold, quoted in publisher's advertisement for *Fathers,* in *New York Times Book Review,* Apr. 2, 1967, p. 23.

15. Several scholars writing recently on Fielding and Coleridge have failed to appreciate fully Fielding's earlier use of the concepts of poetic faith and suspension of belief. See Tillett, Dilworth, Patterson, and the absence of a note where the latter concept appears in the annotated edition of Fielding's *Joseph Andrews,* p. 329. Coleridge himself was probably familiar with Fielding's formulations, for his notes refer to *Tom Jones.* See Coleridge's *Complete Works,* IV, 379-383; Blanchard, pp. 263, 315-322, 566. In *Biographia Literaria,* I, 156, Coleridge refers to a character in *Joseph Andrews.* Coleridge has long been accused of plagiarism. See Bate, pp. 131-138; Fruman, intro, and ch. 20. An early accusation was

made in the anonymous article "The Plagiarisms of S. T. Coleridge," *Blackwood's Magazine,* 1840. Coleridge was aware that some of his ideas resembled those of Friedrich von Schelling. See *Biographia Literaria,* I, 102; editor's notes, II, 317-320.

16. Excerpted in Allott, p. 47.

17. Hardy, *Selected Writings,* p. 139; James, *The Art of the Novel,* pp. 33-34.

8. Literature and Life

1. *Madame de Staël on Politics,* pp. 141, 257.

2. On censorship and freedom of expression in relation to public morals, see Clor, ch. 7-8.

3. On Wilde, "The Decay of Lying," and his review of Whistler's lecture, which appeared in the press the next day, see Ellmann's collection of Wilde's essays, *The Artist as Critic,* pp. 290-320, 13-16.

4. On the anti-art movements, see Egbert, pp. 294-308, 712-716, 721-726; Sontag, pp. 263-274; Kirby; Kerr; Morris, pp. 34-35.

5. Quoted in Chappelow, pp. 88-89.

6. According to R. W. B. Lewis, Wharton wrote an outline for a novel about incest. In a developed scene from this proposed novel, Wharton combined incest with oral sex and sexual intercourse as explicitly as in clandestine pornography of earlier times and in literature of today. The scene, which is uncharacteristic of Wharton, may reveal a suppressed desire to write more freely about the most intimate relations between men and women.

7. Silone, *Emergency Exit,* p. 147. See Glasgow's similar remark in *A Certain Measure,* pp. 81-82.

8. Maurois, pp. 259-260, 275. For a comparable incident about Thackeray, see J. I. M. Stewart's introduction to *Vanity Fair,* p. 13, Penguin Books, Baltimore, 1968.

9. E. J. Delécluze, quoted in Pelles, p. 9.

9. Literature as a Social Science

1. Coser has tried to illustrate this level by presenting short excerpts from novels touching on various domains of social life. The difficulty of the task is illustrated by these truncations, which do not always show clearly what the editor intends.

2. For a recent statement of the same point, see Hoggart, II, 265-266.

3. On hypothesis in literature, see Hoggart, II, 261-264; Hospers, "Implied Truths in Literature"; Guyau, p. 147.

4. On the reinterpretation, holding at least Sacco guilty, see Felix, pp. 144-145; Russell, pp. xi-xv. On the literature inspired by the case, see Felix, ch. 19; Joughin and Morgan, ch. 14-16. A similar case concerns the singer Bessie Smith, about whom Edward Albee wrote a play based on early reports and rumors later shown to be erroneous. It was mistakenly believed that she had bled to death after being refused treatment in a Memphis hospital because she was black. For the versions of her death now accepted, see Chilton, p. 376; Albertson, pp. 216-223.

5. On the cumulative character of science, see Campbell, pp. 46-49; Merton 1968, pp. 27-29; Berelson and Steiner, p. 17.

6. See also de Beer. On "progress" in literature, see Wellek, ch. 19.

7. *Madame de Staël on Politics,* pp. 154-155.

8. *Madame de Staël on Politics,* pp. 261-262.

9. Quoted in Kanin, p. 189.

10. On Dostoyevsky, see his 1869 letter excerpted in Ellmann and Feidelson, p. 311. On Heller, see Ephron, pp. 70, 72.

11. Hardy, *The Life,* p. 171.

12. On the message in Victorian fiction, see R. Colby, pp. 18-19, 303-304; Cazamian, pp. 6-12, 251-252; Aydelotte, pp. 44-47.

13. Coleridge, *Biographia Literaria,* II, 5-6.

14. Wells, *Henry James and H. G. Wells,* p. 154.

15. Bein, p. 395.

16. On the conservative origins of sociology, see Nisbet, ch. 4. On social science in relation to liberalism and reform, the challenge to objectivity, and the growth of radicalism in recent sociology, see Ladd and Lipset, ch. 4.

17. See also Berger, "Thorstein Veblen's Literary Style."

18. Hardy, *The Life,* p. 274.

19. On Utopian communities, see Kanter, ch. 9.

10. The Challenge of Science to Literature

1. Sparshott challenged these arguments in a reply to Margolis.

2. See e.g. Scriven, pp. 185-187; Stern, pp. 213-215; Ross, pp. 6, 215-217; Walsh, pp. 46-49, 74, 128, 136-140; D. Schneider, pp. 319-320.

3. For the effect of science on literature in the seventeenth and eighteenth centuries, see Horne; Jones, pp. 1-3, 20-21, 27.

4. See also Stevenson, p. 38; Raper, pp. 62-82.

5. The usual relation between physical thought and social thought

is to see the first as causing the second. Feuer offers the hypothesis, supported by persuasive evidence, that the true relation may be the opposite. He suggests (p. 58), for example, that Einstein's participation in the socialist, youthful "counterculture" of Zurich and Berne at the turn of the century led him to believe in the "relativity of social laws." This opened his mind to the possibility of "a physical relativity" which would overthrow "absolute space and time" as historical relativity had overthrown bourgeois social laws till then regarded as absolute. Feuer also suggests (pp. 80-81) that Einstein later regarded the physical "principle of indeterminacy" as a "child of contemporary nihilism" rather than the other way round.

6. Contemporary critiques were included in a later edition of Zola's own book, pp. 343-352. See also Guyau, pp. 145, 149-150; Eastman, pp. 156-157.

7. See Sartre, p. 224. On the convergence of philosophy and literature, see Cruickshank, pp. 8-13; Sturrock, ch. 1. On the differences between the "old" and "new" novel, see Steinmann.

8. Several anthologies have recently appeared illustrating the contribution of literature to sociological analysis. See e.g. Coser (1963), Kakonis and Desmarais (1969), Dabaghian (1970), and Milstead (1974).

9. On the 1830s and 1840s, see Tillotson, pp. 123-124.

10. See *The New York Times,* Feb. 18, 1969, p. 36; July 11, 1975, p. 12.

11. See e.g. Roszak, p. 213.

Index